Alain LESCART

THE EXTRAORDINARY ADVENTURE OF THE SACRED CAT OF BURMA

I dedicate this book to my Normand
grandmother, Marie Gibout,
who loved cats and whom I never met;
And to the memory of Java, a Seal-Tortie
Birman, gone too soon...

The Cats

Fervent lovers and austere scholars
Both love, in their mature age
Powerful and cuddly cats, pride of the house
Who, like them, are sedentary and sensitive to the
cold.

Friends of science and of sensual pleasure
They look for silence and the horror of darkness;
Erebus would have used them for his funeral
steeds
If they could, incline their pride to bondage.

While daydreaming, they take on noble behaviors
Of majestic sphinxes stretched out in solitude
Who seemed to sleep in a never-ending dream;

Their fruitful loins are full of magical sparks
And gleams of gold, like a refined sand,
Vaguely be-star their mystical pupils.

Charles Baudelaire *(The Flowers of Evil)*

PROLOGUE

The Sacred Cat of Burma remains one of the most popular feline breeds in France and on the European continent while it gradually declines in the British Isles and on the American continent—in favor of more popular breeds such as the Ragdoll, for example (created from a Birman)—as the number of cats presented at competitions and the births registered by the big feline organizations like the GCCF, the CFA, and the TICA, show for two decades now. One hundred years have passed since the genesis (1921) of this wonderful cat, known for its pleasant, sociable, and affectionate personality.

In fact, the breeding of Birman cats (abbreviation) did not really begin until after the Second World War, in the Fifties, by the dedicated work of a handful of breeders working with the few cats saved from previous generations. It is thanks to the diligent work of French feline technology and pre-war brand promoters/artists, such as Mrs. Marcelle Adam, president of the *Société Française Féline* and writer/actress, as well as doctor-veterinarian Philippe Jumaud, to which we owe the development of this magnificent, princely-looking cat. The origins of the pre-war Sacred Birman Cat (abbreviated SBI) are shrouded in intentional mists.

Greed clearly seems to be the reason behind this artistic vagueness, moreover, but also the latent desire to create an exceptional intermediate cat which would inherit the best of both worlds, particularly popular in between two-wars Europe—Siamese and Persian. The addition of symmetrical white gloves on velvety paws and inverted V spurs under the hind legs (an original Birman trademark) adds a unique additional charm that also allows us to fine-tune the originality of this sapphire-eyed cat. The Birman is a middle cat, if one wants to adapt a Buddhist term that corresponds to its fable.

As the veterinarian Fernand Méry duly noted: "The Birman cat [...] provides the link between Persian and Siamese." This trait was often highlighted by the first Birman breeders (like Mlle Madeleine Boyer of the Kaabaa Cattery) and raises the question of the more recent deviations of certain lines of modern Birmans who lean more towards a Persianized form and have, once again, lost the qualities specific to the Siamese heritage (such as the semi-long silky coat without knots, the size and morphology of the body). The Birman origin is also parallel to that of the creation of the Persian Colorpoint, which uses the same combination of cats but in a fully Persianized type (called Pre-war Khmer cat and also Himalayan). The first post-war breeders of these two breeds—Miss Boyer from the Kaabaa Cattery, Mrs. Simone Poirier from the Crespières Cattery for the Birman, and Mrs. Gamichon from the Grandes Chapelles Cattery for the Persian Colorpoint—worked together for the improvement of their two respective breeds as their pedigrees clearly show. Later, the British followed the same principles in the creation of new colors (chocolate-point / lilac-point for example), always using a Siamese and a Persian Colorpoint, which also has the advantage of already having blue eyes, in addition to the Siamese gene and hair length.

Various books and articles have been written on the mysterious origin of the Birman before 1940, but they lack scientific rigor and still leave glaring inaccuracies here and there which do not satisfy the curious academic that I am. A Birman breeder since 1987 (in Belgium, the south of France, and in the United States on both coasts), I have had the opportunity of meeting and conversing with a number of other breeders since that date. The book by Gisèle Barnay and Simone Poirier, *Les Secrets du Chat Sacré de Birmanie*, in addition to (in English) *The Birman Cat* by Vivienne Smith, remain the best published books on the subject, but they are no longer in print and sometimes contain errors. They also leave behind the mysterious origin of the Birman. It seemed to me, therefore, to try, as much as possible, to fill the gaps or inaccuracies left by the work of my predecessors, all the while recognizing their efforts and the means that were available to them. It is a question of forsaking the golden legend, the peddling of received ideas, in order to collect precise facts from here and there and to allow us to see the evolution of a legend over the years and publications, as with a report. It is also a question of the continued task of precise documentation of the sources, in an academic manner, when the sources exist in the books, magazines, and newspapers of the time. One can also remark that the Internet abounds in whimsical sites about the Birman which peddle and magnify nonsense.

The recent online publication of the pre-war newspapers, digitized by the Bibliothèque Nationale de France, (or Bibliothèque François Mitterrand (BNF)) in Paris, now allows research that was practically impossible until recently. To this must be added, of course, my wanderings in various libraries in France and Belgium for documents inaccessible to the BNF, and the purchase of the contemporary works of antique booksellers.

The discoveries that I made, after years of research and thanks to a sabbatical semester granted by my university (Point Loma Nazarene University) in the Spring of 2019, are unprecedented, and shed a new light on the origin of that which we have called: *The Sacred Cat of Burma*, which is a very French production, if there ever was one.

Whatever its history, incredible as we shall see, the Birman Cat remains an exceptional cat whose personality can only charm and seduce by its devotion, its hieratic side, and its loyalty. What I have written about him tells us nothing about who he really is—an extraordinary cat who subtly slips into the intricacies of your heart and gives you his trust and unlimited love which becomes one with your soul. This remarkable cat was in need of an exceptional legend, which was, in turn, woven together by poets over time ...

CHAPTER 1

THE CORONATION OF A NEW CAT WITH SNOWY PAWS

The genesis of a legend...

The first official appearance of the Cat of Burma, (renamed the Sacred Cat of Burma in 1926), on the occasion of the first International Feline Exhibition in Paris, May 14-15, 1926, at the *Salle Wagram*, caused a sensation and quickly became a media phenomenon that attracted the attention of newspapers and luxury cat lovers. Who was this extraordinary cat with bewitching eyes, sparkling with its royal blue sapphires, who looked somewhat like a Siamese gloved in white and covered in a lace of medium-length hair? Its origin is shrouded in the exoticism of the Indochina colonies and a Hindu legend produced during the Khmer times. Like the rose of *The Little Prince* of St. Exupéry, its appearance required many preparations.

At the source of this oriental tale, three names emerge: veterinarian Philippe Jumaud, Mrs. Marcelle Adam (a renowned novelist who was published in newspaper serials of the time), and Mrs. Léotardi, a high-class adventurer. In addition to this trio, we can also add veterinarian Fernand Méry who published several articles on the topic.

The first published mention of the Birman cat can be found in a three-column article in number 260 of *La Vie à la Campagne* from February 1, 1925, in the *Small Breeding* section. It is titled "Rationally breed and select the cat. Why you need to be interested in the quality breeds and varieties of this domestic feline, by establishing bloodlines and which benefits are possible from this breeding". It is signed by Philippe Jumaud, veterinarian, secretary general of the *Cat Club of France and Belgium*.

This article which encourages the breeding of luxury cats for pecuniary reasons, informs us that this promising activity was already being practiced in France by 1,500 breeders in 1924 and cites as its main example one of the largest catteries of Blues of Persia at the time (Blue Persians today): the Maritza Cattery. This cattery will be one of the first to practice Birman, as we will later see, which belonged to a Mrs. L. Brassart.

In the list of breeds offered for breeding which provide a highly profitable income, Jumaud indicates: "Some rare Cats are very high-ranked, they are the orange, cream, and tortoiseshell, or the extremely rare Birman Cats." (p. 66). This is the first mention of the Birman cat associated with a financial motive. It is important in order to understand the reason for its appearance. This publication indicates that the Birman cat is known to the veterinarian, the founder of the *Cat Club of France and Belgium*, who, beyond the mention of his existence, already had in his possession information which led him to believe in its uniqueness.

Before this article, the Birman cannot be found in cat breed presentations. On November 16, 1924, the newspaper *Les Modes de la Femme de France* published the article "Cats" where it said:

These beautiful animals long neglected by fashion and the favor of women, are conquering our favor. It is fancy to present in your living room, next to the fashionable favorite doll, a beautiful Siamese cat with pale eyes and silky fur. An entirely new science has just created the characteristics of perfect feline types. In short, our cats now have a "standard." The body should be short, low on legs with a broad, round head, large eyes, ears wide apart. Now, you should not ignore that there are two special classes, two unique classes: long-haired or Persian cats and short-haired or European cats. Persians can be single-colored, black, white, blue, orange, cream or fawn. Short hairs include Abyssinian cats, which are very rare today, tailless Isle of Man cats, and Siamese. [...] The most sought-after type today is the blue cat whose esteemed models must be very pale. [...] Who will sing of the eyes, the beautiful eyes of cats? A poet, no doubt ..." (p. 14).

The journalist could not have been more accurate.

The financial motivation for breeding luxury cats was also, for Jumaud, a reason to promote cat shows in France, in order to make the varieties of cats known to the general public, combining pleasure with profit. He also tells us that the first exhibitions of the 20th century in France took place in the south, in Cannes (1910), Aix-les-Bains (1914), Marseille and Perpignan (1924). All under the aegis of the *Cat-Club of France and Belgium*, the *French Club of the Siamese Cat* and the *Club du Bleu de Perse*, in particular. In 1925, several exhibitions were scheduled: in Marseille from February 28th to March 1st; in Cannes on March 13th and 14th; in Lille on April 12th. He also announced plans to create an international feline exhibition in Paris in June (it would be postponed twice and would eventually take place in May of 1926). The latter took place under the aegis of two important journals: *La Vie à la Campagne* and *Fémina* as well as "High Personalities from the world of arts and letters." Philippe Jumaud was the central organizer of these exhibitions. He is well-placed for this kind of activity, having been already, since 1922, secretary of the *Canine Society of France*, within which, he regularly organized dog shows on the Riviera, then went so far as to mix dogs and cats in joint exhibitions, before creating exhibitions solely devoted to felines of which he was, at the beginning, the only qualified French judge.

Here is the report where we find the announcement of the Cannes exhibition of February 1925, in *Le Petit Marseillais* on February 9:

"Cannes Canine and Feline Exhibition. Cannes, February 8. - Meeting under the chairmanship of Baron J. de Meuronnet de Saint-Marc, President of the Canine Society of Rivera Committee definitively decided the list of judges who will judge on March 13, 14 and 15 in Cannes. These are: M. Menans de Corre, Mme Baumann, M. Pezet, M. Ch. De Coppet, M. le Villars, M. Lemaignère, Mme Hélène Saurel, M. Ph. Jumaud for cats. All of these judges are recognized by the Central Society for the Improvement of Dog Breeds and by the Cat Club of France and Belgium. Hence, official certificates of fitness for the championship will be issued to subjects deserving of them. More than 15,000 francs in cash, works of art and valuable prizes will be rewarded to exceptional breeders. With the pledges received, and by the dates chosen immediately after the dog shows in Marseille and Nice, we can expect an exhibition of very beautiful specimens of both canine and feline breeds. All dogs and cats of any breed, whether their origin is proven or not, may be entered into the exhibition. The registration of each animal must be made using entry forms which are sent upon request to Mr. Ph. Jumaud, secretary of the Canine Society of the Riviera, at the Cercle Nautique, in Cannes. Entry forms are also available to potential exhibitors at MM. Gaudin and Lions, veterinarians, in Cannes and at the Cannes Festival Committee." (p. 2).

Number 13 of the review *Chasse, Pêche, Élevage* on July 15, 1924 (Marton), tells us that:

In France, the breeding of luxury cats is still in an embryonic state. We remember having seen once in the past, at the Palmarium of the Jardin d'Acclimatation, a very successful Cat Exhibition, organized by a large Parisian newspaper. But despite its success, this event did not become an annual institution. Cats have their club, however, but its center is very far from the capital, on the shores of the Mediterranean. Its general secretary is Mr. Jumaud, a veterinarian in Saint-Raphaël. In 1923, he succeeded in adding a feline show to the Cannes Dog Show held on March 19, 20 and 21. The notion was a successful one. It deserves to be repeated. A favorable opportunity has offered itself, annually in Paris, for cat lovers, to show their products, this is the great dog show of the Tuileries. There is a hall where the animal painting exhibit is held. Nothing would be easier than having cages in this hall similar to those which are used to exhibit small luxury dogs. An arrangement with the Society of Dog Breeds should be manageable. But the first step is to form a club, because it seems difficult for the southern club to extend its activities to the Paris region. How does one go about founding a club? It would suffice if among the luxury cat breeders, one more enterprising than the others, decided to take the initiative. He would make known, through the various breeding newspapers, that he would voluntarily devote himself to founding a club and that he would be happy to receive the names and addresses of the French cat friends. Once in possession of twenty or even ten names, he would summon his correspondents to a meeting at his home or in a neutral place, such as an editorial office, and the society would be founded during this interview. This experience may be interesting. Breeding Persians and even Siamese is lucrative. They can be undertaken almost everywhere and even more easily in cities than in country residences. This is what we will explain in other interviews." (Francis Marton's article, p. 232).

It will take a year for this creation to see the light of day. The *Paris Cat Club* met in general assembly on June 21, 1925 in the presence of 48 members. The number 37 of *Chasse, Pêche, Èlevage* ("Cat Club of Paris") indicates: "In the absence of Mr. André Silvan, president, the meeting was headed by Mrs. Baronne de Saint-Mars and Mrs. Marcelle Adam, assisted by Mr. Philippe Jumaud, Secretary General." (p. IV). It was decided to create a Feline Exhibition in Paris in January 1926.

Let's go back to Jumaud's February 1, 1925 article. Cats are classified according to precise criteria (following the proposal of the veterinary professor Cornevin of Lyon) which can surprise, judged in one of the current categories: the character of the ears and the tail; skin color; the length and consistency of the hair. The felines are also classified according to their geographic origin. There are thus three categories:

A. Normal-tailed breeds:

I. Small and erect ears.

a. Short coat.

White skin or piebald. Gray coat (Common cat); fawn (Spanish cat); light gray with black underside (Cypriot cat); red and blue (Cape Cat); dress reminiscent of that of the isatis (Icelandic cat).

Black skin. Negro cat (or Gambian cat).

b. Long and woolly coat.

Gray color with bluish reflections (Chat des Chartreux); reddish and uniform (Tobolsk and Korassan cat).

c. Long and silky coat.

a Café au lait color, otter ears, eyes and legs: Birman cat.

b. Various colors: Angora cat; Persian Blue; etc.

II. Drop ears: Chinese cat.

B. Short-tailed breeds (sometimes with a nodosity): Malaysian cat, Siamese cat.

C. The Anoure breeds (without a tail). Isle of Man cat.

As we can see here, the Birman cat is entitled to a very particular class which distinguishes it completely from the others. It has a long normal tail, small, erect ears, a long, silky coat, and a unique café-au-lait with otter-color markings at the ends.

This first general physical description of the Birman cat does not tell us much about its origin, though. A month later, in March 25, 1925, Philippe Jumaud presented this detail in his thesis in veterinary medicine. The content of this thesis is known to us, and is published, like the other theses of the veterinary Faculté de Lyon. Jumaud also published, a little later in Saint Raphaël, a little book of a hundred pages entitled *Les Races de Chats* at the éditions des Tablettes which reiterates the bulk of his thesis. This small book would go on to have four editions (1925, 1926, 1930, 1935) with occasional amplifications, even modifications, in the later editions. This thesis and this book make the veterinarian Jumaud the cat specialist in France.

The Birman Cat takes up only 3 pages of the original edition in 1925. In 1926, its description is increased to 8 pages.

The first version of his thesis and book in 1925 states:

Originating, like the Siamese, from the Far East, the cats of Burma, raised in the temples, are heavily guarded and their transfer is prohibited. However, a few years ago, Mr. VANDERBILT was able to acquire a couple from which the subjects that currently exist originate from." (*Les Races de Chat*. 1926, pp. 40-41). The first version of his thesis stated: "from where did the subjects which served as the basis for our observations come from." (p. 40). There was indeed observation, because found in the text of his thesis there is a list that offers a comparative table of the weights of two male Birman kittens from five to thirty-six days old. This comparative table is omitted from later publications. Jumaud also notes having observed a Birman who was "particularly wild". (ibid.).

This text is important, because it indicates that there was already Birman breeding in early 1925. Mrs. Léotardi is designated as the breeder and affirms that

20

FIG. 7. — Chat de Birmanie

the breeding is difficult and "not to expect to raise one subject out of ten," which indicates that the base cat is crossed with another breed.

This description is literally reproduced in the more extensive book which he published the following year (February 17, 1926) with veterinarian E. Larieux and whose title is *Le Chat: Races - élevage- maladies*. The slightly more precise description of the cat indicates:

The Birman cat, small and short-legged, has an elongated body, a bulging forehead, very long whiskers and, on the ears, long tufts of hair. The coat, cream like with the Siamese, has light bronze hues on the back; the coat is rather long and silky. The tail is decorated with long otter-color hairs on top, gray or beige below. (p. 29).

The head is also described as "long with wide ears," like a Siamese. Contrary to the other races presented, there is no photo of a Birman, but a drawing (see above).

From this first general description of the geographical origin of the Birman cat (the Far East), we retain the name of an American millionaire (another financial association) Mr Vanderbilt who would have acquired a couple from which the 1925 subjects are issued. But this reference to Mr Vanderbilt is not followed by others (see below); we are surprised at first, that the millionaire, so quickly in possession of such a rare cat, apparently got rid of it in good time. The following question concerns just which Vanderbilt is in question. We may think first of Harold Vanderbilt, the well-known winner of regatta races, commodore of the *New York Yacht Club* (1922-24) and single, which we will see, has its relevance. However, my research at Vanderbilt University in Nashville shows that he never went to Burma or that region with his yacht. The other possible candidate is Harold's father, William Kissam Vanderbilt I (1849-1920), the richest Vanderbilt, who was interested in yachting and had a famous stable in France. He was also one of the founding members of the Jockey Club. All the Vanderbilts stayed in France as members of the American troops during the United States intervention in the 1914-18 war. William Kissam Vanderbilt I's stable took part in horse races in France during the first half of 1920 and won, for example, second place at Monte-Carlo, on January 4, 1920, and the first prize of Lupine, in July 1920. Nicknamed "one of the kings of the Parisian turf," "American by origin, but French at heart," he entered his horses in the races in France from January to July and won numerous prizes, echoed every day in French newspapers. However, he died on July 22, 1920 in Paris, at the age of 71, an event reported by these same newspapers. After his death, the stable was sold to the American Macomber for a million dollars; in total, he left his heirs $54.5 million.

Then remains his other son: William Kissam II Vanderbilt, racing driver and yachtman. An important point to emphasize, which we will come back to later, is that he was married to Virginia Graham Fair. In 1918, he published a book about his travels in 1912-13, entitled *A Trip Through Sicily, Tunisia, Algeria, and Southern France.* In 1922, he acquired the luxurious French yacht Ara—measuring 213 feet long—which he kept until 1931. The newspaper *Le Gaulois* on October 14, 1922 said: "Mr. Vanderbilt, who is the president of the New York Yacht Club, intends to sail around the world on his new boat as soon as his armaments are finished." (p. 2). On August 22, 1924, another daily newspaper, *Le Journal,* indicated that his yacht was in Casablanca, and that the millionaire would circumnavigate the Mediterranean, via Morocco, and pass by Paris before returning to the Americas (Note: p. 3).

We have several published accounts by him of his circumnavigation:

First in 1926, *To Galapagos on the Ara.* Then in 1927, *15,000 Miles Cruise with Ara.* And finally, in 1929, *Taking One's Own Ship Around the World: A Journal Descriptive of Scenes and Incidents Together with Observations from the Log Books Recorded on the Voyage Around the World of the Yacht Ara.*

However, these three travel stories around the world refer to journeys that took place too late, between 1926 and 1929, compared to the dating of the beginnings of the Birman legend (1924): the Birman cat had already "arrived " in France.

The Vanderbilt hypothesis does not survive long, moreover, as we will see later. The Vanderbilt family was interested in cats, however, as indicated in an older article from 1899, written by Paul de Bart in *L'éleveur:* "Mrs Vanderbilt owns a purebred cat for which she paid 7,500 francs. Many other wealthy Americans have followed this example; fashion has passed into England, and among the famous amateurs, we have mentioned Lord Dufferin, former ambassador of France, who raises at least a dozen tomcats in his apartments." (p. 278). Would this fact have served as a basis for Jumaud's account?

More interesting: during the same year 1925, another participant came onto the scene: Mrs. Marcelle Adam, a well-known novelist at the time who was also the president of the *Cat Club of France and Belgium*, and who prepared the first major Parisian exhibition in January 1926 (postponed to May because of the cold). She is the first to present a Birman male in a Parisian exhibition, *Manou* (accompanied by the cat's mother, the very mysterious *Poupée*).

She then published in the newspaper serial *Le Matin*, between November 16, 1925 and January 19, 1926, a novel called *L'Amour qui Tremble*, in two parts, "L'Amour dans les Myrtes" and "La Gloire dans les Myrtes". It is there, at the bottom of the fifth page, that the legend of the Birman Cat is presented for the very first time: the Birman makes his appearance in literature before appearing in ceremonial dress in broad daylight.

L'Amour qui tremble, tells the story of three teenagers engaged in complicated romantic relationships: Sylvine Grazielli, an orphan of noble extraction, entrusted to the care of a teacher named Mme Gerboise who teaches her music; the latter's son,

55. — Feuilleton du MATIN du 9 janv.

l'amour qui tremble

ROMAN

MARCELLE ADAM

DEUXIEME PARTIE

LA GLOIRE DANS LES MYRTES

Pascal Gerboise, a small literary genius with a romantic and passionate temper, who is of fragile health since he suffers from one of the symptoms of tuberculosis (Ms. Adam designates her illness by the term hemopthysia [sic] even though this is not medically accurate); and finally, Etienne Augéliaume, son of Pascal's doctor, who will also embrace the medical profession and is jealous of Sylvine's affection for the young patient, Pascal. At the heart of this love triangle that leads to Sylvine's marriage to Pascal, appears *Hiram-Roi*, a Birman cat who belongs to Pascal. Moreover, he offers the "sacred cat" to the girl while telling her the legend. However, Hiram-Roi is only attached to Pascal, his soul mate. The cat then becomes a reflection of the young man's moods.

It was December 26, 1925 that the Birman cat appeared for the first time in literature. Here is the complete reproduction which concerns him.

But now, at the height of the pillow, he [Etienne] sees a small brown mask with blue eyes. Two otter-color legs [sic] with white fingers stretched outside of the bed, a purr unwinds like a spinning wheel. - What! the doctor exclaims, you let Hiram sleep with you again last night. Did I not prohibit you from doing that? He drew the wonderful beast to him. Long ivory bristles, gold

25

streaks on the back, tearful plumes like brown ostrich feathers, dark face lit by two sapphires of an incredible blue. In short, except for the immaculate gloves on the dark legs, the nuances of Siamese cats. But this flexible body, this great wavy fur, this camouflaged nose of a Belgian griffin, this rounded forehead, these intense azure eyes mark the sacred cat of Burma, of which Pascal is very proud. Hiram-Roi, without doubt, is, in France, the only specimen of this precious breed. The writer received the accolade of a British officer. Men of letters and artists delight in the society of pretty penates gods, with moonlit eyes. "O Hamilcar, silent guardian of the City of Books! »... Whispers Sylvestre Bonnard to his clawed friend. Etienne lies on the Hiram-Roi carpet and the water of the azure eyes turns black.

The following day, episode number 42 of December 27, 1925, returns to Hiram-Roi:

Then the young woman goes to the big Japanese couch on which Hiram-Roi was sprawled out like a discarded fur. The beautiful animal! In its face the color of scorched earth, its dark blue eyes are deep lakes. Sylvine spread out next to him, she voluptuously caresses the long cream bristles of the body which stretches up to her face. Hiram-Roi fixes her sapphire gaze on her, meditative and nostalgic, where a secret seems to sleep. He accepts tributes with a patronizing politeness, without delivering anything from the mystery of his azure soul.
"He won't tell you anything," said Pascal at last; he only speaks to me, this sacred cat. There are evenings, I assure you, where his tenderness mingled with mine, I feel that he understands me ... But yes, there are evenings ... when I am particularly sad. We know nothing about beings, or things ...
He smiles and Sylvine thinks that, as a matter of fact, a mystery is hidden in every creature. Pascal, no more than Hiram-Roi, lets nothing surprise the reasons that his reason, maybe, does not understand. He continues:
- I love this feline. I love him for his beauty, for his rarity ... and then, I have the impression that he knows what we are unaware of. He dominates me. By the way, you know that he comes from the Lao-Tsun temple. This unique temple, hidden in the high mountains of Burma, houses the last priests of a religion predating Brahmanism. These are the Kittahs, whose perfect souls are embodied in the bodies of sacred cats, before

26

conquering eternal bliss. Hiram-Roi must have been stolen from the holy men who worshiped him.
- Sylvine laughs.
- I no longer will dare to kiss her.

And the following, dated December 28, 1925, continues:

Madeleine Larsay, still busy with her embroidery, said in a quiet voice: - Pascal did not tell you that the Kittahs threaten the worst punishments on the imprudent who lift a sacrilegious hand to a sacred cat. Fancy that a divine spirit remains in Hiram-Roi. What would he think of his exile among us and your relatives? - Oh! said Pascal, I would believe, in fact, that he would take revenge if I did not feel loved by him. "Beware," said Madeleine, threatening him with a wagging finger. Sylvine continues: - Love him. Love is a talisman. - I like it, replies the writer. Then, turned to the singer, after a silence, he asks: - Do you like it? She answers: - How would I not? So, he said sharply, I'm giving it to you. You'll take him tomorrow. Stunned, Sylvine perked up: - Are you kidding? ... Standing, he obstinately shakes his head. No, no ... I told you that Hiram-Roi looked through my soul with his magic gaze. I give him to you. He will tell you about me. Madeleine, very pale, looks at the singer. - In your place, miss, I would fear the curses of this little expatriated god. Pascal refrains from answering. Sylvine hugs the sacred cat, without even feeling the claws that the animal, in a loving embrace, sank down into her throat.

In this first part of the novel, Mrs. Adam expresses her love for Birmans and for her own specimen, *Manou de Madalpour*, which serves as her inspiration: "I love him for his beauty, for his rarity..." According to an article published a few years later, in December 1931, there was a Birman cat named: Hiram-Roi. The

27

real Hiram-Roi is in fact a well-gloved Siamese with long hair, and also the father of Manou, the aforementioned cat belonging to Mrs. Adam. She therefore expresses her passion with all her lyrical verve as a writer. Note that it is traditional for breeders of the sacred cat to give a name, if not Birman, at least of Asian origin, to Birman kittens, which reinforces the legend of the cat. Thus, Manou de Madalpour, the first Birman male presented, takes his name from Hindu mythology, Manu, being the precursor of humanity, a kind of Indian Noah saved from the Flood.

These passages highlight Mrs. Adam's love for the rare cats she collects. This is how she acquired a Maracajá cat from Brazil around 1929, Dondoca, which she unfortunately had to quickly get rid of, because he did not get along with Manou:

So I adopted Dondoca. The tiger cat began to lay down the law at my place, not tolerating any authority, wandering among the trinkets as if through the jungle, and fixing on us its dark eyes of a cloudy color [...] I tried to get along with 'Dondoca'. I would never have filed for divorce if 'Manou de Madalpour', Sacred Cat of Burma, had not been threatened by the bloodthirsty South American. I was forced to consider a possible drama, and I resigned myself, not to divorce, but to the separation of body and wellbeing.

Let's go back to the first part of the soap opera of 1925: there we come across the first mention of the unique, hidden temple, of Lao-Tsun in Upper Burma and the probable theft of a sacred cat from mythical Hindu priests named Kittahs. We also learn that the cat seems to have arrived in France through the intermediary of a British officer whose name is revealed in the second part, in January 1926.

Indeed, it was not until January that the amplified story of the legend was uncovered. It appeared in episode 55 on January 9, 1926, at the start of the second part of the novel. But it is lined up in the previous episode as follows:

- Hiram-Roi should not be left lying around in the garden. This son of the gods is fragile. He has been losing weight for some time and is sad. - I noticed, replied the young woman. The Asian cat continued his nostalgic reverie on a corner of the lawn; his sapphire-colored eyes seeming to imprison all the sadnesses of exile. Sylvine took him slowly into her arms. - Poor little friend! she whispered, without anyone knowing what suffering she was complaining about in the princely beast. [...] "Hiram-Roi should be tend to," she said. He too is melancholy and I'm worried about that. She added: - Perhaps, you are wrong to let him always sleep at your side, at night. I remember that Etienne was against it. She felt the insistent golden-eyed gaze on her. - Why did he object? For fear of the epidemic? You know it perhaps. - No, she said, but no. With her palms pressed onto the marble top of a pedestal table, she was looking for a soothing freshness. Then she tried to break a silence in which their unexpressed worries were running. - Your mother lingers too much on these mountain paths, when night falls, she said. Bah! he retorted, "she is in Tardeta, she's bringing me some books from there. She will take a car back.

So, trembling upon once again hearing vocalized the fear that was rising in them, she said: - I love Hiram-Roi that you, one day, gave me. But he never stopped belonging to you. His soul remains linked to yours. He is gentle with everyone but he only knows you. He would be dead, for sure, if I had tried to take him from you. "He is mysterious," replied Pascal. What is true in the legend that marks its origins? - This legend, said Sylvine quickly, I don't know. You had to tell me it... It seemed to him that a breath of air was reaching him in a suffocating atmosphere. Pascal had the charming gift of storytelling, a gift where the enveloping music of the voice harmonized with the tender flame of the look, the facial expressions and the delightful little gestures. The words stood out, loudly, in the silence of the house. And from each of them were born living images softer and brighter than reality. The writer, half lying on the daybed, began his story, while

Sylvine numbed under his enchantments that were the dreams of Hiram-Roi.

It was therefore on January 9, 1926 that the legend finally appeared in its entirety, close to later documents:

- Here, said Pascal, the holy legend as it was told to me by Major Lesly, from whom I took my little feline god. Long before the coming of the Buddha, well before the birth of Brahmanism, even before Vyâsa had dictated the immortal words of his divine books, the Khmer people jealously guarded their temples, where the Kittahs, venerable priests lived so close to perfection that their spirit, before conquering eternal ecstasy, spent only in the body of a sacred cat, the duration of its animal existence. But, from the worlds' origin, the saints disapproved of those who did not sanctify themselves in their own way. As did the Brahmans who attacked the Kittahs and devoutly massacred them. However, some of the venerable ones were able to escape through the inviolable mountains of northern Burma and there they founded the underground temple of Lao-Tsun, which means dwelling of the gods.

This temple, Sylvine, is a wonder among the wonders of Indochina. Not far from a lake, it is lost in a chaos of immense peaks, and as if, by an extraordinary favor, my English friend was able to pass through there, it happened to him in order to protect the last Kittahs against the merciless Brahmans. He could then gaze upon the hundred sacred cats of worship and get to know their history.

- I see the scene as if in a beautiful film, murmured Sylvine.

Listen, said Pascal raising his hand with the gesture calling for attention, listen and first of all, hello to you, Hiram-Roi, "When with the malicious moon, came the 'phoums' or, if you prefer more clear wording, the damned Siamese-Thais, when these barbarians came to the mountains of the Lugh, to the Sun mountains, there was, at the temple of Lao-Tsun, the most precious of the precious: the one whose golden beard had been braided by the god Song-Hio himself. The Venerable had always lived in contemplation of Tsun-Kyanksé, the goddess with sapphire eyes who presides over the transmutations of souls, of which the number is counted. He never looked away from his sculpted image. His name was Mun-Hâ. He had an oracle without whom he made no decision: his cat Sinh, whom the other Kittahs revered with fervor."

- Oh wisdom, said Sylvine, to choose an oracle who does not speak!

Sinh, seated near his dreaded master, also lived in contemplation of the goddess. The beautiful animal! Her eyes were golden yellow, yellow with the reflection of Mun-Hâ's metallic beard and the amber body of the sapphire-eyed goddess. One evening, when the moon rose, the Thais approached the sacred precinct. So, invoking Fate threatening his people, Mun-Hâ died laden with years and anguish. He died before his goddess, having his divine cat with him. And the Kittahs lamented such a cruel loss, threatened by the invasion. At that moment, the miracle of the immediate transmutation occurred. Sinh leapt onto the holy throne, braced on the head of his collapsed master, facing the goddess. And the hairs of his white spine became golden and his eyes, his yellow eyes the golden yellow of Tsun-Kyanksé, yellow of the yellow of the beard woven by the god Song-Hio, his eyes became blue. Huge and deep sapphires, like the idol's eyes. Its four legs, the brown of the earth, its four feet which touched the venerable skull became white, to the tips of their toes purified by the contact with the mighty dead. He turned his precious gaze towards the southern door, which interpreted a stern, imperative order, which, pushed by an invincible force, the Kittahs obeyed. Thus they closed the bronze doors of the holy temple against their ancestral enemy. Then, passing through their underground passages, they routed the defilers. Sinh, refusing all food, never left the throne. He remained standing, facing the goddess, mysterious, hieratic, fixing his blue orbs on the sapphire eyes from which he took the flame and the sweetness. Seven days after Mun-Hâ's death, straight on white-purified legs, without lowering his eyelids, he died, taking the soul of Mun-Hâ, too perfect for earthly life, to Tsun-Kyanksé. But one last time, his gaze slowly turned to the southern gate, from which later came the Annamese and Cambodian hordes in full force.

- Hiram-Roi, said Sylvine, what soul watches over you? And, if you love us, why your sadness?

31

- Do we know? ... Ah! I have not finished my legend: Seven days after Sinh's death, the Kittahs assembled before Tsun-Kyanksé to decide on the succession of Mun-Hâ. So, oh wonder, they saw the one hundred cats slowly emerging from the temple in a troop. Their paws were gloved in white, their snowy coat had golden reflections, and the topaz of their eyes had turned into sapphires. The Kittahs bowed down in an attitude of devout awe. And they waited. Didn't they know that the soul of their ancestors inhabited the harmonious forms of sacred animals? These, serious and flexible, surrounded Ligoa, the youngest of the priests who thus knew the will of heaven.

- Poor Hiram! said Sylvine, you probably lament the mysterious paradise of Song-Hio, the god of gold?

- Do we know? said Pascal again. I like the nostalgia that comes with millennia of worship. The blue soul of Hiram-Roi weighs gently on mine, as if to mingle with it.

Then suddenly he laughed.

- How serious you are, Sylvine. You look like Tsun-Kyanksé as Hiram looks like Sinh. Our holy cat man was evidently stolen from the temple of Lao-Tsun by some criminal servant. The Kittahs, lost among their riches, are the fierce guardians of their old religion. Sir Lesly received, one day, this little living god from a native who did not disclose its origins. This native preferred to get rid of, no doubt, a sacred host capable of attracting vengeance from heaven and that of priests. And so Hiram came to me.

Silence continued to surround the house, pushing the limits of all things. You couldn't even make out the furious voice of the river Gave claiming a race to the bottom. A fear crossed Sylvine's mind. So that Pascal did not notice the shadow of it, she hid her face in the soft fur of Hiram-Roi.

- How long your mother is taking to come back! she said.

Clearly, this silence was becoming intolerable to her. She put the sacred cat on Pascal's lap and sat at the piano..." (p. 5).

This first published account of the legend of the sacred cat of Burma puts forward a number of facts which mix myth and reality. It talks about a British officer, "Major Lesly," who is said to have protected the Kittah priests from a Brahmin attack; it talks about the Khmer people, before the establishment of Buddhism in Indochina, but emphasizing the existence of a temple still attached to a Hindu religion which disappeared several millennia ago; this "underground" temple is located in the Lugh mountains and is called Lao-Tsun, which meant "dwelling place of the gods;" it speaks of unknown priests, the last of their race, the Kittahs; there is talk of an attack by the Thais ("phoums") against the temple (but they also later become Annamites and Cambodians); it talks about a god of gold (Song Hio), an ancient goddess with sapphire eyes (Tsun Kyanksé); it talks about white cats with yellow eyes that turn blue; and finally we learn that a sacred cat had been stolen from the temple by a servant who had "given" it to Sir Lesly.

This serial will be republished in a novel eleven months later, on October 28, 1926, under the title of *Eros Vaincu*, published by Albin Michel, but, very strangely, two things changed at the end of the year.

First, the major's name. His name is no longer Lesly, but Russel (p. 224). And above all, the entire extended chapter on the legend transmitted by it has completely disappeared. Only the first abridged description of the legend remains.

The big question that arises then is that raised by Ms. Marcelle Adam herself in the *Matin's* soap opera: "It is mysterious ... What is true in the legend which marks its origins?"

There is in this account a great confusion around the concept of Brahmanism. The Brahmans are a religious caste of Hinduism dedicated solely to the study of sacred books (including the book of Manu) and not taking up arms. Brahmanism, associated with Hinduism, was replaced by Buddhism in the 14th century in Indochina, following the Thai invasions which effectively eliminated the caste system. The religion of the so-called Kittahs, is designated as both pre-Brahmanist, and as still existing in a unique, underground and inviolable temple in Burma.

The legend presented by Mrs. Adam mentions a pre-Vyâsa era. Vyâsa is a mythical Indian sage who would be the first to have written down the ancient sacred accounts, the Vedas, thus being the editor of the Mahâbhârata and the Purânas (the "divine books" mentioned by Mrs. Adam). He would have lived around the third, or perhaps the fifth century, before Christ. The premises of the legend therefore go back more than 2,000 years, to a mythical time. At that time a pre-Hindu religion would have existed giving a large place to the animals, which honors a goddess and has a category of special priests, the Kittahs. There is, of course, no documentation of this existence. This name comes close to the English "kitties" (colloquial name for cats) or, strictly speaking, Low Latin "catus." This religion would have been practiced among the Khmers in Indochina. The advantage of a legend prior to Vyâsa is that it is based on an oral tradition without any written record, since Vyâsa marks the transition from orality to writing.

What then does the notion of "Khmer people" correspond to? Various studies appeared at the time on this subject. The French are present in Indochina: Cambodia, Laos, Cochinchina and Vietnam (Annam), countries bordering Burma, and also mentioned in the legend at the end of the story with the prophetic announcement of the invasion of the Annamese and Cambodian hordes. It is therefore a story that is, in fact, written in the context of the French colonies in Indochina. Most of the newspapers of the time had a daily column, even an entire page, which chronicled events, such as the "Colonial Page" of the *Petit Marseillais*, which published on January 9, 1924 "The

History of Laos, this little-known jewel of French Indochina" (p. 5).

The previous twenty years have seen the appearance of various studies based on the monuments discovered in Indochina (notably with the help of Auguste Pavie which we will talk about later) in particular, in the Cambodian jungle, the extraordinary, abandoned temple of Anghkor. Let us first quote, *The Acts of the French Colonial Congress* and the Debriefing of the 1908 conferences, the first line of Session XVI which deals with "Sociology and Ethnography" in a presentation on "The Indigenous Populations of Cambodia and Laos", by Mr Émile Chauffard. His article is based on the first two volumes of the Pavie Mission in Indochina book, where it is stated that: "Cambodia was once a powerful empire. Its prodigious story has been completely forgotten. Grandiose ruins, some legends are the only vestiges. Today Cambodia is under the French protectorate. Without France's intervention, this fallen country would be no more, where the invading Siam and Annam were already meeting. [...] The indigenous and dominant race in Cambodia is the Khmer race. It is of Hindu origin. The Khmers practice the pure Buddhist religion." (p. 339). Likewise, in Laos, we learn that: "The vast majority of the Laos population are of Thai race, of Hindu origin, like the Khmer race, which it is very close to. [...] In the mountains and the forests live scattered tribes, generally less civilized than the Thais and of very diverse origins, which one confuses under the name of Khas" (p. 344). These Khas live in the mountains and only believe in genies for religion. The article also underlines that: "In Laos as in Cambodia, beautiful ruins, especially mausoleums, dating from the 15th century, remain alone to bear witness to a very old civilization that has disappeared." The conference and the following article of the congress presented on the same subject by Dr Noël Bernard, doctor-major of the colonial troops, add on the Laos that the Khas (also called Penongs) are of Indonesian origin, have 60 tribes and leave in the mountains (thus on the Birman border) a fierce existence. He also mentions the people of the Great River who speak the Thai language, in particular, the white, black and red Pou-Thaïs (according to the color of their clothes) who come from Yunnam and Thibet.

The same year (1908), lectures offered at the Guimet Museum were also published, notably that of M. L. de Milloué on *Le Temple d'Anghkor*. This article on the history of the Khmers indicates that "... from the 14th century, following [a] Thäi invasion [...] the Khmer empire [was overthrown] and [we have] substituted Buddhism for Brahmanism as a state and popular religion." (p. 93). In addition:

According to an indigenous tradition, [...] The Khmers were conquerors who invaded Indo-China at a time which one can place approximately between the third century before and the second century after our era. [...] they would have gradually driven back the indigenous Kam population. [...] The name of Kambodjas appears in the Mahabharata, the oldest poem of India, among the people who take part in the great war between the Pandavas and the Kauravas, and the Manava Dharma Castra or Code of Laws of Manou, also quotes the Kambodjas, in his enumeration of the neighboring peoples of India who, of Aryan origin and of Kchatriya caste, have degraded and have lost their caste as a result of the non-observance of Brahmanic rites and the lack of Brahmins to teach them the Vedic law and make sacrifices. Neither the Mahabharata nor the Manava Dharma Castra specify the dwelling place of these Kambodjas, which appears to be placed in the north of Burma, in the region later called the Pegou kingdom. It is therefore admissible to suppose that the Khmers, conquerors of Cambodia, belonged to this Kambodjas people of Mahabharata and Manou." (p. 94-95).

The article on Anghkor also notes that this ancient monument mixes two religions: "... in these ruins we found a number of statues of Brahmanic deities, gods and goddesses, but none in place, and some Buddhist statues" (p. 98). Anghkor is therefore the temple of transition, built before the arrival of Buddhism in the region. "We have seen that in the 14th century, Buddhism took the place of Brahmanism and, since then, the Buddhist clergy has monopolized the charge of maintaining sacred buildings.... However, Brahmanism has not been completely dethroned, and still today Brahmins officiate, together with Buddhists, in official ceremonies." (p. 113). And further on: "The temple must have been dedicated to the Brahman cult, and it was only later, during the overthrow of the Khmer dynasty by an invasion of Thai Buddhists, around the 14th century, that the victors substituted the images of the Buddha for the mutilated statues of the Brahmanism gods, the religion of the Khmers." (p. 121).

The legend presented by Mrs. Adam in *L'Amour qui Tremble*, takes certain elements from these publications and then mixes and rearranges them into a chaotic mess. The historical tension between the Thai Buddhists having eliminated or supplanting the precedent Brahmanism, and the destroying or abandoning of the Hindu Khmer peoples' temples in Laos and Cambodia in the 14th century, serve as the basis for the story. The legend is displaced by two thousand years and becomes the shift of the Kittahs in the "Lugh mountains" due to the Brahman (and no

38

longer the Thai Buddhist) invasions of Lower Indochina. The flight to the Birman mountains by the Kittahs is also a return to the original land of the first Khmer people. Then comes the survival of a temple hidden for centuries and, at a certain time in its history, the sudden reappearance of the invading Brahmins who are called "phoum-thai" (or Siamese) and the attack of the "well-hidden temple". We recognize here the "pou-thaï" mentioned by Dr Noël Bernard, who lived near the big river, "lower" (in the plains). Although no date is given here for the mythical appearance of the Birman cat, following this attack, it first seems to coincide with the invasion of Thai Siamese in Khmer country and the elimination of Brahmanism, replaced by Buddhism in the 14th century.

The third stage of the legend leads us to the gates of the 20th century, with the British major Lesly who would have helped the last Kittahs resist against Brahman Thai invaders (which is a contradiction of terms) and would have had access to the secret temple to one hundred cats, as thanks for his service. We are then led to believe that we have passed from myth to history when the mentioned enemy no longer exists, since there are only Thai Buddhists left at that time. This major would also have been the one who brought a stolen cat back to France.

Note that the Khas mountain tribes are also etymologically close to the name Kittah. One last word about them: an article from the newspaper *La Croix* of July 12, 1921, on "Laos", says about the Laotian population: "The one that exists is made up of Laotians in the plains or valleys, of Kha [sic] in the mountains. The first are indolent, depressed perhaps by their too-old civilization attested by so many monuments or by the destructive and successive invasions suffered. The Hos come from the north periodically to raid women, the Siamese come from the South to provide slaves. Their last incursion dates only from 1892 when most of the able-bodied population of a province, in the Muong-Khang region, was kidnapped. Out of 10,000 men abducted, 6,000 died of disease and misery before reaching their destination in Siam. Needless to say, since our intervention, these facts have been a thing of the past. The Kha or Moï are still savages, nomadic hunters and great forest destroyers, but it is possible to count on their assistance as conveyors or keepers of cattle or brushcutters." (p. 3).

On the other hand, the name of the deity and that of the temple, both having the form Tsun coupled in suffix or prefix, are also problematic, since it is a completely Chinese term and not Birman. There is of course no historical record of these places or god names. It should first be noted that "Lao-Tsun" is very close to the famous name of Lao-Tse, or Lao-Tzu (as it was written at that time), the wise founder of Taoism. His name (老子 Lǎo Zǐ) means, in Mandarin, "old master" and not "dwelling of the gods." However, according to literature professor and Mandarin scholar Dr. James Wicks, Tsun can also mean "village." So, the other possible translation for Lao-Tsun would be "old village." We are still no closer to the translation offered in the legend. The affix "Tsun" is found in two of the legendary names: Lao-Tsun and Tsun Kyanksé; this affix was used at the time when the Birman legend was written and published.

Indeed, the 1920s were marked by the troubles caused by the Warlords in China. From 1920, newspapers regularly reported the events which agitated China, in particular the military operations of General Wou-Pei-Fou against his rivals near Beijing. One city is consistently cited in connection with these fights, that of Huang-Tsun. We should also note the massacre of missionaries on October 30, 1920 in Tung-Ching-Tsun. "Tsun, in these two cases, means "city or village" and is found in many names of Chinese cities. In 1920, there were also two serials published in daily newspapers at the time, where we find this form "Tsun" in a Chinese context, which was the fashionable literary subject. The first is *The Master of Silence. The Secret of Kou-kou-noor* of Delly, published in the *Journal de Roanne,* and also in the *Mémorial de La Loire.* One of the characters in Shanghai is called "Li-Lee-Tsun". The second is *The Goddess of the Red Lantern* by Edith Wherry, published in 1921 in the soap opera of "L'Humanité". In the April 26 episode, the author mentions that the last empress of China has the nickname "Lao-Tzu-Tsung," i.e. "the great ancestor," or "more respectfully, 'the old Buddha'" (column 5. p. 3).

Finally, it should be added that "Lao" is the name on the maps of the time designating Laos and that the inhabitants of the Laos mountains are called "Lao Sung" ("Lao of Summits").

This faulty translation of the term Tsun as "gods" in the legend of the Birman cat, results in the recurrence of this term as a suffix in the names given to several cats. For example, on February 9, 1929, *Le Petit Journal* mentions the presence of a Birman cat with this suffix:

"Nadi Tsun." Her owner gives the journalist a so-called "translation," "Aimée des dieux" (Loved by the gods).

At this point in the history of the Birman cat in France, in any case, we weren't concerned with the historical truth of what is presented as a legend.

This entertaining tale presents all the characteristics of what was beginning to be called Fantasy—mixing the charm of Eastern religions and magical metamorphoses with the motif of the last survivors of a forgotten mythical people.

Like Conan the Cimmerian, the barbarian of Howard, or the albino sorcerer Elric of Melniboné, invented by Moorcock, the Kittahs are the last of their kind.

CHAPTER 2

FIRST INTERNATIONAL CAT SHOW OF PARIS: MAY 1926

A revelation...

The first mention of the Birman in France that I could spot, is found in the results of the *Féline d'Angers Exhibition* of June 14, 1925. A young Birman cat (entered as Number 317) with a certain Mme Léotardi as its owner won the first prize in the "Birman Cats" category and the third prize in the "Young Cats" category (from 3 to 12 months). The name of this cat is not indicated.

The Parisian public discovered the Birman cat a year later, on May 14 and 15, 1926, in the Wagram Hall among 175 cats exhibited during the first International Feline Exposition. It was during this event that the first press photo of the Birman, showing Manou de Madalpour in the arms of Mrs. Marcelle Adam, was published. This photo, taken by the *Rol Agency* and other photographers, is dated precisely May 14, 1926, and will become the favorite photo of the Birman in a number of newspapers. This exhibition was organized by veterinarians and artists, such as Mr. Fernand Méry (founding secretary general of the *Société Centrale Féline*), and was chaired by Mrs. Marcelle Adam and the Veterinarian Lépinay. *Le Petit Journal* of May 14, 1926 stated:

Mme Marcelle Adam
avec son chat sacré de Birmanie
(Photo Henri Manuel.)

Cats are not made for children and old girls alone. Their deep eyes also move writers and artists. And it is not at all surprising to see, among the members of the *Cat Club of France*, whose feline exhibition opened in the Wagram Hall, Claude Farrère, Mme Colette, Guy de Téramond and many others... What beautiful specimens are gathered there! Siamese, white and blue Persians, real angora, Birman cats, and even the tailless cat from the Isle of Man. There is something for everyone and everyone is admirable." (p. 3).

"Moussi," the blue Persian of Mlle Marcelle Brégy from the *Porte Saint Martin* theater, and the sacred Birman cat by Mrs. Marcelle Adam, shared the photos of the front pages of newspapers *L'Ouest-Eclair*, *Le Petit Journal* for Moussi, and *Le Siècle*, *Comœdia*, and *Le Petit Journal* for Manou.

Pierre Causse of *Intransigent* reported this on May 15:

À L'EXPOSITION DES CHATS

(Photos *Petit Journal*)
Deux lauréats et leurs « mères »
En bas, un joli spécimen de chat de Birmanie

Placed on trestles and aligned in 15 parallel rows, small metal cages contain and let visitors see the most beautiful cat specimens. Lying voluptuously on these embroidered cushions, arranged with maternal solicitude by their owners, the pretty beasts, bear with disdain the examination of connoisseurs. The eyes of gold and jade buried in silky furs turn away, haughty and bored by the human gazes. [...] The members of the jury inspect, one by one, cats from Spain, Holland, Burma or China.

On May 14, *L'Homme Libre* highlighted the presence of "extremely rare cats from Burma" (p. 2), while on May 16, Jean Dorsenne in the *Journal des Débats Politiques et Littéraires* specifically devoted several lines to Birman cats on the first page:

It must be believed that "fervent lovers and austere scholars" are legion in Paris, because the crowd was large that thronged yesterday, Wagram Hall, at the cat show organized by the Cat-Club of France. [...] The cats of Burma, aristocratic and haughty in their moonlight dress, posed languishly on their cushions. Their owners, to best showcase them, have stretched pastel blue, vintage pink or daffodil fabrics over the cages. The stall is transformed into an artist's dressing room. But, in lieu of vases full of precious orchid flowers, here is a full cup of milk or a saucer garnished with small pieces of raw meat. (p. 1).

Emile Condroyer indicated in his May 15 article, "The feline exhibition and His Majesty Fourrée", that the "Cats of Burma, whiter than porcelain, have a wild glow at the bottom of their globes which fill these glaucous reflections enclosed in the moonstones ..." (p. 1). In the May 15 issue of *Comœdia* the journalist "S. R." asked, "Do the most beautiful cats come from Asia?", while Mrs. Marcelle Adam in her article cited how the Sacred Cat of Burma "contemplates with impenetrable eyes a court of admirers." (p. 1).

These Birman cats seem to be only two in number, a female and a male: *Madalpour Poupée* (for Mrs. Léotardi) and *Manou de Madalpour* (for Mrs. Marcelle Adam). But an article from 1927 suggests that there were perhaps three. One of the most beautiful general accounts of this exhibition is that of Gaëtan Sanvoisin, "Le Club des Chats", which appeared in *Le Gaulois* on May 15, 1926. Here are some extracts:

It has been installed since yesterday and for today, in the Wagram Hall. *The Federation of Feline Societies of France* has succeeded in exposing the International of meowing, because, in their respective small boxes, all species are represented; luxury cats from Spain, Holland and China; silver cats from the island of

Cyprus, Gambia, Burma; light chocolate Siamese cats; orange and fawn cats of the Cape of Good Hope; cats ... from Persia. [...]

The great event of the exhibition is *Pharmacy of Mayfield*, a superb breeding male [Persian], white as an ermine, and who, born on January 22, 1922, is worth, it seems, twelve thousand francs! Each of his cubs is listed for eight hundred francs at the time of birth [...] Each cat, moreover, is lying in a circle, on soft and ornate cushions, under a small curtain. Despite the belled collar or ribbon, in which some were decked out as if in a frivolous enslavement, they observed this hieratic and somewhat disdainful attitude which concerned Verlaine and gave Baudelaire reason to celebrate. They rarely fix the gloomy strangeness of their 'mystical pupils' on visitors, and even in front of the female audience, the majority of whom flock to their boxes, they carry on with the indolence of their dreamy rest. However, the sudden points of phosphorus that light up in their eyes are sometimes captivating like a woman's look, and there is a lot of similarity, if not tacit complicity, between these two indefinable versatilities [...] Buyers are not uncommon. They have, it is true, an easy choice among the three hundred and fifty specimens on display. And, through the dense crowd of visitors - a bizarre fact: one speaks almost quietly, as if in secrecy - Veterinarian Hasse, Mrs Natham coming and going, busy. They are the influential members of the jury. The names of committee members are cited: Mr. Claude Farrère, Countess Hocquart de Turtot, Princess Guy de Faucigny-Lucinge, Mrs. Jacques Keller, Mrs. Desjardins, the Marquise de Scey-Montbéliard, Ms. Guzman Blanco, Mrs. Colette, MM. Paul Brulat and Guy de Téramond, the viscountess of the Méloizes. [...]

In front of each cat, a small bowl is placed, containing its minced meat food. The simmering muzzle approaches, fond, delicate and fearful, smells the food and seems to search it before swallowing it up, then, suddenly, the head is raised, and there is, with this movement of withdrawal, a cruel sweetness in the half-closed look and in the humidity of the pink tongue. [...] Sumptuous luxury angoras, companions of the scientists, confidants of the lovers, objects of so many feminine delicacies, you will soon return to your familiar nooks or you will know new homes. To get there, for a few hours you will have to resign yourselves to transport in charmless wicker baskets; but you know very well, from Pliny and Diodorus of Sicily, that we still reserve for you, as formerly in Memphis, the veneration simultaneously uncertain and noble of familiar deities. (Col. 2).

This from the July 1926 report of *Vie à la Campagne*: "We have noted with great pleasure the interest taken in the Persian, of which few people can, until now, appreciate the sweetness and the pleasant character, of the Birman Cat, so rare that those whom the public could admire in Paris are perhaps the only known specimens, to the Siamese, a little more widespread" (p. 276).

As can be seen in the photo of the Siamese and Birman medalists from the 1926 show (p. 277), there is great resemblance in the case of these two cat breeds. Note that the owner of the Siamese above *Poupée de Madalpour*, Mahout, is Mrs. Chaumont, who will also start breeding Birmans later.

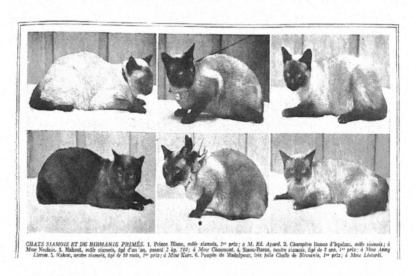

CHATS SIAMOIS ET DE BIRMANIE PRIMÉS. 1. Prince Blanc, mâle siamois, 1er prix; à M. Ed. Apard. 2. Champion Banco d'Ispahan, mâle siamois; à Mme Nochain. 3. Mahout, mâle siamois, âgé d'un an, pesant 3 kg. 760; à Mme Chaumont. 4. Siaou-Rauna, neutre siamois, âgé de 2 ans, 1er prix; à Mme Anny Lierow. 5. Kakou, neutre siamois, âgé de 20 mois, 1er prix; à Mme Kurz. 6. Poupée de Madalpour, très jolie Chatte de Birmanie, 1er prix; à Mme Léutardi.

CHAPTER 3

WHO COMES FIRST? ... THE EGG OR THE CHICKEN?

The origin of the Birman discussed...

The second fundamental article on the Birman cat can be found in number 280 of *La vie à la Campagne*,

dated October 1, 1926. It is, once again, signed by the veterinarian Philippe Jumaud who controlled public opinion on the subject and will even influence the perception of the Siamese cat, a close cousin of this one. Its title is an entire program in itself: "The Birman Cat, sacred animal. Characterized breed, which is said to be the origin of the Siamese and which is clearly distinguished from the long-haired Asian races, with which the subjects do not sympathize." (see Annex).

In fact, this text repeats what Philippe Jumaud had already published in his two books of 1925 and 1926, but notes a considerable change as well. Doctor Jumaud had given on July 31, 1926, on the occasion of the fiftieth session of the *French Association for the Advancement of Sciences*, in Lyon, a conference on "The Cat of Burma", the full text of which is absent from the report published in 1927. Only the title remains. This absence is probably due to the fact that the doctor had already published the contents of his presentation in two books that year and probably requested that his presentation not appear in the volume. However, we do not know if he continued his initial notice, or if his communication to the academic veterinary world already contained what is presented 3 months later, in the article of *La Vie à la Campagne* in October 1926. One can assume this is the case, unless questions raised by the scientific audience at the congress led him to do more research and produce this new amplified version, which would contain data with a stronger appearance of scientific credibility.

This long text would become the canonical document regarding the origin of the Birman cat. At the same time, it is also included in the new edition of *Les Races de Chats* of 1926, replacing the 1925 text. Information concerning the origin of the cat can be found, oddly enough, at the beginning and end of the article.

First, the mention of the American millionaire Vanderbilt has disappeared completely and is replaced by an unknown feminine name out of the blue which constitutes a new intermediate link in the fabricated story: Mrs. Thadde Hadish. In addition, a new character, another British major, also appears in the first part of the story: Major Russel Gordon.

The Birman Cat is native to the Far East. Subjects of this race, raised in temples, are severely guarded, and their removal was prohibited. However, a couple was imported by Mrs. Thadde Hadish (the couple who gave birth to the "Madalpour" family); this couple was probably stolen by a servant of the temple, dazzled by promises and would have fled to avoid punishment, because, for those who know the fanaticism of the Hindus, no one will ever believe that the priests sold, even at a fabulous price, a couple of their sacred animals. Major Sir Russel Gordon, one of the British troops charged with protecting the Kittahs, had the opportunity in 1898 to observe these sacred animals. He drew up a standard which substantiates that which was established in the 1925 doctoral thesis. (p. 402).

Little is known about Mrs. Thadde Hadish, to say the least. This newcomer who replaces Mr. Vanderbilt has a rather exotic name. Hadish is a Persian word which means "heavens". It is also almost the term used to designate the words attributed to the Prophet Muhammad. Associated with a Hebrew forename as extremely rare as the Birman itself, "Thadde" (or "Thaddeus" which is mainly masculine and the name of one of the twelve apostles), it can comprise a Jewish or Persian name. Nowhere to be found is there any trace of this wealthy adventurer who, by sleight of hand, obtained a couple of Birmans, sold/gave a single female from the original couple, Poupée, to Mrs. Léotardi and disappeared from history afterward. This lady would have imported directly from Burma the parent couple of the cat named Poupée. Which would also imply that she was English and traveled to Upper Burma. But how did she end up in the south of France and then disappear? The French population registers do not contain any trace of the existence of this person, neither in Vienne (a city mentioned that will appear later in the legend) nor, moreover, in the rest of France.

Indeed, the name Hadish is extremely rare. There was a family of tailors in New England who emigrated to New York in 1868 with that name. It was a Jewish family of which no member was named Thadde, according to the records. The only mention of the surname in American newspapers of the time dates from December 19, 1922; it appears in several regional newspapers and especially in the *New York Herald,* which had a European edition in Paris. It talks about a certain Josephine Hadisch who narrowly escaped death in a train accident near Boston, in the Providence Express of December 18: "Seven persons were injured [...] Miss Josephine Hadisch of North Bergen , NJ, a passenger, [...] [was] the most seriously injured. [...] Miss Hadisch escaped instant death by a hair's breadth. [...] When the help came it was found the rail had fastened itself in the woodwork of the car wall, this stopping it just as it touched Miss Hadisch's forehead. At a Boston hospital tonight it was said her injuries might prove fatal." (p. 6).

Here was an exotic lady who fell from the sky and not a soul has been able to meet her for verification. She came onto the scene and left directly for the needs of the cause and has never been seen in an exhibition. Next is an explanatory paragraph on the problems raised by this daring appearance and the possible theft of cats from the temple by a servant who fled as quickly as Mrs. Hadish, and therefore cannot be identified. This chain of facts is therefore, as Dr. Jumaud put it, only "probable:" it is a question of conjectures on his part in an attempt to rationalize the elements that were provided to him. Here is what Mr. Marcel Baudoin-Crevoisier, an important Birman breeder of the time (1928-33), said in his article on "Le Chat de Birmanie" published in the July 1931 issue of the *Belgian Feline Review*:

Firstly for information, let's go back to the origin. It seems to me quite confusing. According to some, Poupée is the starting point. This female being full, she was crossed with her children to create the Madalpour strain belonging to Madame Fradich [sic] from Vienne. These cats, supposedly, come from the Lao-Tsun Temple in Burma ... This underground, inviolable and sacred temple, etc ... It is a bit like something out of a novel ... All these origins are surrounded by a certain legend which perhaps sounds very well, but which gives no official information. Others have told me that billionaire Vanderbilt is no stranger to the importation of Birmans into France. Obviously we are in the realm of fantasy. Reality is less funny." (pp. 4-5).

One question leading to another, one can also wonder what happened to the original progenitor couple of the first Birman, Madalpour Poupée. The answer will come later ... but not in this text.

The Abbey Marcel Chamonin, who later took the pseudonym Marcel Reney, another Birman breeder of the time and creator of the Geneva Cat Club, published an article entitled "In favor of the Cats of Burma" in issue 197 of the review *Chasse, Pêche, Élevage* in November 1933. He declared:

If Mrs. Thadde Hadisch (I am not sure on the spelling of this name) really lived, and if she is still alive, would it not be possible to ask her for a complete and detailed account of the arrival in Europe of the first Birmans? And if she is no longer around, relatives will be able to satisfy our legitimate curiosity, because, for animals of such a strange origin, and of such value, the documents have not been destroyed. Besides, one of our readers has letters, perhaps, relating to this subject "(p. 3.931).

And in the book which he published fifteen years later in 1947, "Nos Amis les Chats," Reney-Chamonin adds: "I sought to have new details on the existence of Mrs. Thadde Hadish and on Mrs. Léotardi; it was in vain." (p. 179).

The second newly-introduced character is Major Sir Russel Gordon. The legend of Mme Adam published in *Le Matin* in 1925-26 also contains a major, but with a different name: Major Lesly. He is therefore a newcomer with the same profession. As we saw in the first chapter, the change of Major was carried out by Mrs. Marcelle Adam between January and October 1926. We are thus referring to Jumaud's text and the revised version of Mme Adam's novel *Éros Vaincu* at the same time. I would even say that the change must have been made after February 12, 1926, the publication date of Jumaud's second book, *Le Chat*, which does not show this change between spring and summer. It would not be surprising that the first Feline Exhibition in Paris in May 1926, was the culmination point of questioning and reorganization of the fable, because it constitutes the first great presentation in the world of the Birman cat, and consequently raises the litigations of its origins.

The so-called Russel Gordon, "major stationed in Burma," is therefore the new anchor of the argument and the main "historical" source of the Birman legend. Under cover of this seemingly respectable authority figure, the seriousness and authenticity of the story are reinforced by a series of historical, scientific, and geographical references worthy of the contemporary work of Auguste Pavie. Again, it is impossible to know exactly who this officer is or to find any trace whatsoever of a Russell Gordon (common Scottish surname) in the British archives.

Towards the end of his 1926 article, Jumaud inserted a long paragraph on the major and his contribution to the legend.

To complete this study on the Birman Cat, here are some notes from Sir Russel Gordon demonstrating that the Siamese come from the cross of Annamite Cats and Birman Cats. 'Actually, I think, and the learned explorer Auguste Pavie thinks with me, that the Siamese Cat is a cross between the Sacred Cat of Burma and the Annamite Cats imported during the XVIIth century into the Khmer Empire, at the time when the decline of this strictly-closed empire was taking place under the action of the Siamese and the Annamites. Already in the 6th century, the 'Thai' (Siamese) invaded the Khmers (Cambodians and Birman) and developed their power at their expense. The Khmers have always been resistant to the influence of Brahamic India. Their absolutely closed religion, very secret to the common people and the laymen, was consecrated by all-powerful and very venerated priests, the "Kittahs," These priests were mercilessly massacred and hunted down by the Brahmans during the second Thai invasion, at the beginning of the 18th century. Those who were able to escape took refuge in Upper North Burma, among the inviolable mountains and founded the underground temple of Lao-Tsun (dwelling of the gods).

The Lao-Tsun temple is undoubtedly one of the curious wonders of India that very few mortals have been called to behold. Located east of Lake Incaougji, between Magaoug and Sembo, in a nearly barren region of impassable wall barriers. There, the last Kittahs still lived in 1898, and I was, by extraordinary favor, allowed to observe them somewhat with their sacred animals. Following the rebellion and during the English occupation, at the base of Bhamo– a base very isolated because of its distance from Mandalay–we had to protect the Kittahs against a Brahman invasion, and we saved them from a massacre and a guaranteed pillage. Their Lamah-Kittah, the Yotagi, received me and presented me with a plaque representing the Sacred Cat at the foot of a bizarre deity whose eyes are made of two elongated sapphires (part 4.108 from my Mildenhall collection) and after having allowed me to contemplated the hundred Sacred Cats (a supreme favor), explained to me their origin.'

The legend is pretty, but it doesn't explain anything scientifically. It is certain that a race of Annamite Cats with yellow eyes, with slender and elegant forms, of small size, of the naturally short tail, had been, at some time, introduced in Burma with the invasion. Studies link this cat to that of the Isle of Man (tailless cat), and this animal would have been imported by English caravels in India, around the 18th century. [...] (p. 402).

Several breeders of the time tried to meet Gordon without success. In his 1933 article, Marcel Chamonin questions:

Russel Gordon's story has certainly been published: but in what journal or in what work? In addition, this plaque should have been saved, but in which museum or collection? Wouldn't it have been possible to get an authentic photograph of it? Couldn't our English friends help us in our research?"

There would be no response. Ms. Alwyn Hill, an English Birman breeder, researched this more recently in England, notably in the five volumes of the Gazetteer of Upper Burma. She could not find a Russell Gordon, but a Ramsay Gordon with the same initials who seems to be the only one who could match, possibly, to the time period and the place in the British Indian army. In France, there is no trace of a "Ramsey" Gordon except in Le Gaulois of March 9, 1926 (p. 2), where he was designated as a captain and arrived from Cannes. The rank of Captain is below that of a Major, so he cannot be Major before 1926. However, Mrs. Hill declares that French newspapers were wrong about his rank, which is not impossible, given the lack of rigor of the journalists of the time. She also found on an old map, a village in Upper

Burma called Law-Son, a name phonetically similar to the temple of Lao-Tsun. However, one must coerce reasoning to reach satisfactory conclusions. I am not convinced, while still I acknowledge this fine effort. We also have Robert Gordon, an engineer in the Birman ruby mines, and a spy for the British Empire before the invasion of the north of the country in 1885, but he was not an officer. However, in 1880 he produced one of the first sophisticated maps of Burma which mentions in its part the Lao people (Laotians). Note also that Major Gordon is also reportedly linked to a small English town in Suffolk, Mildenhall; here again, the address does not correspond to anything, but keep in mind the existence of this place—we will come back to this later.

The only thing we can be sure of in this text by Jumaud is that he had in his possession written documents authorizing his assertions on the origin of this cat, which served him as the basis to his doctoral thesis on "Les Races de Chats" of 1925. But documents have never been published independently. There seems to have been a letter from Major Russel Gordon affirming the existence of a temple with Birman cats and reporting a conversation with the illustrious explorer Auguste Pavie; a description of the Birman cat standard established by Gordon; the general text of the legend, probably written by Gordon; and finally, a text or letter from Auguste Pavie on the genetic relationship between the Birman and the Siamese.

Still, according to Jumaud, the Kittahs are from Cambodia and their departure for Upper Burma following the various Annamese and Siamese invasions occurred during the 17th century. There were, indeed, Annamite and Siamese invasions in the course of the 18th century—that of Komping Cham in 1768 for the Annamites, and the annexation of Battamgang, Sisophon and Angkor, between 1795-96 for the Siamese. The addition of these vaguely historical elements purports to corroborate the fable.

At the same time, the presumed place of origin of the Birman Cat located in a territory which had recently become British, is not very well known. The struggle for influence and the colonial rivalries between England and France at the end of the 19th century most likely prevented the French from easily wandering on Birman territory: Auguste Pavie, representative of the French government in Indochina, for example, never set foot there. The border between Burma and Laos is not easily crossable for an official Frenchman, and besides, the situation in the whole region was very unstable due to the frequent revolts against the British. It is therefore necessary to have recourse to an English character. Besides, Jumaud noted that Gordon saw the underground temple and its hundred cats as part of a mission to protect the Kittahs against Thai-Brahmans in 1898, precisely. However, this date does not correspond to any revolt or invasion in the British protectorate, as Gisèle Barnay and Simone Poirier already pointed out in their book Les *Secrets du Chat Sacré de Birmanie* :

The region where Philippe Jumaud situates the legendary temple is in the northeast of Burma, near Mogaug and Myitkyina, not very far from the border located in the Kachin state of the Union of Burma [Myanmar today]. According to Guy Lubeigt, researcher at CRNS and project manager in Burma, where he has lived and studied for eighteen years, the Kachin country was perfectly calm in 1898 and there is no trace of "'Brahman invasions "... Coming from where? [...] Mr Lubeigt also recalls that there are no lamas in Burma "where Buddhism is Tantric," he says, "disappeared in the 18th century." Birman monks bear the name of pondgi or séyado (venerable, superior, abbot). He adds that a Lao-Tsun temple has never existed in Burma and that the cat is not, in this country, a sacred or protected animal. (p. 38).

The scientific backing provided by the alleged Major Gordon is therefore a complete sham which hardly conceals the improbabilities of the legend. Our attention shifts to Auguste Pavie, the text's second scientific and historical authority.

Born in 1847, Auguste Pavie was in charge of Mission for France in Indochina between 1879 and 1895; intrepid explorer of Laos and Cambodia, diplomat, zoologist and vice-consul of France to Luang Prabang in 1886, he sent several specimens of Siamese to France in 1885. As far as Indochina is concerned, it is the authority of reference. In his book: *Zoologie, Mission Pavie. Recherches sur l'histoire naturelle de l'Indo-Chine Orientale,* he noted:

I have unnecessarily sought what in Indochina could be the origin of the pretty species of domestic cat, particularly sweet and caressing that we call the Siamese cat and that the Siamese call the Laotian Cat. The ones I sent to the

Museum came from Bangkok, the only place where we can currently get them.

Auguste Pavie dispatched actually four Siamese cats and two "fishing cats" to the *Jardin d'Acclimatation Museum*, now known as the *Jardin des Plantes*, through zoologist Émile Oustalet. A little further in his mission report he still describes the Siamese cat as follows:

To close the list of predators, we have yet to report a special domestic cat in Siam. The body is a creamy white, slightly yellowish color which turns brown over time, but from an early age, all the extremities (muzzle, ears, legs, tail, genital and anal regions) are soot black which always stands out from the lighter shades of the rest of the body. Sometimes, on semi-adult individuals, we notice, on the external surface of the thighs, vague indications of darker bands, and all along the tail darker rings faintly blurred and regularly spaced. The eyes are constantly very light blue. What is the native wild species of this well-established breed? Does it still exist? These are all unsolved problems; but everything suggests that it differs from that of our domestic cats. (p. 525)

This text completely contradicts Gordon's description which said: "I think, and the learned explorer Auguste Pavie thinks with me, that the Siamese Cat is a cross between the Sacred Cat of Burma and the Annamite Cats." As it were, Pavie emphasizes contrarily his ignorance and his curiosity on this subject. Note that in October 1926, when Jumaud's article came out, Auguste Pavie had been dead for over a year (June 7, 1925). We can no longer consult him to invalidate or confirm his opinions. Jumaud, on the other hand, declared that he knows the origin of the Siamese. How did he come to this conclusion?

First, a number of people are beginning to question the origin of the Birman who is very close to the Siamese and who resembles him in many ways. Rumor has it that the Birman is, in fact, a cross between a Siamese and a white Persian. Then, the majority of Siamese have a knot at the end of the tail, a malformation common at the time and which draws attention to the caudal appendage of the feline.

Chat sans queue de l'Île du Man.

However, at the time, the classification of the cat was also done on the basis of the tail: short, long or anury [absence of tail]. There is a cat which presents a particular feature at the level of the tail: it is the *Cat of the Isle of Man*, (which one also calls the cat *Manx*, of *Cornouaille*, if it has the long hairs, the *Cymric*).

The *Bulletin of the Société Nationale d'Acclimatation* of July 1893 gives the following definition:

Cats without tails. - The Isle of Man, in the Irish Sea, produces a breed of domestic cats remarkable for the almost absolute lack of tail that is not found anywhere else in Europe; you have to go to Japan to find similar animals [Note: This is what we call today the *Japanese Bobtail*]. The authors know only few details on this race which is however mentioned in the accounts of various travelers. It is generally believed that the breed was formed on the Isle of Man itself. Its origin is therefore not very old. It is not unlikely, however, to believe that these cats are descendants from a few subjects brought from the Far East by sailors. Malaysia also supplies its quota of short-tailed cats and William Marsden tells us that the cats of the island of Sumatra have an imperfect tail, tufted at the end and as if not cut from distance to distance.

For his part, Louis-Eugène Louvet, apostolic missionary of the congregation of *Foreign Catholic Missions*, published in 1885 a work entitled *La Cochinchine Religieuse*, the first volume of which reads: "The cat is precious in a country where rats and mice are teeming. The Annamese cat has a rather curious physiological character: its tail seems broken at the penultimate vertebra, and ends in the shape of a hook not rounded, but bent at right angles." (p. 38). But the most complete article on the tailless cat can be found in the report of the January 5, 1893 session of the *Bulletin de la Société d'Anthropologie de Paris*, which appeared in the bulletin of this society: a full article on "The Cat without tail of the Isle of Man" by M.A. de Mortillet:

To find short-tailed cats, we have to go to Malaysia. "In all of the immense space occupied by the Malaysian archipelago, Siam, Pegou and Burma," said Darwin, "cats have their tail truncated to half-length and it often ends in a knot." Unfortunately, we are not much better informed about these cats than about those from Japan. William Marsden, in his Voyage to the Isle of Sumatra (translation J. Parraud, year II), tells us that the cats on this island have an imperfect tail, tucked at the tip and as if indented from distance to distance. In his *Voyage en Cochinchine* [1875, p. 408], Doctor Morice gives the following description [during his stay in Vietnam (Annam) in 1872, at the Cambodian border]: "Its size is smaller than ours, its dress is spotted with black or, more rarely, a spotless white. But the thing about it is the shape of its tail. Barely a few centimeters long, this appendage is several times curled in on itself, as if it had been broken several times in reverse; this arrangement is so pronounced that one of these animals can be lifted by the hook of the tail. This singularity is hereditary." Leon Metchuikoff said cats imported to Java Island would lose their tails from the third or fourth generation.

We therefore know at that time that there were indeed cats without tails in Burma. In fact, a short article on the "Manx Cats," published on June 1, 1865 in the magazine *Hardwicke's Science-Gossip* by a certain David Ross, states:

In the Burmese empire this species of cat is well known, and a military friend, who was with the army in the conquest of that country brought me a pair from Ava, from which I had quite a little family at Madras, and made a most acceptable present of them to an officer on leaving India. You are in error in saying that this species of cat have not tails, for there is a little screw-like knot, which forms a singular little round tuft of hair, being the only tail, if such it may be called. I know the Manx cat very well, having seen them often at Wighton, in Galloway, where I was in early life, and have since been upwards of thirty-six years in India, of which I spent fifteen in Calcutta. (p. 142).

There is therefore a connection between the Annamite cat and the Manx cat. It is generally believed that the race was formed on the island itself. In this case, its origin cannot be very old. Indeed, Mortillet remarks:

Although essentially distinguished by an important osteological character, points out Mr. G. de Mortillet, this breed must only date from a few hundred years ago, since the cat was not introduced in the British Isles until the end of the ninth century. Domestic cats were rare in England in the tenth century.
However, one can also wonder if the cats of the Isle of Man are not the descendants of some cats brought from the Far East by sailors. This hypothesis does not seem implausible. Despite its small population (around 50,000), the Isle of Man, which is quite poor, must certainly provide a large contingent to the English navy. In addition, cats without tails are said not to be very common on the island, while they abound in Japan.

Cats without tails of Japan, mainly spread on the coasts, while those of the interior of the country, have, like ours, a tail, could well have themselves a foreign origin. They may have had ancestors from Malaysian cats with a short tail, knotty and as atrophied, in which this organ would have been further reduced.

We know that in many ways Japan has borrowed more from Malaysia than China." (p. 11-13).

If we come back to Jumaud's text on the Birman, the tail knotted at the end serves as an argument to affirm that the Siamese cat would descend from this Annamite cat which existed in a neighboring state (it is however necessary to cross Cambodia). Then comes this daring assertion that turns the tables: it is not the Birman who descends from the Siamese, but the opposite. The cousin is sort of the uncle. What are the reasons for this opinion which may seem strange today?

It is not uncommon to find Siamese kittens in Siamese lines who have white gloves and a longer coat. The most explicit text on this subject is the comment of Baudoin-Crevoisier in 1931 in *La Revue Féline Belge*: "I know a superb Birman in type, hair, eyes, tail, legs and in addition a perfect parent, which is the product of two Siamese. And it is not accidental, such a case often recurs in the litters of these Siamese." (p. 5) We know that long-haired cats appeared from time to time in the lines of Siamese and were then eliminated by default, until the creation in 1970 of the Balinese cat, which is precisely a Siamese with long hair. However, Jumaud reports in *Les Races de Chats*: "A long-haired Siamese was exposed to the Cat-Club of Newburg by Mr. Harvey who had brought him back from Malaysia. The parents of this cat were, apparently, ordinary Siamese whose products were Siamese kittens with the exception of this long-haired specimen." (p. 84). He adds that one can see in the collections of the galleries of the Museum "subjects presenting small white spots [sic] which mark in the most bizarre way the ends of the legs, towards the birth of the claws of the middle fingers." (p. 85-86). And, two years later, in 1933 therefore, Baudoin-Crevoisier spoke himself of "happy crossing with gloved Siamese females on their legs ..." to vary the parents of Birman cats produced at that time. Since the Birman type appears in Siamese litters, it therefore seems logical to these authors that he was the ancestor.

A number of comments can be made about this dominant discourse.

First, the Siamese imported from the court of the king of Siam in Thailand were not always "pure," as we were sometimes led to believe. Strictly speaking, there was no Siamese breeding at the Royal Palace in Bangkok. Cats were free to come and go, and mated at will, preferably Siamese, but not always. As Jumaud himself recognizes in the 1930 edition of *Les Races de chat*:

The first Siam cats that were exhibited in London were light in color with a dark face and tips. They came from the Palace of Bangkok and had been given to notable Englishmen residing in Siam. It was believed for a long time that the king of Siam maintained catteries at great cost where the royal animals were bred. This was denied by important figures, accredited to the government of Siam. They said that the Royal Siamese cat is a rare variety in all parts of the country, even in and around Bangkok. A couple are sometimes found in the palace, but there is no official breeding and these cats are not regarded as the King's personal property ..." (p. 85).

The genetic background of the Siamese imported into Europe in the 19th century and after, therefore, includes a variety of recessive genes, which are in fact the white glove and the long coat. This means that they must be worn by both parents to reappear in the offspring. The limited number of Siamese imported in the 19th century (mainly females it seems, since the King of Siam was reluctant to let go of whole males) led to a number of consanguineous unions between parents and children which strengthen these recessive traits.

Second, starting Siamese farms was very difficult, because these exotic animals did not adapt well to harsh climates and an impressive number died during the winter as Jumaud also recognized in his book and his articles. All articles on Siamese by other authors also admitted this. The *Jardin des Plantes* made an attempted breeding supervised by Professor Milne-Edwards from the four Siamese sent by Auguste Pavie as well as other cats offered to the Garden, for example by Miss Claire Carnot, the daughter of the president of the French Republic. The archives of the *Jardin des Plantes* that we consulted show that most of the Siamese received as gifts or produced on the spot died very quickly from pathologies linked to the climate.

Arrival	Giver	Siamese	Death
27 Juin 1893	Mlle Carnot	2 (mâle et femelle)	Novembre 1893
31 Juillet 1893	Mr. Auguste Pavie	3 (2 mâles et 1 femelle)	1893
23 Avril 1894	Mr. Robert Mitchell	2 (mâle et femelle)	
5 Juin 1894	Mme Paul Bert	1 (femelle)	28 Juillet 1897
12 Mai 1895	Mr. Robert Mitchell	1 (mâle)	1900

18 Août 1895	Mr. Lefèvre Pontalis (Mission Pavie)	2 (mâle et femelle)	30 Août 1895 2 Septembre 1895
8 Septembre 1895	Mr. Auguste Pavie	3 (1 mâle et 2 femelles)	échange à Mr. Rarubaud. Mâle 1895 / 1900
2 Avril 1897	Mr. Doceuf Fernand	2	
11 Mai 1897	Mme Amélie Lefuri Pontales	1 (femelle)	25 Janvier 1898
18 Août 1898	Mr. Bethmont	2 mâles	September 1898
31 Mars 1899	Mr. Levi Barthou	1 (femelle)	Juillet 1899

Miss Frances Simpson, famous cat breeder in England, wrote in 1928, in her book *Cats for Pleasure and Profits*: "Perhaps the most difficult cat to breed and rear in this country is the Siamese. Some fanciers declare these cats cannot stand our climate ..." (p. 22-23). And in her most famous 1903 work, *The Book of the Cat* (first of its kind), she had already noticed,

Siamese cats seem to be more sensitive than even the most delicate of long-haired breeds, and if attacked by any of the ills that catty flesh is heir to they do not appear to have any stamina to bear up against the ravage of the disease. Their recuperative powers are almost nil, and they rarely pull through a severe illness. [...] I have seen grown-up specimens go out like the snuffing of a candle with acute pneumonia almost before one has realized they were even ailing." (p. 254).

In order to remedy this problem, Siamese breeders will therefore cross their lines with European lines adapted to our climates to produce more resistant individuals. Mrs. Frances Simpson thus mentions the report provided by breeders of the Siamese Cat Club: "An exhibitor known to it has bred prize-winning

Siamese from a cross between a white cat with blue eyes and a Siamese queen. It also mentions another case where such crossing has produced good Siamese kittens, and thinks that many other people have, with more or less success, followed the same tactics." (p. 256).

The rest of the same chapter also reports a number of legendary elements which bear similarities to the future myth of the Birman. Thus, Mrs. Simpson mentions in passing that the Siamese cats "receive the souls of their owner at death ..." Then, further on, she reported that the famous Siamese, Champion Wankee "was bred in Hong-Kong, his mother – 'Nims' – being a stolen palace kitten. This detail is repeated below with regard to other kittens stolen from the Royal Palace of Siam: "There is a legend that these cats were kept exclusively and with great care in the King's palace, as resting places for royal souls. The Siamese are Buddhists, and consequently believe in the transmigration of souls." (p. 260). She also specifies that imported Siamese fall into two categories: The Royal Cat of Siam and the Chocolate Cat of the Temple. This "Temple Cat," she adds, is the responsibility of Jain priests, "who have the greatest reverence for animal life, and whose temple is a sanctuary for all animals". (p. 264).

The idea that the Siamese derives from the Birman is deeply rooted in the argument that Dr Jumaud systematically repeats in all his publications on the two races. Thus, he concluded his article of October 1926:

I therefore believe with some probability that the Birman cat with long hair is the ancestor of a Siamese by a cross with the Annamite cat without tail imported by the English. There are, moreover, quite a few specimens, among the Siamese, of individuals with yellow eyes, more or less brindled chocolate coats and whose caudal appendage is reduced to a few centimeters." (p. 42).

He could be talking about the breed that will be called burmese / tonkinese and which was created from a Siamese named *Wong Mau*, in brown dress, which was brought back from Rangoon in 1930 by the American doctor Joseph Thompson. This is what Jumaud said about this breed:

"It is certain that a breed of annamite cat with yellow eyes, graceful and elegant forms, small, naturally short-tailed, was, at some time introduced in Burma with the invasion. Studies link this cat to that of the Isle of Man (cat without tail), and this animal would have been imported by English caravels in India, towards the XVIIIth century. " (Ibid). And he adds a little further: "There are, moreover, quite a few copies, among the Siamese, of individuals with yellow eyes, chocolate coat more or less brindle ..." (ibid)

In the re-edition of *Les Chats de Race* of 1926 (and also in the later editions of 1930 and 1935), Jumaud suddenly reveals the "sources" of the studies of which he speaks by indicating: "Some studies which Auguste Pavie communicated to me ..." (p. 54). One wonders why he did not specify this detail earlier and why it is the only one missing from the article in *La Vie à la Campagne* in 1926. No doubt this is a reply to critics. We can indeed suppose that Jumaud was in contact with Auguste Pavie, during the writing of his book on purebred cats, in 1924. However, the studies of which he spoke only concern the origin of the Annamite cat. This did not prevent him–in the Siamese cat section–to repeat what he said of the

Birman: "According to the explorer Auguste Pavie, the Siamese cat is the product of the cross of the Birman cat (long haired) with the Annamite cat (without tail) imported in the 17th century into the Khmer Empire." If we read correctly, the author goes from the 18th to the 17th century in a few pages; then he continued: "There are, moreover, in Siamese cats, quite a few yellow-eyed individuals whose caudal appendages are reduced to a few centimeters. In the break or the nodosity of the tail we can again find an indication of the junction of the two Birman and Annamite races." (p. 80). In the 1930 edition Jumaud also offered an amplified version of the origin of the Isle of Man's cat: "According to a legend widespread on the island, this curious animal descends from two specimens stranded on the shore, after the sinking of a Spanish Armada ship." (p. 91).

So, here is a cat that has toured the world several times! From Japan to Spain, then the Isle of Man, and from the Irish island, to Burma, to finish with the Siamese descendants in Bangkok ...

Of course, today we know that all these remarks are pure conjectures. Auguste Pavie had never published anything on the Annamese cat in his list of Indochina felines. The information on this cat in question is limited in fact to that which we quoted above.

The idea that the Siamese descended from anuran cats, imported by the English during the conquest of Burma (between 1824 and 1885), or already during their first contacts with the king of Burma in the 18th century through the company from India, makes no sense.

Siamese cats have existed for a very long time, as proven by the famous collections of poems on cats in Thailand, such as the *Tamra Maew*, composed around 1350, which describes one, or the *Smud Khoi* (19th century) where we meet a Siamese with yellow-gold eyes called "Diamond Cat."

This did not prevent Jumaud from concluding his article as follows, which clearly shows the reluctance of the time to see in the Birman a unique imported breed:

This hypothesis is justified and answers in advance to that expressed by several, claiming that the Birman cat is due to the crossing of the Siamese and the white Angora Cat. Unacceptable hypothesis, as demonstrated by the impossibility of obtaining results for the mating of Siamese and Cats of other breeds" (Idem).

This mind-boggling conclusion brings us back to the central part of the article in the section on breeding Birman.

As we have already seen, Siamese have been united with white cats with blue eyes to ensure the survival of a breed ill-adapted to the harsh European climate—this should in itself suffice to destroy Jumaud's argument. But genetic knowledge at the time was limited, especially with regard to the long-haired (L) and Siamese (C^s) genes.

Now, back to Jumaud's argument in detail. He claimed that Mrs. Léotardi, the first Birman breeder in France, attempted a union of this type without success. Consider this whole passage closely:

The breeding of the subjects observed was particularly difficult. Léotardi, who has had the opportunity to raise several, says that one should not expect to raise more than one subject in ten. Male Birman Cats do not mate with Angora Cats. Mrs. Léotardi having presented a superb Persian to one of her Birman males, this one entered a frightful fury, and it was necessary to cover it with a blanket to prevent it from putting to blood and in pieces the poor beast, while two days later, it willingly mated with a chocolate Siamese. The products of Angoras with Birman Cats have never produced kittens reminiscent of the Birman breed. A female of Mrs. Léotardi, accidentally covered by a tabby Angora, gave birth to ugly kittens, including three tabby males, short-haired, an absolute specimen of the European Cat, and a completely black female, semi-long haired. In this litter, nothing reminded the mother, Birman cat, neither as hair, nor as shade, nor as forms. (ibid).

The information provided is partly true, as far as the litters are concerned. Indeed, a union between a short-haired cat (like the Siamese) and a long-haired cat (like the Angora or the Persian) will only give short-haired kittens to the first generation. On the other hand, if one of these first-generation kittens is paired with a Birman (or long-haired cat), there will be a 50% chance of obtaining short-haired kittens and 50% chance of obtaining long-haired. The same goes for the Siamese gene (C^s). In fact, the marriage of a Siamese with an angora would not give any Siamese kitten, but all would carry the recessive gene in question, which would likely come out in the next generation. Symmetrically, the union of these kittens with a Birman will produce offspring 50% Siamese and 50% non-Siamese. If we also take into account the gene of white gloves (W^g), and that of blue eyes (both recessive) the story becomes even more complicated. In total, we are dealing with four different recessive genes. So, when Mrs. Léotardi said that the marriage of a Birman female with a tabby angora male, did not give a kitten of Birman type, that is correct. But, if she had kept the little black, long-haired female and married her to a Birman, she would have obtained a good proportion of seal-point Birman kittens. The demonstration given is moreover incriminating, because it indicates that, even under the guise of "accidents," Mrs. Léotardi organized interracial marriages between Persians, probably resulting from the cattery of Maritza (production of Mrs. L. Brassart) and Siamese to obtain Birman. She nevertheless claims that Birman males only agree to marry Birman females, while Birman females tolerate unions with Angora males. Although it is true that cats have their own tastes, and may or may not like a partner presented to them, it is not a rule or a genetic principle. But she uses this argument to proclaim that it is impossible to produce a Birman from a Siamese and a Persian.

The remark that we can only raise one "subject in ten" can be explained by what we have just said. Of course, the union of a Birman with a Siamese skips two stages, since the Siamese gene is already present as well as the blue eyes. Only the long coat and the gloves remain to appear. As we said above, there are Siamese already carrying these two genes. It was precisely these Siamese who were united with the first Birman. However, in the first exhibitions in Paris, some Birman without white gloves were presented regularly; moreover, the first Birman had a very short glove, which is another sign of recent origin.

Finally, the article reports that "The Birman cat easily mates with the Siamese, or with the Laotian Lynx cat, but the subjects obtained in this way are rarely gloved regularly and tend to have the coat and shape of the Siamese or Laotian." The question that naturally arises here is: What is this Laotian Lynx Cat? André Chamonin posed it in 1933 in his article "Pour les chats Sacré de Birmanie". Going through everything that has been said about the origin of the Birman, he said ironically:

All of this documentation suggests that the adventure novel that begins at the Lao-Tsun temple and ends with Doctor Prat in Nice is true.
Now, I wrote to Dr. Prat ... I don't know if Mr. Baudoin had taken this precaution by going back on his doubts and admitting that Poupée had been covered by a Laos lynx cat. Because here is Dr. Prat's answer:
'We have indeed had several Siamese cats including Youyou, but we know nothing of its origins ... I do not know anything about Mrs Hradisch [sic], from Vienna.'

Then I asked a great hunter from the Far East who lived in Laos. Mr. Guy Cheminaud whose readers of our review know the sure erudition in such matter, what he thought of the "Lynx cats of Laos." Answer: There are no Laos cats as a different species from the Siamese cat! So, one point is established with certainty: Poupée was not covered by a Laos cat, but by a Siamese whose origin is not even known. " (p. 3931)

The only place where a Laos Cat is mentioned is the aforementioned zoological chapter by Auguste Pavie —he reports that the inhabitants of Siam call the Siamese cat "Laotian Cat." This mystery cat is therefore none other than the Siamese masked under another name, to confuse appearances and feed the legend. Mrs. Léotardi obviously read Auguste Pavie.

Moreover, even the description of the Upper Burma region, where the cat is said to come from ("an almost desert region with a barrier of impassable walls"), is both erroneous and inaccurate. Far from corresponding to field knowledge on the part of the improbable Major Gordon, it confines itself to repeating the vague indications of the imprecise maps of the time.

The crowning glory of the article in *La Vie à la Campagne* is a series of photos of Birman, including the first one we know of *Poupée de Madalpour*, belonging to Mrs. Léotardi and several of *Manou de Madalpour*, belonging to Mrs. Marcelle Adam (whose name is given wrongly like *Manon*).

In 1931, Marcel Baudouin-Crevoisier published in *La Revue Féline Belge* of July 1931, a 2-page article on "Le Chat de Birmanie." He expressed a certain skepticism about the official speech on the Birman:

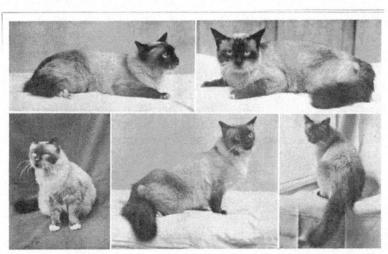

CHATS DE BIRMANIE. 1, 4 et 5. Manou de Madalpour, 1er prix Paris 1926; à Mme Marcelle Adam. 2 et 3. Poupée de Madalpour jolie Chatte, 1er prix Paris 1926; à Mme Léotardi. Les sujets de cette race, au corps allongé, à la tête longue, aux yeux bleu de roi, à la robe garnie de poils longs et soyeux, se distinguent nettement des Chats asiatiques, avec lesquels ils ne sympathisent pas. Moins joueurs que les Siamois, ils sont très sociables, intelligents, gais, mais peu joueurs.

Its origins as a breed are quite questionable. The information collected on this cat is only a few years old and comes only from travelers who, perhaps, did not essentially study this breed as a goal.

According to the documents, the first specimens to arrive in France are only five to six years old [1925-26]; I have before me a genealogical table whose departure is *Poupée*, Birman female who, at the time, was full. On June 20, 1926, she gave birth to 4 young. Lon Golden, Sita II, Nafaghi and Sinh.

It is the starting point for Birman Cats currently in France, some of whose almost perfect specimens still exist.

[...] First of all for information let's go back to the origin. It seems rather confusing to me. According to some, Poupée is the starting point. This female being full, she was crossed with her children to create the Madalpour strain belonging to Madame Fradisch [sic] from Vienne. These cats, supposedly, come from the Lao-Tsun Temple in Burma ... This underground, inviolable and sacred temple, etc ... It's a bit of a novel ...

According to Mr. Jumaud's book, the first couple was imported by Mrs. Thadde Hadish. This couple of cats would have been stolen by a servant of the temple.

All these origins are surrounded by a certain legend which may look attractive, but which gives no official information.

Others have told me that billionaire Vanderbilt is no stranger to the Birman imports into France.

Obviously we are in the realm of fantasy.

The reality is less funny. (p. 4)

And he goes on to the more serious investigation that he himself carried out:

For my part I have documented myself directly with people who, not only frequented Burma, but also the whole region of India, Siam, Indochina, etc ... These people whose profession was the sale, the purchase and the export of wild animals from these regions, usual suppliers of zoological gardens, merchants of exotic animals etc ... told me to have have never met so-called Burma cats. Last year a friend of mine went to the Far East, which he has been visiting for more than thirty-five years to buy animals. I gave him all the necessary documents, photos, standard; he visited an immense region, he saw all his correspondents, those who for him catch animals; none of them could give him any information. It is strange that nobody knows this breed of cat, without even having seen it, having at least heard of it.

On the other hand, for anyone who knows the English, great lovers of everything that is rare, and their 'obligatorily friendly' relations with the great lords of India, it is astonishing that among them, none have received a cat as a gift of such royal origin. Everyone knows that in many places the gifts of live animals are a sign of great friendship or perfect submission.

I am not the only one to have done research on the Birman cat. Other *Cat Club de France* fans have done the same and have not been luckier than me. We must therefore conclude:

In my humble opinion, the Birman cat breed, as the prerogative of a region, does not exist, or rather no longer exists. [...]

I know a superb Birman like type, hair, eyes, tail, legs and in addition a perfect parent, which is the product of two Siamese. And it is not accidental, such a case often recurs in the litters of these Siamese.

[...]

This Birman to which I allude above, covered a Siamese cat, daughter of a Birman; the products obtained were almost all very beautiful Birman, most gloved on all four legs, others only on two legs. Among these is an absolutely perfect male. The following

77

litters were also beautiful. In the Poupée's line, essentially purebred, we have not done better. There are very few gloved Birman in this line and some not even gloved at all." (p. 5).

Four months later, the same author published a second article in the same journal: "Le Chat de Birmanie. II". The first sparked several reactions:

As a follow-up to the article published in the issue of the "Revue Féline Belge" last July, we will deal with the subjects of crossbreeding and reproductions.
First of all, my last article earned me letters from amateurs and former Birman breeders, and I was able to have, without asking, information that I was missing. This information relates mainly to the origin of the Birman in France and I share it with my friends, readers of this review." (p. 6).

Which breeders is he referring to? He did not cite his sources but according to the information which he reproduced one can guess that it is about Mrs. Léotardi or Mrs. Adam, and perhaps also Mrs. Brassart?

For the first time, this article contains the name of the alleged mother of Poupée (and a return to Vanderbilt):

The first couple was indeed imported from Burma from the Lao Tsun temple by Mrs. Thadde Hadish. These cats were called Sita and Madalpour. On the yacht of Mr. Vanderbilt which brought them to France, the male Madalpour died accidentally. The single female arrived in France. Sita covered by Madalpour gave birth to a female *Poupée*, which we consider pure, since daughter of two Birman. *Poupée* was then covered not by a Birman cat since there was no longer any in France, but by a Laos lynx cat belonging to a doctor from Nice. This cat was called "Youyou". This crossing was motivated because of the resemblance of the Laos cat with the Cats of Burma. The same experience could have been made with a Siamese cat, because the Laos cat is similar to the Siamese, a little higher on hind legs and much darker blue eyes, like the Birman. The product obtained, named

Hiram-Roi, was entirely of the Laotian type. At the next litter, Poupée was covered by her son Hiram. The products were always Laotians. Until this time, therefore, no Birman type except Poupée. At the next litter, Poupée, still covered by Hiram-Roi, gave birth to a superb Birman *Manou de Madalpour*, very similar to her. So here is a Birman after Laotians without having changed breeders, and this is how the Madalpour line was created in France. In all its different litters, Poupée had only one girl who did not live. For the litters which followed, always by Hiram, were born Timour, Uru [sic], Birman. Subsequently, Timour covered Poupée.

This is a well-established point, this information is official and the pedigree of Manou son of Hiram-Roi and of Poupée carries the No. 7002 C.C.F. dated June 13, 1925. " (p. 6).

Baudoin-Crevoisier then talked about his own breeding, in which he had created a new line:

For my part, I obtained my superb subjects by crossing Birman males with Siamese females gloved in white. The products were impeccable, Dieu d'Arakan, Reine de Rangoon are descendants of these crosses; but that selection didn't happen overnight, and it took four years of work to complete it. [...] I advise the amateurs who would like to make Birman to always try with a Siamese female gloved with white. I prefer the male of the breed for that we want rather than the female, although for Madalpour, it is the female who was of the desired breed. In the selection, preferably look for the nature of the coat and the dark blue of the eyes rather than the white of the paws. I know that amateurs are looking for these snow mitts, as Mr. Steens says so well, but this glove appearance, so difficult to obtain, even with gloved reproducers, is in my view a fantasy of nature which in any case don't produce it abundantly" (p. 6).

The following year Baudoin-Crevoisier published another article in the special issue "Races de Chats" of the review *Jardins et Basses-cours* of August 20, 1932:

"Le Chat de Birmanie, sacré animal". He wrote about the general Birman breeding:

The lack of new blood in the litters inevitably brought waste due to inbreeding. Trials made by crossing Birman and Siamese females have given the best results. The honor of maintaining this marvelous breed belongs to the first breeders; unfortunately, none of them continued it. Some names, however, must remain in the annals of the Birman breeding: Mmes Léotard [sic], Marcelle Adam and Brassard [sic] were the first to have these extremely rare cats. Since Poupée de Madalpour, beautiful subjects have figured in the prize list of this sacred race; these are: Manou, Miram-Roi [sic], Lon Golden, Ubu, Bijou, Djaipour, Lon Saïto, Nafachy [sic], Sita II, Sita III, Idjadi-Tsun, Yadi." (p. 376).

So much for the list of Madalpour. To this is added the lineage of Birman from the gloved Siamese: Sun of Arakan, Bouli of Arakan, God of Arakan, Prince of Rangoon, Queen of Rangoon, Poupée of Rangoon, Zaquelle of Mandalay.

The last major article on the origin of the Birman can be found in the exceptional number 92 of *La Vie à la Campagne* dated April 15, 1935. Entitled "Le Chat de Birmanie ou Chat Sacré", and subtitled "German cousins of the Siamese by their origin as by their appearance, the quality and very typical subjects of this breed are quite rare, which increases their value, while their originality and their beauty justify an amplification of their production". It is also signed by Baudoin-Crevoisier and will be cited later under the title "Sa Majesté le chat" (His Highness the Cat) (p. 19). And here is the article:

The Birman cat, sometimes called *The Sacred cat of Burma*, has been known in France and Europe since 1925. The first specimen imported into Western countries would have been in France.

Currently, livestock production appears to be in decline; the majority of fine specimens produced over the past 10 years gradually disappear without always being replaced. This state of affairs justifies an effort at reconstruction.

ORIGINS. The origins of the Birman Cat are discussed, despite its precise name. Several authors have made it a legendary animal and it would be in the Lao-Tsun Temple, in Burma, that the origin of these superb animals should be sought.

Apart from the writings of Sir Russel Gordon and Auguste Pavie, no document has come to specify the origin of these Cats. After 6 years of personal research and 10 years of breeding in France, the Birman Cat remains as mysterious as it was originally, and no new imported product has been seen and, therefore, studied.

The first couple of Birman cats, brought to France around 1925 by Mrs. Thadde-Hadisch would therefore come from the temple of Lao-Tsun, where these animals are jealously guarded. The male died on the boat during the crossing, and the female, who fortunately had been covered, gave birth in Nice to a litter of Birman kittens. Among these kittens, a female Poupée was noticed as having the most perfect Birman type.

This female was then covered by a Siamese cat, who at that time had been baptized for the occasion Cat of Laos ... For lack of Birman male, it was necessary to try a test. This one partially succeeded. From litter to litter and from selection to selection, the descendants improved. Preference was given to youngsters whose appearance most resembled the first breeders. Thus was formed the Madalpour strain, named after the first male to perish before reaching France.

Assuming that Poupée had been covered by a Siamese cat, other breeders crossed Birman Cats from the Madalpour strain with gloved Siamese cats, that is to say with the tips of their white paws. Frequently renewing the blood of the breeders, they obtained more vigorous subjects and conformed to the first Birman types. It was another branch of Birman, far superior to the old. Currently, the Breeding seems to have remained in these first trials.

It is not impossible that the Birman Cat is the ancestor of the Siamese Cat, or at least a close relative. There is, in fact, a lot of analogy between these two races: type, coat color, eyes, ease of crossing, habitat, resemblance of the cry. The Birman Cat was once able to cross with Anuran Cats from Indo-China and produce Siamese Cats whose broken, twisted, truncated tail proves the blood supply of Indochinese cats. The white paws which are sought in the Birman cat are frequent in the Siamese cat. Long-haired subjects sometimes appear in Siamese litters. These phenomena are only homecomings to the ancestor and indicate a common origin between these two races. Finally, it should be noted that a Birman and Siamese gloved crossing gives, at the end of the second generation a high proportion of Birman type [sic] and that these again crossed between them, give type Birman kittens in the proportion of at least 80 to 90 percent.

Then, to conclude, Baudoin-Crevoisier declared dithyrambically:

The Birman Cat is one of the aristocrats of the feline gent. Its indisputable beauty, especially its rarity, have made it one of the most expensive Cats to acquire. Its breeding can therefore be reasonably remunerative, if patience [réussite] and success smile at you.

Subjects have reached fabulous prices. Young people at weaning (2 months) are worth 1,500 to 2,000 francs. Adults vary according to the beauty and perfection of the type. A specimen very well gloved and perfect in all respects can be worth 15,000 to 20,000 francs. An average subject pays for around 5,000 francs." (P. 19).

Indeed, Marcel Reney (aka Abbé Chamonin) confirmed in 1947 that "Sacred cats in Burma are practically unobtainable and were sold before the war at astronomical prices." (p. 128-29).

CHAPTER 4

THE BIRMAN'S LEGEND: PUBLICATIONS-EVOLUTIONS

The First texts

LA LÉGENDE DES CHATS SACRÉS DE BIRMANIE

bleus, immenses et profonds comme les yeux de la déesse. Et comme il tournait doucement la tête vers la porte du Sud, ses quatre pattes qui touchaient le crâne vénérable devinrent d'un blanc éclatant, jusqu'à l'endroit que recouvrait la soie des vêtements sacrés. Et comme ses yeux se détournaient de la porte du Sud, les kittahs obéissant à cet impératif regard chargé de dureté et de lumière, se précipitèrent pour fermer sur le premier envahisseur les lourdes portes de bronze... Le temple était sauvé de la profanation et du pillage... Sinh n'avait pas cependant quitté le trône, et le septième jour, sans avoir fait un mouvement, face à la déesse et les yeux dans ses yeux, il mourut, mystérieux et hiératique, emportant vers Tsun-Kyanksé l'âme de Mun-Hâ, trop parfaite désormais pour la terre...

« Et quand sept jours plus tard les prêtres rassemblés se consultèrent devant la statue pour décider de la succession de Mun-Hâ, on vit accourir tous les chats du temple... Et tous étaient vêtus

Veterinarians and breeders have incidentally set up the main lines, but they are primarily interested in the animal itself. From 1927, however, journalists and writers took over the legend itself and more or less reworked independent versions of it. It was indeed on September 18, 1927 that the journal *Minerva* in its number 110 published the first of these independent texts. Here is the whole text:

The curious legend that we reproduce here was collected in Burma by an explorer. He explains the origin of the special veneration that the inhabitants of this country devoted to their magnificent cats, of which Mrs. Marcelle Adam presented a very pure specimen at the last cat show.

In order to shed light on certain passages in this legend, we believe it useful to recall that Birman people believe in the transmutation of souls. But it is only among priests (lamahs) and divine officiants that this soul emerges from the embryonic state. Also, only the priests have the power to revive in a sacred animal, such as the cat, before taking over a body for total perfection. The Lamahs Kittahs, which are discussed here, must spend their lives in contemplation of the divinity to whom they have devoted their service.

"When with the malevolent moon came the Phoums army, the army of the accursed Thai Siamese, then lived, in the mountains of the sun, the precious among the precious, the one whose god Song-Hio had himself braided the golden beard: the lamah Kittah Mun-Ha.

The venerable had always lived in contemplation of Tsun-Kyanksé, the goddess with sapphire eyes who presides over the transmutations of souls whose number is counted, and had never looked away.

The revered Kittah Mun-Hâ had an oracle without which he made no decision: his cat Sinh, whom the other Kittahs revered with fervor. This magnificent cat was pure white: only its ears, its nose, its tail as well as its four legs, all of its extremities, finally, were earth-brown in color, in order to demonstrate that everything related to earthly impurity must hide its defilement under a dark shade.

Sinh also lived in contemplation of the goddess, seated near its dreaded master. Its eyes were yellow like the reflection of Mun-Hâ's golden beard and the golden body of the sapphire-goddess.

However, one evening, at the rising of the moon, as the "Thais" approached the sacred precinct, and while he was invoking with all his soul threatening destinies, the venerated one died, loaded with years and anguishes, in front of his goddess and having with him his divine cat. He died, leaving the Kittahs overwhelmed by the loss of their great master in the midst of the cruel ordeal of the invasion. Then came the miracle of immediate transmutation.

Sinh leapt to the throne of gold arched, to the head of his bent master, facing the goddess. Afterward the hairs of its white spine became golden and its eyes became blue, huge and deep sapphires, like the eyes of the goddess. Next it turned its gaze to the South Gate, and its earth-brown four legs turned white to the place that had silken sacred garments. It turned its precious eyes to the South Gate, bright, harsh, imperative, and the Kittahs, obeying an invisible force, quickly rushed to close the bronze doors on the Brahmin enemy. And passing through their underground passages, they were able to exterminate them and rout them, thus saving their temple from profanation, plunder and destruction.

Sinh never left the throne, refusing all food; facing the goddess, eyes in her eyes, sapphires in sapphires, mysterious and hieratic. Seven days after the death of Mun-Hâ, upright on its legs purified of white, its precious eyes riveted on the goddess, Sinh died at the time of the opening of the temple, taking the soul of Mun to Tsun-Kyanksé Hâ, too perfect, therefore, for the earth. One last time, its sapphire gaze slowly turned and fixed forever on the north door, from where, later, came in numbers the Annamese and Cambodian hordes. And when, seven days later, the Kittahs were gathered before Tsun-Kyanksé, to decide the succession of Mun-Hâ, they saw advancing little by little all the cats of the temple, and, in great amazement and respectful terror, found that their paws were gloved in white, that their white coats had reflections of gold, and that their eyes of gold had turned into sapphires.

The cats surrounded Ligoa, the youngest of the Kittahs, and all the kittahs thereby knew the designation of their ancestors reincarnated in the bodies of cats sacred by the will of the goddess.

Therefore, when a sacred cat dies at the temple of Lao-Tsun, it is the soul of a Kittah who returns forever to the mysterious Paradise of Song-Hio, the golden god. Woe to him who, even involuntarily, hastens the end of these dreaded and venerated felines: the worst torments are reserved for him to appease the soul in pain, separated from its body before the term fixed by the gods." S. R. (p. 14).

This first account differs somewhat from that of Mme Adam's soap opera published in 1926 which will itself be reviewed and republished in number 5 of *La Revue Féline Belge* in December 1929, then taken up by Dr Fernand Méry in number 386 of the review *Minerva*, January 1, 1933, and finally copied verbatim that same year in the *Revue Féline Belge*. Who is the author? Is it Fernand Méry, who signed the 1933 version? But then why these initials S. R. ? We find the signature of Fernand Méry in other articles of the journal *Minerva*, in 1928 for example, and moreover, his version of the legend was released in January 1933, following an interview with Mrs. Marcelle Adam.

The text we have just quoted is presented as a story "collected in Burma by an explorer." We can conclude that this is the original text from which Mrs. Marcelle Adam would have made successive revisions, from her 1925 soap opera to the 1929 article. The explorer mentioned would then be the major stationed in Burma, and renamed Russel Gordon in the latest version. This being the case, what are the differences, or the cuts of this text compared to that of Mrs.

Adam? For starters, it is missing the entire introduction that explains that the Kittahs practice a pre-Brahman religion. We have a shorter text, less literally worked, which generally corresponds to an older text. Then, both the introductory paragraph and the course of the text indicate that the Kittahs are Lamah priests. This poses a problem, of course, since the lamas are part of Tibetan Buddhism: as we have already seen in connection with the remarks in the book by Poirier and Boyer, this was not the name given to priests in Burma.

In addition, contrary to what happens in Adam's text, we are not talking about the Lugh mountains, a name which is unknown in Southeast Asia, but simply the mountains of the sun; the army attacking Lao-Tsun Temple is "exterminated" in this version, while the attackers apparently less organized, are just "routed" from Mrs. Adam's home, making the Kittahs more peaceful victims. Finally, it is specified that the Sinh cat certainly died seven days later, but also at "the opening of the temple." Basically, however, the story is the same.

It is necessary to refer to the final version of Mme Adam, published in December 1929 in the *Revue Féline Belge*, to observe more significant changes. Here is the text.

Here is the holy legend, as it was told to me by those who entered the land of my little feline god.

Long before the coming of the Buddha, well before the birth of Brahmanism, even before Vyâsa had dictated the immortal words of his divine books, the Khmer people jealously guarded the temples where the Kittahs, venerable priests lived, so close to the perfection that their spirit, at the moment of conquering the eternal ecstasy, passed only in the body of a sacred cat, the time of its animal existence.

But from the beginning of the worlds, the saints disapproved of those who did not sanctify themselves in their own way. So did the Brahmins who attacked the Kittahs and piously massacred them. However, some of the Venerables were able to escape through the untouched mountains of northern Burma, and there they founded the Lao-Tsun underground Temple, which means *Dwelling of the Gods!*

This temple is a wonder among the wonders of Indo-China. Not far from a lake, it is lost in a chaos of immense peaks and if, by an extraordinary favor, Auguste Pavie and Major Russel-Gordon were able to enter it, it is because they happened to protect the last Kittahs against the relentless Brahmins. They were therefore able to contemplate the hundred sacred cats of the cult and learn their history.

You know that Auguste Pavie, this hero, conquered us, step by step, Cambodia and that his great benevolence born of his intelligent goodness, brought us more victories than the force of arms.

From Cambodia he went to Burma and the Kittahs instructed him about this legend:

When, with the malevolent moon, came the Phoums, or if you prefer a clearer language, the cursed Siamese Thai, when these barbarians came in the mountains of Lugh, in the mountains of the Sun, Mun-Hâ lived in the temple of Lao-Tsun. Mun-Hâ, the most precious among the most precious, the one whose god Song-Hio had braided the golden beard. The venerable had always lived in the contemplation of souls, whose number is counted. He never looked away.

He had an oracle which dictated his decisions, his cat Sinh whom the Kittahs revered with fervor.

O wisdom to choose an oracle who does not speak!

Sitting near its dreaded master, Sinh also lived in contemplation of the goddess. The beautiful animal! Its eyes were golden yellow, yellow from the reflection of Mun-Hâ's metallic beard, yellow from the amber body of the sapphire-eyed goddess.

One evening, when the moon rose, the Thais approached the sacred precinct. So, invoking the threatening fate of his people, Mun-Hâ died laden with years and anguishes. He died before his goddess, having his divine cat with him. And the Kittahs lamented such a cruel loss.

At that moment the miracle of immediate transmutation occurred.

Sinh leaps onto the holy throne, braced on the head of its sagging master in front of the goddess. And the hairs on its white spine were golden in color. And its yellow eyes color of the golden yellow of Tsun-Kian Ksé, yellow of the golden yellow of the beard woven by the god Song-Hio, its eyes became blue, immense deep sapphires, like the eyes of the goddess. Its four paws of the earth brown, its four paws which touched the venerable skull became white from the nails to the end of the fingers purified by the contact of the powerful dead.

Sinh turned his precious sight towards the South gate, as the reading of an impregnable order, to which, pushed by an invisible force, the Kittahs obeyed. Hence, they closed on the ancestral enemy, the bronze doors of the holy temple. Then passing through their underground passages, they routed the profaners.

Sinh, refusing all food, never left the throne. It remained standing, facing the goddess, mysterious hieratic, fixing its blue gaze on the sapphire eyes from which he took the flame and the sweetness.

Seven days after Mun-Hâ's death, upright on its white-purified legs, without lowering its eyelids, it died, taking the soul of Mun-Hâ, too perfect for the earth, to Tsun-Kyanksé. But one last time, its gaze slowly turned to the South Gate, from where later the Annamese and Cambodian hordes came in numbers.

Seven days after Sinh's death, the Kittahs assembled before Tsun-Kyanksé to decide on the succession of Mun-Hâ.

So, oh wonder, they saw the hundred Temple cats coming in a slow troop, their paws were gloved in white, their snowy coats had golden reflections and the topaz of their eyes had turned into sapphires.

The Kittahs bowed down in an attitude of devout dread. And they waited. Didn't they know that the souls of their master [ancestors] inhabited the harmonious forms of sacred animals? These [monks], serious and flexible, surrounded Ligoa, the youngest of the priests who thus knew the will of heaven.

When a sacred cat dies at the temple of Lao-Tsun, the soul of a Kittah returns forever to the mysterious Paradise of Song-Hio, the golden god. Woe to those who hasten the end, even involuntarily of these dreaded and venerated felines, the worst torments are reserved for them, in order to appease the soul in pain.

Apart from the change of orientation of the door which logically means a change of invader, the essential modification is that we go from one explorer to two, whose names are given: Major Russel Gordon, but also Auguste Pavie. This is a bold addition, as we know that Pavie never set foot in Burma – it would have caused a diplomatic incident. Presumably, if he had seen the temple and its cats, he would have mentioned it in his reports. In addition, he left Indochina in 1895; but in 1929, he was dead for 4 years and could therefore only turn over in his grave!

Of course, at the time, these changes went almost unnoticed, since previous publications were scattered in varied and hard-to-read journals. The latest text – which will become the canonical version – is that of Fernand Méry, published in number 388 of the journal *Minerva* dated January 1, 1933, and reproduced exactly in the Revue Féline Belge, the same year. Here is the text:

"The Legend of the Sacred Cats of Burma"

Little is known about these precious cats which are, in general, the highlight of any self-respecting cat show. It is true that by counting well there might not be twenty in Europe. What do I say, not twenty? Not ten, not five... not one (as Marie Dubas sings)... let's get on! Not one who can boast of its authentic nobility ... not one who can be said to come from a real couple of sacred felines directly imported from English Indochina.

Those who currently exist with us have only a Birman ancestor "Poupée" that had to be mixed with a kind of Siamese: the Laos lynx, so that the Birman blood does not completely die out. What religious care and solicitude it has taken since, to preserve through the generations of mixed blood, the gold fur and the sapphire eyes of these marvelous beasts, and especially the four immaculate gloves, symbol of their divine essence.

But if we know little about Birman cats because they are rare, we know even less the beautiful legend that told us one summer evening near the Spanish border a blonde friend of animals and poets ... Would I know, now tell it to you as it should be...

"At that time–our friend began gently:–in a temple built on the slopes of Mount Lugh, lived in prayer the very venerable kittah Mun-Hâ, great precious lama among the precious ones: the one whose god Song-Hio himself braided the golden beard ... Not a minute, not a glance, not a thought of his existence which was not devoted to adoration, contemplation, the pious service of Tsun-Kyanksé the goddess with sapphire eyes, the one that presides over the transmutation of souls, that which allows the kittahs to reincarnate in a sacred animal the duration of its animal existence, before resuming a body haloed by the total and holy

91

perfection of the high priests. Beside him meditated Sinh, his dear oracle, an all-white cat, whose eyes were yellow, yellow with the reflection of its master's golden beard and the golden body of the goddess with sky eyes... Sinh, the advising cat, whose ears, nose, tail and extremities of the limbs were of the dark color of the ground, marks of the stain and the impurity of all that touches or can touch the ground.

Now, one evening, as the malicious moon had allowed the cursed Phoums from abhorred Siam, to approach the sacred precinct, the high priest Mun-Hâ, without ceasing to implore cruel destinies, slowly entered the dead, with his divine cat at his side and before his eyes the despair of all his overwhelmed kittahs ...

It was then that a miracle occurred ... the unique miracle of immediate transmutation: with a leap, Sinh was on the golden throne and perched on the head loaded with years, and who for the first time did not looked more at his goddess ... And as it slowly turned his head towards the South door, its four legs which touched the venerable skull became bright white, to the place covered with the silk of sacred garments. And as its eyes turned away from the South gate, the kittahs obeying this imperative gaze charged with harshness and light, rushed to close the heavy bronze doors on the first invader ... The temple was saved from desecration and pillage ... Sinh had not, however, left the throne, and on the seventh day, without having made a movement, facing the goddess and looking into its eyes, it died, mysterious and hieratic, carrying the soul of Mun towards Tsun-Kyanksé-Hâ, too perfect now for the earth...

And when seven days later the assembled priests consulted each other in front of the statue to decide on the succession of Mun-Hâ, all the cats of the temple ran in ... All were dressed in gold and gloved with white, and all had changed the yellow of their eyes into a deep sapphire ... And they all surrounded, in silence, the youngest of the kittahs, therefore designated by the ancestors reincarnated by the will of the goddess."

And now, said the storyteller, every time a sacred cat dies in the temple of Lao-Tsun, the soul of a kittah resumes forever its place in the paradise of Song-Hio, the golden god. But woe—she also concludes—to the one who hastens the end of one of these sacred beasts, even if he did not want to. He will suffer the

92

cruellest torments until the troubled soul he has disturbed soothes ... " (p. 14).

This latest refined version of Fernand Méry, eliminates any mention of the explorers Pavie and Gordon. It only seeks to tell a legend and does not bother with any "historical" detail. The story's author is simply referred to as "a blonde, animal and poet lover." It is rather vague. However, in "Sa Majesté le Chat" which appeared more than twenty years later, Fernand Méry will specify: "It is the Sacred Cat of Burma which legend served men's imagination. Legend every day a little more embellished, a little more enriched by poets, but whose essentials, if our memories are correct, was told to us well before the war, in 1926, by the priestess of 'Son Altesse *Manou de Madalpour*', Mrs. Marcelle Adam, who then chaired the *Central Feline Society* and was the first in Paris to make public this very beautiful and extremely rare cat from the Lugh mountains" (p. 133). So, we always come back to Marcelle Adam influence.

CHAPTER 5

MISS LEOTARDI: "HIGH ADVENTURER"

The mysterious Mrs. Léotardi, first breeder of Birman cats.

Mme LEOTARDI

Who is Mme Léotardi? What do we know about her from documents relating to cat shows in general and the Sacred Birman Cat in particular? Her name is there from the very beginning.

The first text concerning the Birman which appeared in Philippe Jumaud's thesis, *Les races de Chats* (March 25, 1925), is based on his observations, or on the data he obtained from Mme Léotardi between the end 1924 and 1925: "The breeding of the subjects that we observed was particularly difficult. Léotardi, who has had the opportunity to breed several litters, says that you should not expect to breed more than one in ten." (p. 41).

In a table concerning four cats, Jumaud focused on two male Birman cats whose weight he tracked, in one case from 5 days to 5 months, and in the other, from 5 days also up to 36 months—which brings us back to a date of birth in 1921-22 for the oldest. We cannot determine whether the curve that stopped at five months corresponds to the death of the kitten in question or when Jumaud wrote his report. They were probably two kittens with different litters, the most recent of which dates from 1924. The mother is *Poupée de Madalpour*, the only Birman cat likely to reproduce at this time if we believe the medals she received in various exhibitions.

It was not until the summer of 1925, and more particularly June 14, that the name of Mrs. Léotardi was mentioned during the Angers exhibition. It is on this occasion that the Birman appeared for the first time on display with a transcription error: *Birmamie* instead of Birmanie. Mrs. Léotardi won two prizes with the same cat, numbered 317, which was a young female, that is to say, by the standards of the time, aged less than 12 months, and therefore born between 1924 and 1925. On this occasion, Mrs. Léotardi rubbed shoulders with Mrs. Brassart, vice-president of the

L'EXPOSITION FÉLINE
A DISTRIBUÉ SES RÉCOMPENSES

L'exposition féline a clos ses portes, mais non sans avoir distribué les traditionnelles récompenses.

C'est ainsi que *Poupée de Madalpour*, à Mme Léotardi, décrocha la palme de la catégorie birmane, ajoutant une cinquième médaille à ses précédents trophées. Parmi les siamois, *Amour de la Roseraie*, à Mlle Donnety; *Ko-Ki-Nos*, à Mlle Darrieux; *Mousmée*, à Mlle Uffoltz, emportent le premier prix, et aussi *Mamy*, un magnifique chat de Turquie, et *Dimitri de Slootendries*, à M. Gevaert, pour les chats des Chartreux.

Club du Bleu de Perse, who had already exhibited in England and France and was the owner of the Maritza farm in Aire-sur-Lys, in Pas- de-Calais. In Angers, she exhibited several Persians and won 6 prizes. But it may have also been on this occasion that she became interested in Birman and decided to start breeding it in addition to her Persians. She had experience in the breeding industry and sufficient financial means to buy specimens at a high price.

> *Chat de Birmanie* (femelle)
> 917. 1. Prix. — Mme Léotardi.
> *Chat de Birmanie* (jeune)
> 317. 3. Prix. — Mme Léotardi.

The Birman cat had three promoters who guaranteed its success: Philippe Jumaud, president of the *Cat Club of France and Belgium* and promoter of French cat exhibitions since 1913; Marcelle Adam, president of the Paris Cat Club; and Mrs. L. Brassart (her first name does not appear anywhere), one of the largest cat breeders in France. Each of these three people was in direct contact with Mrs. Léotardi.

Mrs. Léotardi is then mentioned in connection with the first international feline exhibition to be held in Paris on May 14 and 15, 1926. However, the name associated with the Birman was that of Marcelle Adam, of whom we know several versions of her first photograph. Then came (as we already mentioned) an article by Philippe Jumaud in the October 1926 issue of *La Vie à la Campagne*. It provides new information and alludes to new revelations from Mrs. Léotardi concerning the breeding of Birman; she claimed to "prove" its exceptional origin. As we have said, this text is found in the 1926, then 1930 and 1935 editions of *Les Races de Chats* of Jumaud. There is an anecdote from Mrs. Léotardi presenting Persians and Siamese to her Birman with varying success. Note that despite the official story that Birman chocolates appeared in the 1970s, there must have been some before the Second World War since, according to what this article states, Ms. Léotardi favored the mating of a Birman with a chocolate-point Siamese, which would also bring the Birman closer to the Siamese " Temple Cat," with a more rounded head, rather than the Siamese known as "Royal." In fact, the article in *L'Ouest-Éclair* published on May 28, 1927 reports the existence of "chocolate from Burma" cats. It is, moreover, by using a chocolate-point Siamese that English breeders later create, the chocolate-point Birman and the associated diluted gene, the lilac-point. One can also wonder where Mrs. Léotardi had

LE CHAT DE BIRMANIE

A l'Exposition féline de la salle Wagram, Mme Marcelle Adam, membre du jury, expose ce magnifique chat sacré de Birmanie.

found the "superb Persian cat" which she first presented to her male Birman (who rejected her). Again, it seems that the most plausible answer is the breeding of Mrs. Brassart who was one of the main Persian breeders in France and who would produce the beautiful birman cat *Lon Saïto*. In any case, what this article demonstrates is that Mme Léotardi did not hesitate to make daring crosses between races.

The photos illustrating the article designate Mrs. Léotardi as the owner of *Poupée de Madalpour* who won the first prize for Birman females at the *International Feline Exhibition* in Paris in May 1926. (*Manou*, the son of Poupée that Mrs. Adam acquired, won the first prize for Birman males.)

The following year—in the report given by *Le Petit Parisien* of January 16, 1927 of the International Cat Show in Paris on January 14 and 15, under the title "The Cat Show distributed its awards"—the name of Mrs. Léotardi is again mentioned to indicate that Poupée de Madalpour "belonging to Mrs. Léotardi" obtained a fifth medal. That year, there were three Birman cats presented. But this was the last year in which the press talked about Mme Léotardi and her cat

Poupée. She then seems to have disappeared from circulation and from that moment, the Birman is associated with Mrs. Adam and other breeders whom we will talk about later.

THE LÉOTARDI AFFAIR

Mme Léotardi à son arrivée au Palais.
(C'est en vain, comme on voit, qu'elle a tenté de
se dérober à l'objectif de nos photographes.)

However, in the newspapers between the two world wars, one can discover a series of extraordinary documents concerning a Mrs. Juanita Léotardi who circulated between Paris and Nice. It appears on the front page of all the newspapers, from the end of December 1922 to the beginning of January 1923, about what is called "The Léotardi Affair" which kept the French public in suspense among the twists and turns at the final judgment in 1924, and even until 1931 with other cases. As I will demonstrate, she was indeed the creator of the Birman cat.

On December 22, 1922, France learned of the existence of a vast scam which was called "The Léotardi Affair," and which is very similar to the Crawford-Humbert Affair that took place almost twenty years before (cf. Annex).

The plot reveals itself on December 16, 1922, when Mr. Bangue—a Parisian banker in the ninth district (arrondissement)—filed a complaint against Mr. and Mrs. Léotardi, for having obtained from him an advance of funds on inheritance of 35,000 francs, sensibly intended to pay the costs of the succession of a certain Lilian Fair Heller, who died on July 21, 1921 aboard her yacht Old Chap, during a cruise in the Mediterranean. This alleged American billionaire was said to have instituted Mme Léotardi as her universal legatee. As the affair dragged on for more than 17 months without success, the banker feared that this legacy was "more than problematic." The complaint was withdrawn due to a prompt refund made by the Léotardi. The suspicious prosecution nevertheless decided to continue the investigation and uncovered a most incredible story. Here is the starting point:

In 1910, Mrs. Léotardi says to have made the acquaintance of a certain Mrs. Lilian Fair-Heller, American billionaire who adored animals, and shared this adoration with Mrs. Léotardi, and purportedly left her a fabulous inheritance—the amount varies according to the newspapers between 85 and 700 million dollars (between 1 and 9 billion French francs of the time). The will was registered in Marseille on July 6, 1921, just two weeks before the presumed death of its author; here is the text:

I leave to Mrs. Jane Manchado, now Mrs. Albert Léotardi, my jewelry and all my fortune. She will have to take care of my animals, all my animals. I also name my cousin Wilbur Heller Ryerson of Boston to carry out these wishes and leave him my yacht in remembrance, the Old Chap, with what is contained. These wills must be the only ones which are executed and which nullifies the others. Signed: Lillian Fair-Heller. Boston, U.S.A."

At least, that is what the *Paris* newspaper of December 22 claims under the ironic title "The Rolling Billion. A file that contains the Gotha of nobility and the mob".

LE MILLIARD QUI *ROULE*

Un dossier qui contient
le gotha de la noblesse et celui de la faune

Mrs. Léotardi not only had a holographic copy of the will (a written copy - the original of which is invisible), she also had a large file of almost 700 pieces. Among these was the list of animals collected by Mrs. Fair-Heller. There were all species: dogs, cats, monkeys, fish, crocodiles, giraffes, bears and even elephants. On the same list were the names of the zoos or acclimatization gardens which had custody of them: most in Bermuda (a totally inaccessible place) and, more curiously, in Valencia, Spain. Questioned on this subject by the investigating judge, Mr. Barnaud, Mrs. Léotardi confessed (according to the *Paris* newspaper) that this list "is almost entirely the product of her imagination or of the researches she has done in Natural History – it was to amuse my husband, she added, that I made this list. I affirm, however, that Ms. Fair Heller had a complete collection of live animals that could be domesticated." (p. 1). But three days later, on December 25, in a direct interview with the representative of the big national daily newspaper *Le Journal*, she proclaimed with indignation in the article "The legacy of 9 billion. The Léotardi spouses protest in good faith": "It has been said that I confessed to having invented the famous lists of animals, continues the heiress; it's wrong. All the documents in the file are authentic" (p. 2).

In this file, the name of Mrs. Cattauï, wife of the banker who was involved in the Thérèse Humbert affair, the famous presumed heiress of the alleged fortune of the Crawford untraceable, also appears (see Appendix). She is designated there as a relative of the deceased millionaire, who would try to buy back "at low cost" the inheritance to Mrs. Léotardi with the help of the hypothetical cousin, Wilbur Heller. Another part of the file is a letter signed by a well-known Japanese lawyer, originally according to versions of Yokohama or Tokyo, and named "Kadohara" by the newspapers, who outspends the history of the inheritance by saying that thirty million yen belonging to Ms. Fair-Heller would also go to Mrs. Léotardi. Contacted by French police, the unfortunate Japanese man reported that he had never heard of this heritage or of the two women in question.

Among the personalities mentioned in these seven hundred documents, we find generals, admirals, senators, chamberlains of kingdoms, ministers of South American republics, without counting Vanderbilt, Ford and Pierpont Morgan. Their letters are addressed to Ms. Fair-Heller, Mrs. Léotardi or even Miss Manchado. However, when asked about these personalities, Mrs. Léotardi said that they were simply "modest homonyms" and not characters known to all.

Going back to the will—the central element of the file—the question arises about the identity of Mrs. or Miss (the newspapers are not fixed on this point) Lillian Fair-Heller. In fact, it probably had no real existence. At the origin of this imbroglio, we find the history of the Fair heritage: in 1902, an American couple of this name, Charles and Caroline, related to the Vanderbilt family, died on August 14 in a car accident on the way to Pacy-sur-Eure, in France. Obtaining their inheritance in the amount of 50 million francs, was the subject of a dispute between the husband's family (his two sisters, Ms. Virginia William K. Vanderbilt [2nd] and Theresa Herman Oelrichs, children of the Californian senator James G. Fair (of San Francisco) and that of the wife (his mother Mrs. Abraham-Nelson). The question arose: Which of the two died first? With false testimonies and disinterestedness agreements, the case was dragged before the courts for two years before being finally judged in favor of the sisters of Charles Fair on May 5, 1904. However, Mrs. Abraham Nelson received the sum of 1,250,000 francs, not a negligible amount. It will be noted that, contrary to what Mrs. Léotardi claimed, no niece of the Fair spouses could be called Fair-Heller, if judged by the genealogies exposed during this trial. And any nephews and nieces of Caroline Fair could not bear this surname.

However, Mrs. Léotardi dodged this existential question to focus on the circumstances of the death of Lillian Fair-Heller. She explained that she could not come into possession of her inheritance (which justified her different loans), because the notary who held the will refused to make it public until he had received a death certificate. However, it was unknown, and for good reason, where Lillian Fair-Heller died (at sea? Or in Barcelona?) and where she was buried.

The Léotardi couple continued to keep the banker Bangue and other lenders in suspense on the pretext that the investigation was ongoing in America and France. Of course, the witnesses and participants in this story were continuously impossible to meet, for all kinds of pretexts, the accumulation of which becomes very unlikely.

After Mr. Bangue's complaint, the police investigation could find no trace of Mr. Wilbur Heller or of a yacht named *Old Chap*. Thereupon, on December 23, 1922, they learned that a French official, who remained anonymous (M.R.), had also lent Mrs. Léotardi a considerable sum (40,000 francs), in order to allow her to obtain her inheritance in exchange for sumptuous promises—that of the marriage of his daughter with the famous cousin, Wilbur. Unfortunately, the official was never able to meet the latter and wondered "if he has not been the object of a hoax". At the same time, we discover that under her maiden name, Juanita Manchado, Mrs. Léotardi was the subject of two convictions in Nice. Then, in the process, we learned that Mrs. Léotardi was mandated by Ms. Fair-Heller (which indicates she had the notarized power of attorney signed two years prior), to buy real estate and land on the Côte d'Azur (French Riviera) and in Paris—up to 20 or 30 million francs. Of course, this money never materialized, which was a striking reminder of Thérèse Humbert's case. Meanwhile, the Marseille notary, Maître de Gasquet, who had been a problem, admitted that he did indeed have the original will, but had never met Lillian Fair-Heller personally. She had been seriously ill when she

Mme Léotardi

sent him this document, and died soon after. Maître de Gasquet did not question the existence of Ms. Lillian Fair-Heller, but imperatively demanded a death certificate to proceed with the opening of the will. But the consul of France in Boston, contacted for this affair, concluded that there existed, in his district, no Miss Heller.

Nor did the Fair-Heller family forge or steelworks exist in the city of Boston, contrary to the rumor circulated by Mrs. Léotardi. The American consul, based in Marseilles, for its part, carried out similar research and came to the same conclusions, stating there was no trace of cousin Wilbur.

It should be noted that on December 23, an article in the New York Herald published in Paris and entitled

"Police of Paris Scoff at Story of Fair Estate" (p. 7), confirmed that the French police doubted the legitimacy of the claims of Mrs. "Marcel Léon Tardi" and wondered if she was the victim or the organizer of a scam concerning the fortune of "Mrs. Lillian Fair Heller of Boston." This text was quite confused, and riddled with errors, (starting with the one that bears the name of Mrs. Léotardi). Nonetheless, it was relayed two days later in an article by *Le Petit Parisien* entitled "The Fabulous Heritage." Incorrect translation or abusive extrapolation, the information contained in this French version of the facts, did not really correspond to the note of the *New York Herald*. But the *Petit Parisian* categorically engaged in controversy through a short article which states that: "Mr. Charles L. Fair [sic] of New York, who is related to the Fair family of California, has never heard of Miss Fair Heller." (p. 3).

Police of Paris Scoff at Story of Fair Estate

Say Marcel Leon Tardi Is a Joke Victim or a Dreamer.

Special Cable to THE NEW YORK HERALD.
Copyright, 1922, by THE NEW YORK HERALD.

New York Herald Bureau,
Paris, Dec. 22.

The French police, after further investigation, are convinced that the fantastic story told yesterday by Mme. Marcel Leon Tardi, the professed heiress to the estate of Mrs. Lillian Fair Heller of Boston, is without foundation; but they are doubtful whether Mme. Tardi is the victim of a joke or herself fabricated the story of the will bequeathing her the Heller fortune. nevertheless a document purporting to be the will of "Lillian Fair Heller" has been found in Paris, and charges of fraud brought by a banker, who advanced Mme. Tardi 20,000 francs, have been withdrawn.

The Paris police, however, on the supposition that the Charles L. Fair estate, the bulk of which went to his sisters, Mrs. Herman Oelrichs and Mrs. W. K. Vanderbilt 2d, might be the subject of an attempt to swindle, decided to check up Mme. Tardi's declarations more closely. They found that already she had altered considerably her first story.

On the same day, judge Barnaud indicted the Léotardi spouses for fraud and aiding and abetting fraud. But three days later, Mrs. Léotardi retaliated by blaming the delays and hesitations concerning the inheritance on a sister of Miss Fair-Heller, Ethel Cattauï of whom

HÉRITAGES. — Je vous vois recueillant une succession de neuf milliards !...
— Ça va... Prêtez-moi donc 500 francs dessus.

we spoke above, who tried to prevent her from coming into possession of what was due to her. This Mrs. Cattaui was supposedly first the divorced wife of a Cairo banker involved twenty years earlier in the Humbert affair; but then Mrs. Léotardi altered her story, declaring that this lady, who offered to buy her inheritance for 40 million, was the widow of an Armenian cotton broker from Boston. Ordinarily resident in Tunis, she was currently in Armenia. However, the information fluctuated extremely since Mrs. Léotardi contradicted herself several times about the identity of this lady, her place of residence and her marital status, while Mr. Léotardi's statements did not fit this timeline.

The same issue of the December 27 Journal also offered a first photo of Mrs. Léotardi as well as a caricature on the situation.

On December 28, the press published details on Mrs. Léotardi's life in Nice, the city where she stayed between 1914 and 1919. In particular, two significant incidents occurred there: First, in 1914, while she was the wife of Maurice Vesian, authorized representative of the *Compagnie Algérienne de Nice*, she was prosecuted for having sold a piano bought on credit. Since she managed to get along with the complainant, the case was dismissed. Second, in 1917, when she divorced and returned to being "Juanita Manchado," and tried to buy the villa "Aurore" from a certain Mrs. Capelle. To this end, she declares that she had a current account with the Algerian company of her ex-husband and produced a check book confirming her statements. But Mrs. Capelle then realized that Mrs. Manchado did not have the necessary funds, although she was already installed in the villa and sold the furniture (which of course belonged to Mrs. Capelle). This time, she was sentenced to six months in prison by the criminal court. Finally, under her pen name, Marcelle d'Urlac, she borrowed large sums from her cook by promising her miraculous rewards. After being sentenced to one year in prison by default, she was in fact acquitted on opposition proceedings. After these revelations about Mrs. Léotardi's past, we revisit the Fair-Heller affair, when, on December 29, 1922, we learned that her heir should have been an American "Mr. Vanderbilt who had been her fiancé." However, Lillian Fair-Heller had then changed her mind and made Mrs. André Léotardi her universal legatee. These emotional ups and downs serve to explain the fact that Mrs. Léotardi tried to cash four checks, for a total amount of 550,000 francs, signed by Mr. Vanderbilt, who of course refused to honor them. Mrs. Léotardi's argument was that these checks constituted compensation spontaneously offered by Mr. Vanderbilt during a brief reconciliation with her fiancée, during which he became her heir again. After another, definitive break, Mr. Vanderbilt had no reason to be generous. On the same day, the newspaper *Le Populaire de Paris,* opened the way to new speculation by claiming that Mr. André Léotardi had in fact married Juanita Manchado "to make it easier for him to take possession of American dollars" (p. 3); this poor man would therefore also be an innocent victim of his wife.

Let us continue to dig into Mrs. Léotardi's past. The *Paris* newspaper reveals on December 29 that in 1919, before her remarriage, Juanita Manchado lived in the suburbs of Marseille, and had power of attorney established in the name of one of her neighbors, Miss Olivier, so that she may receive in her name a pension from the "King of Spain." Of course, the documents provided were false, but they nevertheless enabled Mme Manchado to extract 1,500 francs from Miss Olivier. The stories did not stop there but continued: *La Presse* (p. 1) announced that Mrs. Léotardi would also be the beneficiary of another inheritance, that of the Norman family of Royer-Plasson, all deceased in a few months, after having made a donation of 40 million to William or Wilbur Heller Reyson (cousin Wilbur), on the condition that he gives a life annuity of 20,000 francs to the Leotardi's family. But as of December 30, a dramatic change occurred, because these people were unknown in Lisieux and in fact did not exist. Of course, Mrs. Léotardi declared that she never touched any of these enormous sums. This additional legacy was not even the last, since another document in this inexhaustible dossier mentioned talks between Mrs. Léotardi, a certain Mr. Derrick Beaconfield from Country-Castle, Barton Mills near *Mildenhall* (in England therefore), and Mrs. Léotardi. Mr. Beaconsfield was said to have agreed to pay the Léotardi family at the end of 1920 the sum of

1,200,000 francs, as compensation for a failed real estate transaction.

Overall, the newspapers were very skeptical from that date. *Le Journal* writes in its December 29, 1922 issue, under the title "Mrs. Léotardi explains to the judge about the fabulous legacy":

Certainly, everyone agrees, very much agree – except the Léotardi spouses – on the non-existence of this magnificent American whose presence on the French Riviera has so far been manifested only by the deposit of a power and a will in the study of a notary in Marseille. Well worthy, indeed, of the land of "galéjades" [exaggerated stories in Marseilles' tradition] this extraordinary story of will created from scratch by the fiery imagination of Mrs. Léotardi. Nothing is missing in truth: the blue sea, the Old Chap yacht with white sails, the fiancé with a well-known name, the Japanese lawyer, etc." (p. 1).

This skepticism increased even more when, on January 5, 1923, *Le Petit Journal* unearthed a 1917 judgment: Madame Leotardi reportedly told Judge Bourgueil of Nice that she was "under the dependence of a Hindu prince who hypnotized her with the help of a precious stone embedded in a ring and whose facets plunged her into a state of somnambulism: she then obeyed his orders with morbid passivity." Following this statement, she was examined by an alienist doctor, Dr. Roques de Fursac, who established that she was a "hysterical morphine addict capable of extraordinary fables, half-conscious but still responsible for some of her actions and neurosis." (p. 4). This diagnosis in 1917 led to the suspension of the proceedings against Mrs. Léotardi. The same physician was therefore invited to examine her again in 1923, and he confirmed that "Mrs.

Leotardi's stories are pure inventions. She needs to lie like a morphine addict needs to prick herself." (p. 3).

On January 9, 1923, a new complaint was filed with the parquet floor of Paris by Mr. Delbost, director of the real estate agency *Paris-Publicité*. The Léotardis swindled him out of 23,000 francs under the pretext of the purchase of a castle having belonged to queen "Marie Antoinette," La Ferté-Vidame. He explains to *Le Petit Parisien* (p. 2) the ins and outs of his mishap. He introduces himself as an old friend of Mr. Léotardi and tells:

I had known Léotardi for a long time. I saw him from time to time, in agricultural exhibitions, for example, where he placed artificial incubators. At the end of 1919 he came to my house one evening. He was in deep misery and was coming out of the hospital. I gave him some subsidies and, in conversation, told him that I had to sell large properties in Eure-et-Loir, including the 900 hectares of the historic Château de la Ferté-Vidame, residence of Marie-Antoinette. Léotardi replied that he knew a buyer in the person of an American billionaire, Miss Fair Heller, who was specifically looking to acquire in France for 30 million properties. My friend added that he could be in touch with this person by the intermediary of a delightfully pretty woman with whom she was in touch. But to be on the safe side, he had to marry this woman and it was an important investment for him. Thinking that my castle was going to be sold through Léotardi, I advanced the necessary amount to him to make a suitable wedding and the marriage took place. I was all the more reassured that soon after, Léotardi showed me letters and dispatches from the American lady where she promised to acquire the Carabancel Palace in Nice. In order to propose the case to Miss Fair Heller, I left for Nice. But the latter was no longer there ... [...] the American had left for Florence where she was busy buying a palace belonging to the court of Italy which she paid 15 million. She sold it almost immediately to Mrs. widow Gordon-Bennet, who lived in Beaulieu. At least that's what Léotardi told me. [...] even if the money is not paid, there is an indemnity of 3 million, which is provided for and guaranteed by Morgan, Vanderbilt and Rockefeller." (p. 2).

In the middle of this soap opera, a journalist who worked for the important daily newspaper *L'Intransigeant*, Gilbert Gile, gained entry into the Parisian apartment of Léotardi and discovered a letter of wishes addressed by Mrs. Cattauï, sister of Mrs. Fair-Heller, to Mrs. Léotardi, January 1, 1923. He quoted large excerpts from it in the January 12 issue of his journal, and cruelly concluded: "In this letter, presumably dictated by Mrs. Léotardi's sick brain, we notice with what attention to detail she does her staging, pushing accuracy – even exaggerating it – to the heaviness of style." (p. 2).

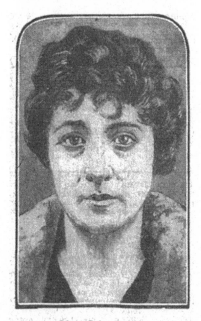

MME LÉOTARDI

At the end of the year, Mrs. Léotardi was finally arrested, on November 6, 1923. A writing expert, Mr. Rougemont, examined all the documents in the Léotardi file and concluded:

"They were faked and by the hand of Mrs. Leotardi." Investigations in America, Spain and everywhere else came back negative. There is definitely no Miss Edith Alix Lillian Fair-Heller, who would have been born on April 23, 1896 in Bolivar, Venezuela and would have lived in Boston, "if not in the imagination of Mrs. Léotardi [...] Mrs. Léotardi, née Juanita Manchado [sic], brought in the afternoon before Mr. Barnaud, the examining magistrate, cried a lot when she heard the judge say that she would go to sleep in Saint-

114

Lazare prison. She declared herself sick and sought medical attention. Dr. Paul, a medical examiner, will go and examine her and say if she can support the prison regime." (ibid.).

The newspapers then make the comparison between this affair and that which moved the press 20 years before. "A new Humbert affair," headline *La Libre Parole* of November 7, 1923 (p. 2) and the same day edition *Le Journal* speaks on the front page of "Mrs. Léotardi, born Juanita Manchado, this emulator of the 'Grande Thérèse'." But twenty days later, on November 26, 1923, Mrs. Léotardi was indeed released on bail for health reasons and the case fell asleep for more than six months; it was not until June 24, 1924 that the matter was brought before the 11th Correctional Chamber, and not until November 12 of that same year that Mrs. Léotardi finally appeared before this chamber. She was accused of fraud, but then tried to shift all responsibility for the case to her husband, who had since died. Her lawyer, Maître Alcide Delmont, stated very precisely that Mrs. Léotardi was the victim of a "daring hoax" and that her husband was the only intermediary in all financial transactions. While the information on Mrs. Léotardi continued to lack precision (for example, according to sources, she is between 38 and 46 years old), the accused continued to affirm her story was true; for example, she said about the multiple false documents: "So, sir, here are fourteen different writings that I am charged! How can we demonstrate such a thing! One or two scriptures would be defensible, but fourteen!". We also learn, incidentally, that the famous bogus checks deposited by Mrs. Léotardi at her bank bore the signature of bachelor Harold Vanderbilt, which would prove important. Finally, after multiple referrals due to the fact that the accused was sick, she obtained release on bail for almost a year. The judgment was pronounced on November 26, 1924: Mrs. Léotardi was sentenced for fraud to one year in prison without a suspended sentence and to a fine of 500 francs.

Apparently, journalists were no longer interested in the Léotardi case. However, as we will learn later, in another case, it seemed that Mrs. Léotardi still managed to delay the inevitable by appealing the judgment of November 1924. It was only on January 17, 1927 that would have been rendered the final judgment of the court of appeal, which condemned her to two years in prison and a thousand francs fine, double the initial sentence. We must therefore conclude that Mrs. Léotardi was imprisoned between November 1924 and January 1927. She returned to the front of the stage seven years later, January 14, 1931 this time: on this occasion Mrs. Léotardi claimed that during the information of the previous trial, a pearl necklace with a value of 225,000 francs was seized and handed over to the Paris registry. But the necklace deposited at the registry was only worth 150 francs. Mrs. Léotardi claimed that it was not the same one (she had only 64 pearls instead of 74 and had lost its precious clasp) and filed a complaint against persons unknown in the context of an accusation of corruption against the Paris registry. Le Journal of January 14, 1931 quoted her testimony in court.

During the investigation opened by Mr. Barnaud, the magistrate, she said, I "had a pearl necklace seized from my home on Boulevard Haussmann by Mr. Ameline. This necklace, bought for her in 1917 at the Gompers house in Monte Carlo by a friend, had been purchased for 225,000 francs and consisted of 74 fine pearls with an olive clasp formed by an opal and two circles of diamonds".

An expert in jewelry's making–expertise made during the necklace appraisal–described it and estimated it at 70,000 francs, that is to say at a sum well below its value.

However, some time ago, Mr. Joutel, administrator, appointed receiver of the necklace, noted at the time of delivery that my necklace had been replaced in the sealed with a necklace of false pearls worth 150 francs. " (p. 1)

However, this necklace was used as collateral for a new loan of 145,000 francs granted to Mrs. Léotardi by Mr. Richard, former notary (this loan was intended to allow the exercise of a real estate option on the French Riviera, including Mrs. Léotardi who claimed to be in possession). Mr. Richard had asked Mr. Joutel to put the collar in receivership because of his doubts about the alleged option. After Mrs. Léotardi's complaint, Mr. Richard's recent widow also filed a lawsuit against persons unknown, for the substitution of a fake for the high-value original. However, on March 13, 1931, in an article entitled "The mystery of Mrs. Léotardi's necklace is clarified," the newspaper L'Œuvre revealed that "Mr. Moser's investigation established that the seals affixed to the necklace were intact and that in addition, at the time of the seizure, Mrs. Léotardi had spontaneously indicated to the police commissioner Ameline that the necklace was worthless. During the investigation, she said that the necklace had been repaired in Marseille and had then been the subject of an expert. All of these facts were found to be entirely false. On the other hand, the investigation made it possible to verify that no substitution was possible at the registry where the objects are kept securely." (p. 2). While "The necklace affair" may be incredible, it is less so than the Fair-Heller heritage; Mrs. Léotardi's last appearance on the public scene was even more modest. On November 29, 1931, the newspapers reported a final scam. Mrs. Yvonne Boudard and Juanita Léotardi wished to buy old lace from an antique dealer, Mrs. Baroness de Camont. Mrs. Boudard attested to her credit worthiness by declaring that she owned large properties in Nièvre, a fact apparently confirmed by a letter from a notary in Clamecy. Mme de Camont therefore agreed to a 2,500 franc lace sale on a draft, but naturally did not manage to get her money's worth. According to *Le Journal*, the thirteenth chamber of the Paris court sentences Mmes Boudard and Léotardi to three months in prison for fraud (p. 4). But the title of the article only mentions Mme Léotardi. She was absent during the conviction and would never be talked about again.

All these cases testify to the audacity and the coolness of Mrs. Léotardi who did not hesitate to produce false documents, to create imaginary characters, but also use the names of well-known people whom she had of course never encountered. Her charisma and acting skills allowed her to maintain the mystery for years, which we will also see in the story of the Sacred Birman Cat. Indeed, Mrs. Léotardi happily reuses some of the ingredients of these inheritance affairs in her feline history.

First, it must be recognized that both the different stages of Mrs. Juanita Manchado's public career and the first data concerning the Birman are located on the Côte d'Azur and precisely on the Nice side. In particular, it is in Nice that the first Birman are supposed to disembark, and it is there too that the famous *Youyou* Siamese of Doctor Prat is found.

But the legendary adventurer was also happy to take on some of her characters from one fiction to another: this was the case, for example, of poor Harold Vanderbilt. On the one hand, he was the alleged signatory of the false checks addressed to Mrs. Léotardi; and on the other, he was also the man who helped a servant of Lao Tsun to acquire a couple of sacred cats. In addition, this version was quickly replaced by a scenario which stages two complete strangers: Major Russel Gordon and Mrs. Thadde Hadish, whose exotic names conform well to the tastes of Mrs. Léotardi, without counting her alleged interactions with the widow of James Gordon-Bennett, when she lived in Beaulieu-sur-mer, near Monte-Carlo. However, Gordon-Bennett, who was not content to finance the Stanley expedition in the footsteps of Livingstone (and the vain quest of the ship "Jeannette" to reach the North Pole), also traveled a lot around the world on his yacht "Namouna" and went, in particular, to India and probably Southeast Asia. He was therefore able to easily inspire Mme Léotardi with the name of Major Russel-Gordon.

More specifically, Mrs. Léotardi also made use of her scenarios in a little-known town in Suffolk, *Mildenhall*. This one, very improbably, was mentioned by Major Russel-Gordon when he described the famous plaque number 4.108 (representing a feline admiring a deity with sapphire eyes) which constituted the highlight of his collection of memories of Burma. But this was also the place where the residence of Mr. Derrick Beaconfield was located, which was involved in a dark story of forfeiture in the amount of 1,200,000 francs due to Mrs. Léotardi in place of a real estate transaction which did not happen. The newspapers which alluded to it, on December 20, 1922, were quite incapable of explaining clearly what it was all about but repeated many times that same Mr. Beaconfield's address: "Country-Castle Barton Mills Mildenhall (Suffolk)."

But the parallelism between the two main fictions woven by Mrs. Léotardi culminates with the recurring interest which she showed for animals. Not only did she mention during one of her hearings having researched "Natural History," as *Le Journal* of December 25, 1922 quotes it, but she repeatedly stated that her friendships with the mythical Lillian Fair-Heller came from their common passion for animals. In fact, the counterpart of the legacy of the American millionaire would have been the care that Mrs. Léotardi had to give to her friend's menagerie, a menagerie which, of course, included cats. Better yet: on Saturday December 23, 1922, in an interview with the newspaper La *Liberté* Mrs. Léotardi had the "first Birman cat" served to demonstrate her intimacy with Lillian Fair-Heller:

'During a cruise with Miss Heller aboard her yacht Old Chap, we bonded quite intimately with her.
- Is it true that she had a lot of animals around her?
- My God! She owned small dogs and cats, including **the Birman cat** here ... '

And Mrs. Léotardi shows us a superb cat very similar to Siamese cats, except that it is marked very curiously with white on all fours paws. (p. 1)

We have here the confluence of the two favorite inventions of Mrs. Léotardi and, in a way, the first appearance of a Birman cat on public documents. Contrary to the legend that she had spread elsewhere, Mrs. Léotardi says with impunity that this cat came to her from Lillian Fair-Heller. It is quite probable, if one can add faith to the rantings of Mrs. Léotardi, that this cat is in fact Poupée, and therefore was already an adult in 1922. In any case, the journalist's testimony proves the existence of a conforming cat Birman standard. But this version of the facts had nothing to do with the romantic information that Mrs. Léotardi provided to Philippe Jumaud as well as to Marcelle Adam who spoke of Birman in their respective publications before officially launching Birman on the forefront of the world feline at the first *International Feline Exhibition* in May 1926.

However, it seems that the Birman is not at the center of Mrs. Léotardi's machinations. As the alienist doctor Roques de Fursac says and already quoted, "[she] needs to lie like a morphine addict needs to prick herself," she could not resist the temptation to invent incredible stories; but the Birman remains in the background. During the Fair-Heller affair, she concealed her face with such care that journalists called her "the Tuareg," published nothing on the Birman, and shone by its absence on the posts of the winners of feline exhibitions. She encouraged Philippe Jumaud and Marcelle Adam to publicize the legend of the Sacred Birman Cat, but she was not directly

ON DIRAIT UN TOUAREG

Mme Leotardi dérobant son visage à l'objectif indiscret.

involved in this endeavor. After successfully delaying the execution of her judgment for years, Mrs. Léotardi disappeared from the scene after 1931, probably to the great regret of journalists. But as for the Birman, it was already in 1927 that she passed out of the scene.

It was Marcel Reney (alias Marcel André Chamonin) who had the last word on the subject in 1947. In *Nos Amis les Chats*, he wrote:

There was also, in their tale, a certain Mrs. Léotardi, a high-class adventurer, it seems, who had possessed the Birman after Mrs. Hadish ... Mrs. Marcelle Adam, who surrounded the last days of Manou de Madalpour with her tender affection, certified to me in Paris that Madame Léotardi, before disappearing quite mysteriously, told the story of the Birman as Jumaud and Baudoin wrote it". (p. 178).

The term "adventurer" was in fact also that which had been used by the substitute Siramy at the time of the judgment of November 24, 1924, as *Le Petit Journal* noted it: "the alleged inheritance of Mrs. Léotardi is only a fable invented by an adventurer already twice sentenced for identical crimes". (p. 2).

Mrs. Léotardi was therefore the source of all the information available on the origin of the Birman and all the other authorities she cited are in fact characters of her invention. Frustrated, Marcel Reney added a little further: "I sought to have new details on the existence of Mrs. Thadde Hadish and on Mrs. Léotardi. It was in vain." (p. 179). In addition, he published in 1957 a new 64-page book, small format, entitled *Chats* in which he was even more skeptical about the role played by Mrs. Léotardi:

Extraordinary stories have been told about these cats since a certain Mme Léotardi introduced them to France in 1924. Are they really from Burma where they were severely kept in temples? I cannot vouch for this fabulous origin any more than the legend once written by Mrs. Marcelle Adam to sing the surprising beauty of "Manou de Madalpour," the first sacred cat from Burma exhibited in France. After this splendid cat, there was yet another extraordinary cat of this breed, "Dieu d'Arakan." The war made them all disappear. Since then, attempts have been made in Germany and France to reconstruct the breed, but breeders have not yet obtained the golden color of the fur, any more than the purple blue of the eyes." (p. 42).

Aside from outright mythomania, Mrs. Léotardi's motivations were likely to be financial. The Birman cat was the most expensive cat of the time, due to its extreme rarity, and the breeder was able to amass a small fortune by selling the kittens to wealthy amateurs seduced by their mysterious legend. Large sums of money were actually at stake, as Baudoin-Crevoisier clearly explained in the special issue of *Vie à la Campagne* in "Sa Majesté le Chat", published on April 15, 1935:

The Birman Cat is one of the aristocrats of the feline gent. Its indisputable beauty, especially its rarity, have made it one of the most expensive Cats to acquire. Its breeding can therefore be reasonably remunerative, if success smiles at you. Subjects have reached fabulous prices. Young people at weaning (2 months) are worth 1,500 to 2,000 francs. Adults vary according to the beauty and perfection of the type. A specimen very well gloved and perfect in all respects can be worth 15,000 to 20,000 francs. An average subject pays for around 5,000 francs. These prices are fixed in francs and cannot be compared with the prices of such Cats of other races, sold in England according to the pound value. However, to balance values, carefully divide British prices today by three. Conversely, compared to such prices of Persian cats sold in England, a quality Birman would be worth around sixty-thousand francs across the Channel. Which is obviously a very big achievement price. (p. 19).

In fact, in the 1920s and 1930s, several breeders would embark on the lucrative business they believed to be the production of Birman cats.

One can see the picture of Number 17 on Boulevard Haussmann, in Paris, near the *Galeries Lafayette*, where the Léotardis lived in a plush apartment with *Poupée* in 1922-23. Ironically, the pediment says ... "Transatlantic Bank."

In conclusion, we can now say that the creation of the Birman cat took shape during the Léotardi Affair and the miraculous heritage invented by the non-existent Ms. Liliane Fair-Heller. It is very likely that cats sold under the name of "Burma" by Mrs. Léotardi already existed at this time around 1922 as indicated in the article in the newspaper *La Liberté*. In the delirious imagination of Mrs. Juanita Manchado-Léotardi an additional legend was formed, based on the fact that Miss Liliane Fair-Heller would have had a collection of exotic animals scattered all over the world. In this elaborate tale, she would have acquired a cat stolen from Burma in an imaginary temple thanks to the intermediary of her supposed lover of the moment: Harold Vanderbilt, who would then have offered this cat to his invented fiancée. After the trial and the revelation of the inexistence of this Miss Fair-Heller, Harold Vanderbilt remained as importer and Miss Fair-Heller was then replaced by a new imaginary character: Mrs. Thadde Hadish and further, as an accompaniment, British major Lesly ... and Russell Gordon.

CHAPTER 6

THE FIRST BIRMAN BREEDERS

The efforts made to create the breed

Among these first breeders were Mrs. Marcelle Adam and Mrs. Brassart. However, it is not at all certain that Marcelle Adam, president of the *Société Féline Centrale de France*, would have raised Birmans and, if she did, it was probably briefly. She was rather, indeed, a collector of rare cats belonging to a wide variety of breeds; this is in any case suggested by the articles dated before the Second World War which mention these cats: cats from Burma certainly, but also Persians, Chartreux, and even more original, Maracaja cats from Brazil and cats from Tibet. On the other hand, we know from the article in *La Vie à la Campagne* published in July 1929 that her famous Birman *Manou de Madalpour* was castrated and therefore could not have been used as a breeding male for breeding Birman cats. In any case, after 1929: "Let us quote two cats, unfortunately neutered, belonging to Mrs. Marcelle Adam, and whose beauty put them out of competition: *Manou de Madalpour* and *Li-Lhio*." (p. 293). It also appears that she did not have a Birman female since only these Birman males are mentioned.

Marcelle Adam first heard of Birman cats through Philippe Jumaud, who probably introduced her to Mrs. Léotardi in 1925 during a cat show on the French Riviera. At the first International Feline Exhibition in Paris, which was held on May 14 and 15, 1926, the names of Marcelle Adam and Mrs. Léotardi appeared in the newspapers. Number 277 of *La Vie à la Campagne*, published in July 1926, presents the first photo of Poupée and writes: "CATS OF BURMA. The subjects of this race are rare, but those which were exposed were very pretty, in particular *Poupée de Madalpour*, to Mrs. Léotardi, female presenting all the characters of the race"(p. 276). For its part, the May 15, 1926 issue of the newspaper *Comœdia* presents the first photo of Manou with, in the course of the article, the comment: "'The Sacred Cat of Burma,' by Mrs. Marcelle Adam, contemplates with impenetrable eyes a court of admirers." (p. 1). As we have noted previously, Marcelle Adam staged the Birman cat in her novel, first entitled *L'Amour qui Tremble*, then republished under the title *Eros Vaincu* on October 28, 1926; but that doesn't prove that she was breeding them.

From there, the sacred cats of Burma were present in almost all the cat shows of 1926 in France: after Paris in May, Lyon in November, and Bordeaux in December. But, we also see allusions to Birman cats appear in articles that have nothing to do with the world of feline breeders. In fact, in an article in the *Petit Journal* published on November 17, 1926, the diplomatic journalist George Martin spoke with a famous French explorer, Robert Chauvelot, son-in-law of famous French writer Alphonse Daudet, who had just been charged with a mission in the Sahara. It begins by describing its interior as follows:

M. R. CHAUVELOT

A quiet apartment in Neuilly, where under the eye of our host's father-in-law, Alphonse Daudet, painted in a chiaroscuro, moving and almost tragic manner, curious wonders abound: tapestries, furniture, old knick-knacks and, hanging on walls or placed in display cases, fetishes, weapons, Puppets, exotic beasts. We are at the home of Mr. Robert Chauvelot, a man of letters and an explorer, who has just been charged by the Ministry of Colonies with a mission in the Sahara.

While his well-behaved, daughter, plays on a chair with Birman cats with purple eyes, the author of *Mysterious India, Smiling Japan* and *The Paradise Islands*, pursues a lively monologue, struck, interrupted by searches for papers in drawers and deploying cards, with the index pointing to the Great South ..." (p. 4).

The intimate touch provided by the reference to Mr. Chauvelot's Birman cats is repeated, in more detail, in a very serious article on foreign policy published three months later, on February 27, 1927, in *Comœdia*:

Mr. Robert Chauvelot comes and goes, nervous, his fine face expressive and reflecting every nuance of his thought; there are two adorable young Birman cats Isis and Istar who climb the heavy red curtains with the devil's agility; he gives them flicks, while he defines Japanese diplomacy to me. [...] Before I left him, Mr. Robert Chauvelot showed me the countless and precious memories of his travels; and around us the Birman cats prowled, feline and tender, with their eyes fresher and velvety than violets". (p. 2).

Robert Chauvelot, "man of letters," was like Marcelle Adam, member of the *Committee of the Syndicate of French Novelists*, as attested by the article of June 11, 1926 in which *Le Rappel* provided the list of writers who awarded the Syndicate prize French novelists (p. 3). It is therefore likely that, having befriended Marcelle Adam, he obtained Istar and Isis through her. In February 1930, it was discovered that he was a member of the Honorary Committee and the Board of Directors of the *Société Centrale Féline de France*.

It is not entirely certain that Marcelle Adam was involved in the organization of the big cat show in January 1927, but Mrs. Brassart was part of the organizing committee. It was an imposing exhibition, with, according to Mme Férard who reported on it in issue 284 of *La Vie à la Campagne*, about 210 cats exposed, including 98 Siamese. She also specified: "The varieties of Cats other than the Siamese and the Persians, especially blue, were few in number and did not seem to interest either the public or the breeders, except the Birman Cat. [...] three beautiful Birman Cats, whose hair could be described as half-long, already exhibited in 1926." (p. 56). This account, however, was very prosaic compared to that of Mr. Lucien Farnaux-Renaud, in *Le Gaulois*:

A society of noble lords, coming from the Orient of the Caliphs and from the most Extreme, that of the Mandarins, therefore all subtle and savvy, preferred the muddy cushions of lodges to the muddy asphalt, to the dull rain of this beginning of January well decorated. There, with half-closed eyes, they examined without emotion the women with short hair and the men with vain ideas who passed before them, ironed. What a more perfect method to study a breed than to consider it evolving in freedom on two legs while one remains oneself immobile and in the quietest comfort! So, they were all there. The blue Persian princes or chinchillas with a broad forehead, with a thoughtful look, and the white ones with pink eyes who stretch slowly as well as living snow, and the pink Turkish cats projecting from a cup of raha loukoum. Devilish, the Siamese held out their black ears and stared at you so abruptly, with eyes so clear that one suddenly felt the anxiety of being perfectly ridiculous before an ironic genius. More serious, the Birman remembered that they were sacred. But their neighbors in China, probably disgusted with this western civilization, purely movement-based, turned their backs on the visitors and resumed the dream of inertia to the point where their ancestors left it. A few European tabby or tortoiseshell, a gray chartreux seemed to do the honors of the capital to these Asian hosts to whom, black, a tailless cat from the Isle of Man extended a friendly paw.

While their faithful maidservants, the old ladies, whose weary hands and measured gestures they enjoy, watched over their well-being, the humans, frozen in the street and feverish from the tumult of the modern city, began to speak to low voice, then were silent and circulated silently, secretly intimidated by these nonchalant observers where all that was the wisdom of the past centuries took refuge the day when the sons of Sem and Japhet began to prefer glory to the sweetness of life and the money to love." (p. 1).

Definitely, this exhibition, as well as the sacred cats of Burma, inspired commentators; Madeleine H. Giraud took pleasure in describing them in *Le Siècle* on January 17:

It was a nice innovation, that of the decorated cages, but which had been little followed. Some were very successful. A cage decorated with orchids was splendid and we did not know what to admire the most, the magnificent cat or its luxurious house ... The sacred cats of Burma had to shelter their majesties insensitive to the tributes of the crowd, the leaves red, green and yellow ... Electric bulbs lit them with a mysterious, orange, soft light, while next to an empire green cushion, a Siamese was sleeping under the green light, dazzling with small cruel bulbs. (p. 2).

It was at this exhibition that Mrs. Léotardi won her fifth medal with Poupée de Madalpour.

From then on, Marcelle Adam was systematically associated with her Birman, even in articles that were not dedicated to cats. Thus, number 75 of the *Minerva* Review of January 16, 1927, devoted an article to "Gastronomy and Writers" where we find the famous photograph of Mrs. Adam with her cat Manou. The legend reads: "Mrs. Marcelle Adam the excellent novelist of *Moune, Artist's Wife*, with one of her sacred cats from Burma." We find the same photo again, three months later, in number 86 of April 3, 1927, in a similar article by Gaston Derys this time entitled "Literature

132

and Gastronomy" The photo is accompanied by a text in which Marcelle Adam reveals the recipe for a panache with ragweed:

Marcelle ADAM
et « Manou de Madalpour », son chat birman.

Mrs. Marcelle ADAM, the inspiring novelist of Moune, Artist Wife, secretary of the *Syndicat des Romanciers français*, president of the *Paris Cat Club*, and owner of the illustrious Manou de Madalpour, magnificent Birman cat, holder of a first prize at the cat show, Mrs. Marcelle Adam is also an experienced gastronome. By his subtle care, a simple panade becomes an ambrosia."

Doctor Méry signs further, in issue 102 of July 24, 1927 of *Minerva* another article entitled: "Writers 'Cats & Artists' Cats," in which Marcelle Adam appears alongside the most famous women of letters of the time:

It is curious to note that writers, poets and prose writers, novelists and philosophers, like painters and sculptors, prefer cats. The cat's enigmatic personality, the harmony and nobility of its attitudes, its cleanliness, its discretion, have always made the charm of this ideal friend of the intellectual. In the silence of the studio, in the fancy decor of the workshop, perched on the library or coiled on the couch, isn't the cat very often the only witness that we tolerate? [...] Among the women of letters can we separate the name of COLETTE from everything related to literature or feline psychology. And Mrs. Marcelle ADAM who breeds extremely rare white gloved Birman cats. Mrs. Jeanne LANDRE, Raymonde MACHARD, Claude DAZIL, RACHILDE, TITAYNA, Madeleine GIRAUD, Gérard d'HOUVILLE, Miss READ, spiritual heiress of Barbey d'AUREVILLY from whom she collected "Demonette" with the cats of François COPPÉE and Mrs. Lucie DELARUE-MARDRUS finally, who often fixes on the canvas the harmonious attitudes of his favorite.

The reputation of the Birman cats grew; about the following exhibition, organized by the *Société Centrale Féline,* which took place on May 27 and 28, 1927, *Le Figaro* wrote: "Imperial, the Birman cat stares, without detour, on the visitor with splendid eyes of this sapphire blue that over the centuries, on the terraces of the Orient, it has received beautiful nights from the sky." (p. 3). As for the report given by *Comœdia,* he emphasized an important innovation:

Mrs. Marcelle Adam, who prides herself on a splendid sacred cat from Burma several times awarded, and who will also be part of the jury, has proposed to group all cats belonging to writers: this will be the section of 'Cats of Letters' where we will see the favorites of Colette, Francis Carco, Charles Derennes, Jeanne Sandre, etc. Facing this "Letter Cats" section, there will be "Theater Cats" and Artist Cats." sections (p. 2).

Other men of letters were also present: Paul Brulat, René Fauchois and Raymonde Machard – the link between writers or intellectuals and felines became increasingly close. Between these two exhibitions, the *Club du Faubourg* organized on May 9, 1927, a special literary evening in the Wagram room: "Tonight: Colette on 'Les Chats.'" The program was tantalizing: "contradictory conference by Professor Lépinay from the 'School of Psychology: Cat Trial!" With the intervention of the famous woman of letters, Mrs. Colette, MM. Paul Brulat, doctors Bérillon, Blier, Vachet etc, on the *Psychology of Cats. Are they smart? Cats, woman and love.* (p. 3). If the central subject of the debate seemed rather to be the frivolity of

Parisiennes, from a successful but controversial novel, *L'Amour à la Parisienne* by Clément Vautel, it is significant that cats occupy the stage during the first part, highlighting their link with fashionable women. In addition to Colette, mention is made of Claude Frémy, Marcelle Adam, the Countess of Erly, Maud Gipsy and the text adds "etc".

A little later, *L'Ère Nouvelle*, in its section "Feuilleton" of October 14, publishes a special article by Gaston Derys on "Les Chats des gens de Lettres" which lists:

Among today's writers who are in love with cats, let us quote Colette, to whom they inspired masterpieces; Marius Boissard, who wrote pages of them with a sagacious observation; Claude Farrère, who studied them so well in 'Beasts and People Who Loved Each Other;' Charles Derennes, already mentioned, and Francis Carco, and Arthur Bernède, and J.J. Frappa, who has beautiful Siamese, and Pierre Benoît, who subjects his pussies to the operation of the oophorotomy, and Paul Brulat, and Mrs. Jeanne Landre, and Mrs. Marcelle Adams [sic], justifiably proud of her wonderful Birman, and Gaston Picard, author of the Confession of the Cat, and many others still that I forget ..." (p. 2).

Colette, of course, was frequently associated with cats. At the May exhibition, she "and her chartreux cats won a first honorary prize" as the report by *Comœdia* says, which goes on: "Other honorary prizes are awarded to a black Persian, a little Birman cat, to a Siamese family." (p. 1). This "little Birman cat" seems to be *Nafaghi de Madalpour*, who is mentioned in the long article of 1931 by Baudoin-Crevoisier. She was the daughter of Poupée de Madalpour, and, exceptionally, we have her date of birth: June 20, 1926. The review *Chasse, Pêche, Élevage* of November 15, 1927 confirms this hypothesis with a photo with the caption: "1st

prize. Cat show in Paris (1927), belonging to Mr. and Mrs. Max Gibert. "

Additional proof of the success of the Birman: Mrs. L. Brassart, known internationally for her breeding of Persian cats in Pas-de-Calais, added the Birman to her catalog to apparently become the first (and only?) large breeder of Sacred Cats of Burma as suggested by the advertisements she placed in the review Jardins et Basses-Cours in the fall of 1927 which stated: "Unique cattery of the Birmans."

7966. Chatterie unique des Birmans. Élevage de Maritza, Aire-sur-Lys (P.-de-C.). Chatons à céder, quelques persans adultes, champion noir.

The development of the Sacred Birman Cat continued in the years that followed, at the same time as its association with a type of woman in fashion at that time. For example, the various articles concerning the 4th *International Feline Exhibition of Paris* which takes place in May 1928 mention the number and the beauty of the Birman exposed, signal the appearance of new breeders, or rather breeders, and renew a certain number of photos on the bond between beautiful cats and pretty women. Thus, The *Intransigent* of May 3rd sticks to a factual observation: "We will salute illustrious animals there. The two Chartreux of Mrs. Coletty [sic] will be next to the four Persians of Mrs. Paul Morand And we will also see some of these extremely rare Birman cats which have tender colors and long hairs, and whose legs are gloved in white." (p. 2). The issue 140 of April 15, 1928 of the journal *Minerva* in fact inaugurates a new section entitled "Women and animals" which would appear once a month. This introductory issue to the theme, signed by Doctor Méry, justifies this new section in the following way:

Who is the woman who does not like animals? Is there one that has never been moved by the warm caress of a small dog, the playful grace of a young cat or the fragility of a downy chick? All women love animals, as all animals love women because they trust their sweetness and appreciate their kindness. But it is not enough to cherish the animals to make them happy or to draw from their presence with us the maximum of material or emotional satisfaction.

To make animals better known in order to make them love more and make them better appreciated, this is the goal we are pursuing. For this we will try to document you on all the domestic fauna which can animate, dear readers, your apartment or your country house, populate your garden or your farmyard. We will study in cats, dogs, birds, etc., psychology, hygiene, breeding, diseases specific to each breed, to each variety. The subject, as we can see, is immense. How to choose a dog or a cat, a bird, rabbits, ducks, etc. Which breed to choose? Where to buy it? What price? How to feed it? Have it reproduced? How to raise the little family that we have created? How to sell the subjects? etc ...

We will endeavor at the same time to keep you informed of animal news, because there are for animals, exhibitions, competitions, fashion, a stock market even values that vary with the vagaries of the hour and for purely utilitarian reasons. [...] The cat which one considers as a worthless animal in the countryside, because one has the bad habit of letting it procreate at the whim of the purest fantasy, is on the contrary a prize animal as long as we take the trouble to select it and keep it from all misalliances. A purebred animal costs no more to care for and feed than another; it performs exactly the same services and its market value like that of its products is far from being disdained.

This entire page of the journal includes no less than three photographs of Birman. We find there

Chat de Birmanie.
Hiram, Roi de Madalpour, mâle de 30 mois,
n'atteint que le prix de 3 à 4.000 fr.

Madalpour Poupée, of course, but also the only photo of *Hiram-Roi de Madalpour* and a prototype drawing of Birman which is largely inspired by Poupée. Under the photos, there is, in particular, an indication of the value of the Birman represented: the price of *Poupée* would be estimated at 7,000 - 8,000 francs, while *Hiram-Roi* (male 30 months) would reach only 4,000-5,000 francs. Generally speaking, a perfect Birman sells for between 8,000-10,000 francs.

If women were taken to task in this section, the article by Jean Lasserre in *Le Figaro* of May 5, 1928, entitled "Promenade chez les Chats," focused rather on the female presence within the framework of the feline exhibition, with a tone of irony:

Those who, confident in the poster announcing the Feline Exhibition, will enter the Wagram Hall to see tigers and panthers, will be disappointed. It is, in fact, only felines in miniature who ring out from their meows this closed field of electoral battles and popular balls. But the curious will, on the other hand, have the pleasant surprise of finding, in place of the tamers powdered in gold and covered in leather, very beautiful ladies with fresh voices, who only wear leather - and fine - at the feet, and gold that flowed in a ring or mesh around their white wrist.

Pretty women, in fact, like pretty beasts, like beautiful dresses and cars with harmonious bodies. Horses if they are purebred, dogs if they have a good look, and birds if their plumage is bright or their song of love is in favor with them. But what animal more than a cat can please them? The cat is silent, its velvet streak is muffled on the carpet, it is soft and familiar like a fur. Finally, it is ungrateful, it ignores recognition and it abandons its master at the first call of a moonlit night in spring. The cat is attractive and fickle like a gypsy. It is full of grace and desires. There is a prince and a thug in him. It likes caresses and disdains the fine hand that gives them to him. What more to rule the hearts of women?

It is not possible to believe that women have a hard soul when you catch the maternal and tender look that they can have for a cat.

Such love makes equal the modest guardian of the Wagram Hall whose skinny tomcat is a regular in gutters, and the lady who came from Passy with the flexible and perverse feline, with beige coat, which they brought her from Siam.

Yesterday, however, the beautiful mistresses of the animals on display exchanged between them these jealous glances from mothers who compare their child to the children of others, or from lovers who extol the qualities and merits of those who love them ... They also wondered:

Chat de Birmanie à Mme Brassart

-- What do you give him in the morning?
-- Milk.

LES PRINCES DES CHATS

-- And the night ?
-- Milk still
-- And at noon:
-- Always milk.

And the cuddly and superb cat passed, arching its flexible kidneys, a pink tongue between its tiny teeth, dreaming of birds chirping on the roof and whose bones are tender and crunchy.

All the clichés of ambient misogyny are found in these texts where cats serve little more than a pretext. On the other hand, the report of *La Vie à la Campagne* of June 1, 1928, signed by Mrs. A. Férard, is much more precise: "about 180 subjects, including 88 Siamese, 70 Persians and 8 Birman," and goes as far as to list the Birman who have received an award: "The Birman: Lao Yo de Madalpour CAC and Lon Saitodi [sic. This is an error, the name Lon "Saito de" is distorted.] Madalpour C.A.C. to Mrs. Brassart; Bijal de Madalpour (young male) (to Mrs. Max Gibert); females: Nafaghi de Madalpour (to Mrs. Max Gibert); Yadi (young female) (to Mme de Marigny) are magnificent subjects, many of whom lacked gloves." (p. 216). It was an important year for the Birman, moreover, of the two photos published by *Le Matin* on May 5, 1928, under the title "The Princes of the Cats," one is that of a Birman: Lon Saïto de Madalpour, whose name was also distorted in the article in *La Vie à la Campagne*. This cat was undoubtedly a celebrity.

Mrs. Brassart had been known for a long time, but in the list of owners of Birman champions were two new arrivals, Mrs. Max Gibert and Mrs. de Marigny. The first is the wife of a jurist and investigating judge who had no predisposition to take an interest in cats, the second was known for her breeding of Irish Setters, but she suddenly seemed to commit to cats from Burma, if we believe an article in *L'Intransigeant* published in 1930: "We have seen the sacred cats of Burma whose breed may not disappear in Europe thanks to the efforts of Mme de Marigny." (p. 5). However, this hope would remain vain: after a few years, Mme de Marigny disappeared completely. It is also the period of the big crash.

The success of the Birman is confirmed during the two annual exhibitions of February and May 1929. The first organized by the *Cat Club of Paris*, the second by the new *Société Centrale Féline* which was created in December 1928 and of which Mrs Adam was the president. The report of the first, fifth exhibition of its kind, published in *Chasse, Pêche, Élevage* of March 15, 1929, indicated the presence of 300 cats of all breeds, including a new pair of cats from Burma: "unique in the whole world, in terms of perfection, admired the visitors: Lon Saïto (God of light) and Ijadi Tsund [sic] (Loved by the gods)" (p. 4). For the exhibition of May 1929, veterinarian Dr. Taskin, member of the organizing committee of this event, wrote the report published by *La Vie à la Campagne* on July 1, 1929. He expressed a keen interest in the breed, and the details of the standard:

Always very much admired, and rightly so, are the Sacred Cats of Burma, pretty beasts that are reminiscent of the Siamese in color, but have the long, silky coat of the Angora. In addition, the characteristic of this breed is the presence of white spots encompassing the fingers or even the hands and feet. They are "gloved," they say in technical terms. The great rarity of specimens of this species means that very beautiful subjects are not numerous. However, let us cite two cats, unfortunately neutered, belonging to Mrs. Marcelle Adam, and that their beauty put out of competition: Manou de Madalpour and Li-Lhio. Let us also mention Lon Saito, to Mme Brassart (1st prize), and Mouki, to Mme Lorenzo (1st prize). " (p. 293).

Mouki (by Mme Lorenzo) was not otherwise known; on the other hand, Lon Saïto, frequently quoted, held the imagination of journalists. In the work of February 9, 1929, Henri Simoni wrote a bit oddly: "I became acquainted with Lon Saïto yesterday, which means, in Birman, God of Light ..." (p. 1) and in *Le Figaro* of the same day, Georges Ravon to add: "There are cats which bear [...] religious names: Lon Saïto, God of Light, and Ijadi Tsund (sic. Tsun), Loved by the gods." (p .3).

In the same issue of *Vie à la Campagne* as the one in which the general report of the exhibition is found, Mrs. Marcelle Adam slipped a small article on her cat Manou, which took up at leisure the exotic elements of the legend:

The grandparents were abducted from the Lao-Tsun temple in Upper Burma. There live, honored and served by priests, a hundred sacred cats who reincarnate the soul of the best of the servants of the cult. It is a religion before Buddhism and a wonderful temple defended by the sheer peaks. The little feline gods are jealously guarded. They are revered in strange ceremonies. Their coat with very long hair is white with golden reflections. Their mask, their plume tail, their legs are a dark brown as with the Siamese. And their wonderful eyes are dark blue for having contemplated the sapphire-looking goddess, the exquisite Tsun-Kyanksé, who presides over the transmutation of souls. At the end of the otter-colored legs, the fingers are white, because Sinh, their ancestor all, landed on Mun-Ha, who was holy, before reincarnating his spirit.

Travelers have told me the ritual of this amazing feline religion. They do not understand that two of the sacred cats could have been removed from the temple. Such sacrilege must be punished with death.

Forgotten about his divine origins, "Manou" lives comfortably in my studio. He continues to be revered there. In her small brown face live the two sapphires of the goddess Tsun-Kyanksé. Alas! No matter how I contemplate them, the miracle is denied to me. My eyes do not take the unfathomable azure. (p. 284)

Minerva number 200 of June 9, 1929 offers a new photo of Manou de Madalpour who remained the main promoter of the breed.

« Manon de Madaïpour », Chat sacré de Birmanie à Mme Marcelle Adam.

On the other hand, *L'Intransigeant* of May 29, 1929 did not really get caught up in the exotic charm of cats in general, and the Birman in particular: it published a long caustic article by Henry de Montherlant in which the writer combined his love of cats and his well-known misogyny:

The cats are each in their stall. They tried to ridicule them as they could: by huge showy silk ribbons tied at their necks, by the decoration of the stalls, where the guesthouse style triumphs: branches of lilac, small ribbons, paper flowers. Sometimes the tomcats are locked up with inside their cage, a real display of the medals they won, like the dead of archaic Greece locked in their graves with their trinkets; it used to be their photograph, and there they are, like the man of letters who works in front of his portrait in his office.

Some cages carry signs, "For the sake of the cat, please do not touch." In others is hung a small doll, or rattle, which these ladies call a cock (zizi). Everywhere we see baby bottles, jars of milk, baskets from which towels come out, all the instruments of maternity; because the tone of the exhibition is that of a nursery, where however the characteristic of the "mothers" would be to have never given birth.

They, with all due respect, seem to not care... royally. They are lying on cushions, on small luxury fabrics, or even on the Intransigeant newspaper (perhaps you are not aware that it is the great pleasure of cats, to be seated or lying on an unfolded newspaper). They breathe quickly, because of the heat, and from time to time, we see them breathe a big sigh. We recognize the males immediately by the beauty of their eyes, with deep dilated and dark pupils. Above all, there is a certain irregular Persian 'whose eyes would have driven Omar Khayyam crazy. I don't know why it is irregular, but it's not surprising when you have such beautiful eyes.

To each of them I say a few kind words in Spanish. Some affect not to look at me. Others, on the contrary, seem to recognize me and are touched that I smile at them: we had probably met, once, in the primitive forest, them jaguars and I orangutan. They stare at me for a long time, finally close their eyes to indicate that they have seen enough of me for today.

We also see, in distant corners, somewhat neglected cats, who have had no luck, cats who are not lying on the *Intransigent* newspaper, but on the bare wood of their stalls, and with whom I sit down as before with the not-so-pretty young girls, whom the dancers dropped during the party favors. There is an old lady there who I made cry when she praised her tomcat, with whom people did not stop. In this isolated corner, there is a cat from Central Africa. I do not know why it is always before him that the ladies, by the way, exclaim: "The cat is too hot!"

Exhausted by these delicacies, I went to sit at the buffet to drink a lemonade. There, these ladies are installed. We recount the prowess of Moumoune, Minet, Minou, Pompon: these are the names of the "darlings," if you find better, I'll pay you. I learned how Pompon does when he asks for permission to sleep, at what age he knew how to say: 'Mom'. Some ladies have brought the darling, who climbs on their shoulder, where it performs acrobatics. And if you practice cats, you know the one and only goal of the acrobatics of a cat which is mounted on your shoulder, and it is, putting up the tail, to put its behind under the nose.

A young boy comes and goes offering you insecticide. A gentleman, as in M. de Pourceaugnac, walks around brandishing a large clyster, from which a few threatening drops are already escaping. Hold on tight, constipated darlings! But I soon understand that it is a vaporizer. Because some cats ... emotion ... but hush! Finally, they do not smell good, poor little ones.

And, seen with a little hindsight, from this group of 'mothers' where I find myself, I have better distinguished the aspect of the room which, even more than in a nursery, reminds us of a charity sale. It was when I heard people around me praising their chaste offspring and throwing their heads at the prices offered by wealthy amateurs that this idea came to me. I thought I saw, in place of cats bobbed and wrapped under their sign 'For sale', the poor young girls to marry, also bobbed and wrapped that their mothers make come and go in said charity sales, like a filly in tattersall, under the rich amateur's cold eyes. All this in the same noise of figures. But in sales, you know how to live and you don't put up a sign." (p. 1).

This piece of journalistic bravery is titled "Pass-Time. Feline Exhibition." This was not the only literary use of cats in 1929: a colleague of Mrs. Adam in the *Syndicate of French Novelists*, Mrs. Jeanne Henri, published in serial in *Le Matin*, and under the presumed male pseudonym H.G. Magog, a novel titled *Dot Runner*; the 31st episode, dated August 18, 1929, mentions a Birman cat: "A Birman cat, lying in front of the radiator, dreamed while purring at the sacred places which had seen him born." (p. 4).

We continue in the same tone in 1930. *Paris-Midi,* in its issue of March 12, 1930, on its "Woman's Page" devoted an article to "Salon Cats" in which the writer gave himself up to enthusiasm, but also a touch of social criticism:

The most beautiful specimens of cats imaginable were imported from Asia: Persian blues, flexible and light; the majestic angora, the fawn-like Siamese, with forget-me-not eyes, and finally, the most beautiful of all felines, the Birman cat, with such a strange golden look and silky coat. Now who is the woman who does not own one of these price beasts? You buy a purebred cat like you buy a valuable potiche. And then it's so nice to see, on the piano or on the couch, this disdainful and familiar companion, in hieratic poses, that nothing can force to obey, who, with an air of supreme indifference, watches you live.

The Egyptians had deified it: would we have been influenced?

This living trinket is now taking its place among our big gods.» G. de B. (p. 7).

More laconic, *L'Intransigeant* of April 19 announced the following exhibition with a certain sobriety: "We will see the rarest animals there, such as seven cats from Abyssinia, two sacred cats from Burma, two ocelots, pink cats from Turkey, etc."

A L'EXPOSITION FELINE

Trois des animaux exposés
En haut : *Chat tigré du Brésil.* Au milieu : *Chat sacré de Birmanie.* — En bas : *Chat sans poils*

Le Petit Parisien of April 26 presented several photos of cats from the exhibition, including a Birman cat. The author of the article, Yves Dautun, commented: "The Siamese are the number. Fashion has installed in our homes these wild animals with short coats and disturbing eyes. They are all racy, but also all bad guys. Only the cats of Thibet, meditative like lamas in prayer, and the sacred cats of Burma retract their claws and make good apostles: they are not of this world" (p. 1). The *Petit Journal* of the same day also offered a photo of the same Birman cat in another position, enthroned between a tabby cat from Brazil and a hairless cat (Sphinx).

The profits from the May 1929 exhibition were used to renovate the Menagerie of the Museum of the *Jardin des Plantes*. Under the pen of Georges Ravon, one of the lions of the *Jardin des Plantes* expressed himself in *Le Figaro* on May 25: "Thanks to their cat brothers, the kings of the desert will no longer be poor cousins here." (p. 3). It must be said that the director of the Museum, Mr. Louis Mangin, is an honorary member of the exhibition. We find as a member of the jury Marcelle Adam, but also the famous Robert Chauvelot who had two Birmans. From the same scientific perspective, this exhibition was also an opportunity to study the psychology of cat breeds with interventions from veterinarians like Dr. Hasse, from Belgium, and Dr. Lépinay from France, but also by Mrs. Adam.

However, interest in Birman seems to diminish from 1930. Already on the occasion of the 6th International Feline Exhibition of Paris, organized by the *Cat Club of Paris, L'Œuvre* of February 15, 1930, underlines the rarity of the Birman cat: "Cats take on nonchalant or noble attitudes on the golden and embroidered cushions. There are European cats, Persians with sumptuous furs, Siamese with black ears and, above all, extremely rare Birman. There are four of these Birman people on display. There are only six of this species worldwide" (p. 6). The *Intransigent* of February 16 confirmed the specialists' concerns by quoting Fernand Méry who hoped that: "the race may not disappear in Europe thanks to the efforts of Mme de Marigny", which I mentioned above. (p. 3). At the following exhibition, this time organized by the *Société Centrale Féline*, in April 1930, only two Birman cats were announced (out of a total of 147 cats exhibited). *L'Echo of Paris* highlights this rarity in its article and makes it its main title, "In the midst of the rarest cats," published on April 26:

Mrs. Marcelle Adam and Mrs. Guignaud, who are the organizers of this event, were kind enough to introduce me to the rarest cats.

First here are the sacred Birman cats. They have a legend. There are only a very small number. One hundred exactly, who live in a Birman monastery with one hundred monks. When a monk dies, his soul is reincarnated in the cat. These cats do not breed in our climates, or very rarely, since we do not have at their disposal souls of Birman monks ready to reincarnate." (p. 2).

In view of the marked resemblances between the articles published that day, it seems likely that Mrs. Adam gave a press conference to introduce the romantic legend of the Birman to the world. Nevertheless, journalists did not really get caught up in the charm of this whimsical tale. Thus, in *L'Intransigeant*, André Malève took up almost word for word the ironic comment concerning Birman monks likely to reincarnate and went even further by denying any special beauty to the Birman:

The sacred cats of Burma, who have worthy representatives of the Wagram Hall, have a legend: there are only a very small number in the world - a hundred exactly - who live in a monastery in Burma, which has a hundred monks. In other words, each monk has a cat. These animals do not reproduce, or very strenuously, in Europe, probably because we do not have in our climates souls of Birman monks ready to reincarnate.

Physically, these cats, to a layman like me - and I'm going to make the judges cry - look like angora siamese with a less thin head. (p. 3).

The skepticism of the April 26 *Journal* is expressed in a different way by questioning the specific origin of Birman cats: "Here are the sacred cats of Burma, exported we know not how from the monastery where the monks raised them: they obviously have a

149

common origin with Siam cats which, rare a quarter of a century ago in Europe, are now acclimatized to the point where you can even see them playing in the snow in winter without risking the slightest cold." (p. 2). On the other hand, *Paris-Soir* cheerfully takes up well-known folk elements:

But as rare as they are, there are none, Persians, Siamese or Abyssinians, who can compete with these strange and admirable beasts that are the sacred cats of Upper Burma. They descend from a very precious race which, for centuries has been preserved in the Birman temple of Lao-Tsan [sic] In this temple live a hundred priests and a hundred cats and tradition dictates that when a priest dies his soul is reincarnated under the appearance of a cat which, for this reason, is sacred.

Maum and Lou-Saïto de Madalpom [sic], these are the names of the two Birman cats which appear in the Wagram Hall, the only ones of their breed in Europe. Each is said to be worth a whopping 25,000 francs! ... ". (p. 1)

But the Birman rating remains fairly high if we are to believe "La Tzigane," (the gypsy) an interesting female pseudonym adopted by the author in the article in the issue of *La Femme de France*, which, although published on July 13, 1930, contains the report of this April exhibition:

Friends of the felines, there were many of you at the Wagram Hall Exhibition. What were your favorites? These kitties were as exhilarating as you could want, and we wanted to give everyone the price. However, I stopped longer at Dondoca, the Brazilian ocelot with the big eyes of a sulky child; the snowy theory of Persians with blue pupils; the charming little house of chinchilla angora; and especially the duo who jealously guarded the tiny altar of the Buddha: a marvelous bluish gray Persian with copper pupils and a cute sacred Birman cat who seemed so proudly invested in its mission. (p. 792).

But it should be noted that the sacred Birman cat shares the "jealousy" worship of the Buddha with a Persian! The last show of the year, which took place in December, introduced into the feline circuit a new young Birman male who would become famous. The

Excelsior of December 6, 1930 published the photo with the caption: "Djaïpour, to Mme de Marigny, sacred cat from Burma". In all probability, it is this same Dajipour which gave rise to the lyric flight of *L'Illustration* of December 1930 in the full page, decorated with sketches taken from the feline exhibition: "And here are [...] wild Birman whose tail grows like that of a squirrel ... " (p. 580).

It was however during this year 1930 that the brand-new *Revue Féline de France*, created in February with a quarterly frequency. The official organ of the *Société Centrale Féline Française* presented in its number 2 (April 1930) the Birman standard, of which here is the full excerpt:

The body is elongated, well proportioned. Quite low on legs. The adult weight varies between 5 and 6 kilograms. The head is short, with broad ears, the bulging forehead, the nicely raised nose. The eyes are large, dark blue, iridescent, extraordinary. Their expression is sweet, childlike, a bit nostalgic.

Coat: The hairs are quite long, separated on the back, as if by a comb. Those of the tail are very long, very bushy and form a large plume that the animal carries erect in the manner of squirrels. The color of the dress is creamy white, with golden tones at the collar. The mask, the tail, the ears, the legs are the same dark brown as those of the Siamese. But the otter's kicked

legs have pure white fingers. The tail never shows any lumps. These cats are very social, very intelligent, very cheerful, very caressing. They are jealously attached to their master and cannot bear to leave them. Breeding is difficult, perhaps because of the renewed unions between animals of the same blood, since we know so far in France and perhaps in Europe, only one family of Birman Cats. These sacred cats, raised in a temple in Upper Burma, are severely guarded by priests who believe that their souls are reincarnated in them. Their transfer is therefore prohibited. A lady, who returned last year from these regions with her husband, was surprised to recognize a sacred cat at our exhibition. Some naturalists see the Birman cat as the ancestor of the Siamese cat resulting from a cross with the Annam cat. (p. 15).

The article also included the photo of Manou de Madalpour which had already been published several times. We note the intervention of a new character, a traveler whose alleged surprise gives the legend increased legitimacy.

An article by Dr. F. Schwangart published in the *Revue Féline de France* of April 1931, nevertheless considered the Birman as a simple crossbreeding and not a new import product:

As regards the shape characters, they already reveal two ancient noble races: the Persian race and the Siamese race. The Persian race only depends on the form (of the body and the hair system); in the Siamese, it is of decisive value. The newly introduced Birman cats seem to me to demonstrate that even in cats, the creation of breeds can be based not only on selection, but also on crossbreeding.

Anyway, Marcelle Adam continued to repeat the legend of the Birman cat by embellishing it a little, each time. This is what she did, for example, on the occasion of the feline exhibition of May 15 and 16, 1931 in an article published on May 16 by *L'Intransigeant* which is nicely titled "The Tiger in the House. " Once again, she spoke there of Birman:

The sacred cats of Burma remain extremely rare, for lack of new contribution. We know that the monks, refugees on the high plateaus of their country, rigorously guard from the laymen these divine animals which must reincarnate their souls. Dress with long, frothy hairs, the same hue as that of light siamese, pure white fingers on otter boots and, in the brown mask, the sapphire eyes of the goddess Psun-Kyanksé [sic]. (p. 11).

But this time, the highlight of the exhibition is not a Birman but an albino Siamese. Moreover, *L'Intransigeant* of May 19, 1931 also drew attention to the Siamese, mentioning, as if by the way, that Paul Doumer, French Governor General of Indochina between 1897 and 1902 "was one of the first to bring back to France Siamese cats, which were so rare at the time and which have become so fashionable." (p. 2). In fact, Marcelle Adam herself chose that year to present her Tibetan cat, *Pi-Litt*, at this exhibition.

However, the cat remains the fashionable animal. Suzanne Normand, novelist—who will write in 1966 "My Stories of cats, four without pedigree"—published on May 23, 1931 in *Paris-Soir* a vibrant praise of the cat entitled, "The Cats Powerful and Sweet...":

... I do not believe that there is anything alive on earth which reaches perfection in grace, in pride, in the eurythmy of movement. [...] The cat, him, gives to the glance the most complete satisfaction. It is perhaps the only one who can move its lines without our regret or dissatisfaction. Because a moving cat is pure beauty. [...] I knew a big cat lover who called them "pocket tigers". [...] Only, if the cat, reduced model of the wild animal, kept from this wild independence, it added to it, paradoxically, the fidelity. It is, according to Kipling's term, the one "who always goes away by himself," But it is also the one who returns to its home, and to its master, with an attachment, and a perseverance in affection, worthy of the canine race. [...] However, the best quality of the cat, its most charming grace, it is perhaps that it is silent. We said, we sang, but we will never say, we will not sing enough, the sweetness of a feline tenderness. Is there any company preferable to this one? I bet that a cat is, on its own, capable of populating the worst solitude: this presence, both tyrannical and discreet; that touch of velvet; this selfishness well understood which requires the best care, the most ingenious attentions; this gentle despotic invasion, which however still respects your dreams, your work, soothes your sadness, by some distraught purring, some tenacious caress ... Is this not the best expression of tenderness? [...] For we are so made, that we cherish nothing more than souls who hide ..." (p. 2).

Similarly, a certain H. de V. who is perhaps (if one believes the caustic tone of the article) a pseudonym of Henri de Montherlant, praised the cat in the relatively new journal *Je Suis Partout*. He prided himself on chronicling worldly and literary life. This text dated May 30, 1931, and entitled "Chez les Bêtes. Their Majesty the cats," does not just report on the feline exhibition which just took place that May, but reflects on the nature of the relationship between cats and humans and does not hesitate to quote French poet Baudelaire:

It has become a rite. Each year, catophiles or ailurophiles (the latter term is more correct, being of purely Greek origin, while the former represents a hybrid of Greek and Latin) [...] require a feline exhibition. [...] Does the cat appreciate being exposed to the sight of the eager visitors of the Wagram room, where two days he is sitting? What does he think of the adventure? Not much good. The other day, a Birman cat made vehement demands. Something interested him powerfully in a cage behind his, separated by a curtain. None of us knew what he wanted - not understanding the Birman "meow:" but the animal wanted it with energy. Even with passion. Many cats view cat exposure as a chore. And they take refuge in the bottom of their cage, stubbornly turning the rump in the face of visitors. And yet they have the best intentions in the world: they bring love and visitation. Many quadrupeds, however, do not allow themselves to flex. They don't want to know anything from the public. And take it for granted that if the roles were reversed and if in the world of cats we had organized a human exhibition, many of these felines would not visit it. Our antics would not interest them. Some are philosophers. And the mothers who raise their broods continue the work undertaken. Softly abandoned, they suckle their delicious and voracious kittens who drink until refusal. [...] during the Feline Exhibition, everything is at peace and harmony through the prestigious virtue of the charm of the exquisite beast, also dear, if one believes Baudelaire, to fervent lovers and to austere scholars" (p. 10).

More modestly, Pierre de Trévières, stuck to Colette and Lucie Delarue-Mardrus, in his report of the same exhibition published in *La Femme de France* of July 12, 1931, under the more encompassing title of "Love of Beasts":

Of course, women have always loved animals. A veiled affection sometimes tinged with fantasy but always faithful. There was a huge crowd at the recent Cat Show which took place in the Wagram Hall. It may be that this strange animal had the clever whim of seeking its admirers among all social classes. Faithful guardian of the concierge's lodge, the cat can climb the ladder of a policed hierarchy and penetrate to the boudoir of the fashionable woman or the artist in vogue.

It is rather curious to note that the love professed with regard to these felines does not involve mediocrity. Dogs can be slightly affectionate. But cats, we hate them or we love them. From Mrs. Philippe Berthelot to Colette and Mrs. Lucie Delarue-Mardrus ... And their eyes, pers where strangely evil, accept with disinterested air these fervent tributes, be it the Siamese cat with the double velvet dress, the common gutter tomcat, the pearl gray Chartreux cat, the tailless Isle of Man cat or the angora with a silky livery. (p. 22).

These articles are very general, it is necessary to await that of Paule Malardot in *Les Dimanches de la Femme* of July 12, 1931, to return specifically to the Birman: there are several, according to her, but especially, a Birman albino.

Here, the sacred cats of Burma. With their black coffee faces, their café au lait mittens and their blue eyes - blue, says the legend, for having contemplated goddesses - they seem to look down on their admirers. But even more haughty, Bouddhabis, an albino Birman with pale agate eyes, a broken tail in question mark, dreaming, frozen in a hieratic pose of an idol. A discreet sign warns passersby that "Buddhists love and worship white Birman or albino people, because Buddha said he would rather appear on earth in this form ...". But no one, after reading, seems to believe that Bouddhabis may be a god..." (p. 5).

Bouddhabis, however, is not the one who receives the priority attention from the recent *Revue Féline de France*, whose account of the exhibition of May 15-17, 1931 was much more detailed: we learn the presence of Lon Saïto and de Manou (out of competition), next to two "half-bloods" (undoubtedly Birman-Siamese hybrids), three new males, Bouli to Mme Lorenzo; Allah and Mouck to Mrs. Chaumont and Taboo, a female to Mrs. Chaumont. We are therefore dealing with two new breeders, Mrs. Lorenzo and Mrs. Chaumont. The latter is known as a Siamese breeder. Associated with Siamese champions from 1926, she is particularly mentioned, for example, in number 277 of *La Vie à la Campagne* (p. 204-207) with regard to her cat Mahout whose photo is right above that of Poupée de Madalpour. The following year, still in *La Vie à la Campagne*, about Poussy "aged 10" (p. 109). The special article devoted to "Siamese cat, luxury breed" published by Philippe Jumaud in the May 5, 1928 issue of *Jardins et Basses-Cours*, contains another photo of his Siamese male Mahout, one year old (p. 211). And moreover, at the cat show in Paris in 1928, she won with a 12-and-a-half-year-old Siamese female, named Am-Rhaou. However, the results of the May 1929 cat show revealed that she was also raising Persians, since she is cited as the owner of Boule de Neige (Snowball,) a black Persian. We therefore see that it is well placed to diversify by starting the breeding of Birman; we will find her later as owner of the affix of "Madalpour."

About Mrs. Lorenzo, we don't know much except the name of her cat Bouli. She appears to have spent only a year or two raising Birman, although she is mentioned in a few pedigrees later. On the other hand, Baudoin-Crevoisier, who started breeding in 1929, began to be known from 1931, when he produced the very beautiful *Dieu d'Arakhan* (God of Arakan). The review *Chasse, Pêche, Élevage* in May 1931 indicates in particular that he exhibited two cats at the second Feline Exhibition in Rennes which was held on April 11 and 12, 1931: "We also noticed the splendid cats of Burma: *Reine de Rangoon* (Queen of Rangoon) and *Dieu d'Arakan*. Prize of esthetics to Reine de Rangoon, Mr. Marcel Baudoin, she obtains her C.A.C., Prize of male Birman, Dieu d'Arakan, Mr. Marcel Baudoin, Prize of female Birmans, Reine de Rangoon." But above all, apart from these exhibitions which are not necessarily the most important, he wrote five articles between 1931 and 1935. In the one which appeared in June-July 1931 in the *Revue Féline Belge* under the title: "The Sacred Cat of Burma" he

34. Dieu d'Arakhan, *l'un des plus beaux chats sacrés de Birmanie.*

specifically mentions several Birman, Lon Saïto, Dieu d'Arakan, Manou de Madalpour, Bijoux and Djaïpour, and gave a fairly detailed description of each. However, the results of the feline exhibition of May 1929, reveal that she raised also Persians, since she is cited as the owner of Snowball, a black Persian. We therefore see that she was well placed to diversify by starting the breeding of Birman:

These cats are very sociable and intelligent. In the apartment they follow their masters like dogs. Small, they play a lot. Older, they have moments of calm followed by periods of frantic excitement. Their approach is reminiscent of that of big cats in cages. These cats are very gentle with each other. I put together young kittens with whole adult males; the latter played with the little ones like mothers. [...] The coat, and this is the most beautiful trait, is silky, wispy; I bring it a little closer to the swan down. It is half-long on certain parts of the body and long in other places: tail, attachment of the latter, and neck. At the neck, in particular, it forms a real collar which gives it remarkable beauty. This collar on the front of the head returns in the form of "favorites" which makes it look like a tiger. All the originality of this cat is in this natural adornment. The hair is the color of light Siamese. The brown parts are very dark but the rest of the body is almost white. It darkens slightly with age, but should never be darker than the crème brûlée color. The four paws are as if gloved in white, those behind higher and rising behind the leg. Between the claws there is a little longer white hair. The tail is quite long and very bushy. The Birman cat often wears it straight, for example when walking, and the hairs fall out in a plume. The effect is wonderful. Under the neck and the belly, the hair is slightly wavy. The eyes are very blue and very big." (p. 4).

Baudoin-Crevoisier also pointed out with a slight irritation that the Birman are easily confused with the Siamese in the exhibitions: "when there are Birman, you hear laymen say: Well, long-haired Siamese ... This exclamation erroneous has a semblance of truth. Indeed, at the first aspect these two varieties are similar. The color, the eyes, and the tail, when it's a long-tailed Siamese. A closer look shows the difference." (p. 5). Nowadays, we would tend to confuse them with the derived Ragdolls. Baudoin-Crevoisier went so far as to detail the perfections of a particular Birman; although it does not give the name, it is probably about Dieu d'Arakan:

I know a superb Birman like type, hair, eyes, tail, legs and in addition a perfect parent, which is the product of two Siamese. [...] This Birman [...] protruded a Siamese cat, daughter of a Birman; the products obtained were almost all very beautiful Birman, most gloved on all four legs, others only on two legs. Among these is an absolutely perfect male. The following litters were also beautiful. In the Poupée line, essentially purebred, we have not done better. There are very few gloved Birman in this line and not even gloved at all". (p. 5).

And finally, he concludes with an enthusiastic hymn to the Birman: "Let us continue to consider this breed of cats as the most beautiful in the world. Its rarity makes it a very valuable breed. By its mysterious origin, the beauty of its coat, its attitudes, its somewhat enigmatic whole, the qualifier of 'sacred' cat which one gives to the cat of Burma is not exaggerated." (p. 6).

But it was from 1932 that Marcel Baudoin-Crevoisier exploded on the feline scene with his splendid Birman who were already international champions: Lon Saïto de Madalpour, Dieu d'Arakan, and, in the words of *La Vie à la Campagne* from February 1932 "the amusing Reine de Rangoon" were present in Reims for the exhibition of the *Cat Club of Champagne* in January 1932. It therefore seems that he bought Lon Saïto de Madalpour from Mme Brassart, who disappeared as a Birman breeder from that point on. As for Dieu d'Arakan, he could well be "The little cat very

photographed" of which The *Intransigent* of January 24, 1932 published a photo. In any case, he won the first prize for males at this same exhibition on January 22 and 23, 1932, and Lon Saïto de Madalpour obtained the 2nd prize. Reine de Rangoon was in open class, which shows that she was still very young, and in the same category we notice Zaquelle de Mandalay who

Le petit chat très photographié

was brought up by Baudoin-Crevoisier but belonged to a certain Miss Rousselle who we will talk about again.

In the process, Baudoin-Crevoisier published in March 1932, an article in *Chasse, Pêche, Élevage*, which has become since January the official organ of the *Cat Club of Paris and Champagne*, and which includes a magnificent photo of Dieu d'Arakan which was intended to go around the feline world. Under the title

"The Birman Cat," this text is in line with the breeder's crusade in favor of the Birman:

Chat sacré de Birmanie
« DIEU D'ARAKAN », Champion international à M. Baudoin (C. C. P.).
Un des plus magnifiques parmi les très rares spécimens de cette race mystérieuse actuellement en Europe.

If there is one breed that has been able to please everyone, it is the Birman cat breed. Without being exaggerated, the Birman cat won all the votes and was able to attract admiration not only from cat friends, but also from people who generally have no feelings for cats. It is not a fashion, this cat is not yet widespread, it is rather the consecration of an absolutely perfect type, attractive par excellence and of total beauty. He is Persian and Siamese at the same time if we consider on the one hand his hair and on the other hand his color, but he is neither Persian nor Siamese from the zoological point of view. " (p. 3554).

Then the author continued by repeating a certain number of well-known elements of the legend, but supplementing them with additional details. They may have been communicated to him by Marcelle Adam, unless it was Mrs. Léotardi:

The male accidentally died on the boat that brought him back to France, and the female, Sita, happily full, gave birth in Nice with a litter including a perfect product, a female: Poupée. The male, Madalpour, having given his name to the descendants of imported Birman, all the lineage of Birmans existing in France are therefore "Madalpour". (ibid).

From there, Baudouin-Crevoisier lists the main descendants of this lineage: "Manou, Uru, Pijou, Hiram-Roi, Lon Golden, Djaïpur and Lon Saïto", for males. And for the females: "Poupée, Nafaghy, Sita II and III, Idjadi-Tsun, Yadi." These were direct descendants of Poupée, but it is well specified, even if the names mentioned are also distributed, that the females were much less frequent in the litters. To this original list, the breeder adds another, made up of the offspring of descended stallions of Poupée and gloved Siamese supposed to be more resistant; these crossings which aim to eliminate the problems of inbreeding, were a great success, to believe the conclusion of Baudoin-Crevoisier: "we have managed to create absolutely perfect types of Birman, of course stronger, very marked, the main ones of which are: Soleil d'Arakan, Roult d'Arakan, Prince de Rangoon, Reine de Rangoon, and above all Dieu d'Arakan, absolutely marvelous type international champion." (ibid). So, we end up with three lines, maybe four, if we add to the Madalpour, Arakan and Rangoon, the Mandalay. The Madalpour are the direct descendants of Mme Léotardi's Poupée; but the three other affixes, two of which belong to Baudoin-Crevoisier, correspond to branches from Siamese females gloved in white. In all these cases, it may be that the stallion is Lon Saïto de Madalpour [note: Which we saw that he went from Mrs. Brassart to Crevoisier] whose more Persian type was, according to the photos, relatively close de Dieu d'Arakan, unless the services of Djaïpour were used. Baudoin-Crevoisier insisted on these lineage manipulations which bring Birman and Siamese together, to the exclusion of all other races:

These crosses with Siamese were motivated on the one hand by the very origin of the reproduction of the Birman, which took place, as indicated above, with a cat lynx of Laos; then by the resemblance between these two breeds, especially with regard to the gestation time of females. It follows an ease to have Birman with only one breeding of the race, as much as possible the Birman male. Obviously, apart from the Siamese type, no crossing is recommended if we want to keep or acquire the Birman type. [...] This white legged, which is a quality for the Birman and a fault for the Siamese, is sometimes seen in the latter which would prove a common origin. Besides, in the Far East, you will find long-haired Siamese, some with bushy tails, or without tails, or simply a kind of rudimentary stump. [...] This immaculate white, placed quite irregularly, should preferably go higher on the hind legs than on the forelegs, taking only the whole of the fingers, while the whole of the feet, and even going up behind the point-shaped leg. The large, round eyes, worn very slightly obliquely, are of an intense blue. [...] The strong jaw, the upper canines extending beyond the lip and giving the mouth this half-open appearance. This distinctive sign is essential, very few Birman currently have it." (Ibid. p. 3555).

As a serious breeder, he dwelt on the key elements of the standard, such as gloves or a parted mouth. He went so far as to quote English comments on the subject, but did not forget the financial aspect of Birman breeding: "The Birman cat, which the English call 'Gold Cat', is well named thus, although this name has rather to do with its coat. It is a valuable animal, and it is deserved. It is currently the rarest breeding cat that exists; and setting prices for champion breeders would be very difficult ..." (Ibid). Although he emphasizes how difficult it is to assess the market value of a champion, he is no less a wise businessman when he publishes, at the end of the same newspaper, in the section "Small Ads," his own:

163

"CHATTERIE DE BIRMANIE. M. BAUDOUIN-CREVOISIER, Breeder. Covered by international champions. 500 francs on Birman, 300 francs on Siamese."

Note that there is also, a little below, another announcement concerning Birman, published, this one, by Mlle Rousselle, of Liège, in Belgium: "FOR SALE: 2 kittens, half-blood Birman, 3 months: male and female excellent to form Birman race." Miss or Mrs. Rousselle is in fact the first Birman breeder in Belgium, and her cats came to her from Baudoin-Crevoisier that same year, 1932. It is even possible that the father of the kittens mentioned here is Lon Saïto de Madalpour, that Baudoin-Crevoisier, after having bought it from Mme Brassart, hastened to sell to Mlle Rousselle: the poor beast knew three owners in less than two years!

The following big Feline Exhibition, organized by the *Central Feline Society,* was held from April 1 to 3, 1932. And as usual, it received strong attention from the newspapers, which were particularly interested in the Birman cat.

The *Intransigent* of April 2, 1932 opened the ball with an account titled: "At the Wagram Hall. The Triumph of Exotic Cats": "A sacred Birman cat, a sort of long-haired Siamese with a bulging front, close to a Tibetan cat who is his close and no less sumptuous parent." (p. 5). On the same day, *Paris-Soir* and *L'Écho de Paris* published photographs, including one in particular, taken from above, where we see a cat literally taken by storm by photographers, who could be this famous Birman cat. As for the *Petit Journal* of April 4, it praised "this mysterious sacred cat from Burma; whose purple

LA GLOIRE !

Quel homme célèbre, quelle star attireraient autant de photographes ? Ce chat minuscule a lui seul mobilise les objectifs. C'est qu'il appartient à une espèce rare et vous le pouvez voir à l'Exposition féline qui s'est ouverte aujourd'hui.

pupils still seem to contemplate theories of prostrate priests in a cloud of incense " (p. 4)

Collection de l'Institut zoologique. Ed. Noyer.   Photo Férard.

Chat sacré de Birmanie

The interest in purebred cats, evidenced by the success of cat shows, was also reflected in a unique publication: at the end of May 1932, the president of the *Cat Club of Paris*, Léon Boilève de la Gombaudière, produced a relatively luxurious album on the various feline breeds, abundantly illustrated, which he entitled "Nos Compagnons les Chats." For the sacred Birman cat, there is obviously the beautiful photo of Dieu d'Arakan, as well as a photo of Zaquelle de Mandalay, and another of an unknown cat (pp. 11-12), accompanied by a short description on the breed: "Birman cat. Still extremely rare in our countries, the sacred Birman cat, raised in the mystery of the Hindu temples, is a splendid animal, with a robe woven of burnished gold, with an attitude full of dignity, as if it were conscious of its nobility and its divine character. Fairly tall, with a long, silky coat, sapphire eyes, deep and melancholy, and white-gloved legs, tapered with brown. Affectionate, intelligent, cheerful, he exclusively loves his master, whose absence plunges him into sadness and dreams. Its breeding is particularly difficult." (p. XI). Of the two photos of Birman, one represents a clearly Siamese cat, with a very triangular head, but still with fairly visible gloves, (collection of the Zoological Institute), while Zaquelle was much closer to the standard developed at the time, with a round head and very dark eyes.

Anecdotally, we realize that the possession of a sacred Birman cat becomes synonymous with a certain social status and human qualities. "The woman of letters" Yvonne Ostroga completed a very serious article published in *Le Figaro* of July 20, 1932, under the title "Philanthropy and Commerce," with a paragraph of

Chatte amrée de Birmanie
« ZAQUELLE DE MANDALAY » À M. Baudoin, de Saint-Denis (C. C. F.).

completely different tone. After describing the exemplary career of the American "Mrs JF," who came to France a little by force but remained by taste and who worked for a Parisian fashion house, she recounted her presentation to the "child" of Mrs J.F., a "magnificent Birman cat":

It's time to leave Mrs J. F ...: her occupations call for her and it is not her habit to be late for her schedule. It keeps me for a second yet, however, the time to place a charming note in all this seriousness, this virile energy. "You have to see my child," she said, opening a door. And the child immediately looks at me gravely with his big round and clear eyes. It is a beautiful Birman cat with very dark short hair, with small straight and black ears. Only the blue stone of the necklace puts, with the eyes, a pale note in this dark harmony. While his mistress looks at him with pride, I call him, but he remains frozen in a lazy and quite oriental impassiveness. Is it by contrast that this living American loves her so much? (p. 4).

167

Fig. 398. — «*DIEU D'ARAKAN*», Chat de Birmanie, *Champion international; à M. Baudoin-Crevoisier.*

In a more frivolous fashion, the worldly chronicler Horatio reported in his "Echoes of the City and the Fields" of the newspaper *Comœdia* the curious mores of a young provincial sub-prefect who happened to have, there again, a "young Birman cat":

The sub-prefect ... In the city. On the balcony of a hotel in Western Paris, a young woman spends her days in pajamas. She erected an umbrella ... against the rain, installed a table where she takes her meals, makes her correspondence, plays with a young Birman cat ... Some stranger, it is thought; an actress, original by nature's inclination ... No. It is quite simply the small wife of a young sub-prefect of a department of the littoral who comes to practice in Paris the hygiene which the administered by her husband prevent her from following, it seems, in her department ... (p. 3)

On August 20, 1932, *Jardins et Basses-Cours* devoted a special section to "The Classification of Domestic Cats" (pp. 361-82); there, Baudoin Crevoisier published the new article on "The Cat of Burma, sacred animal. Characterized breed, said to be of Siamese origin and clearly distinguished from long-haired Asian races, with which these subjects do not sympathize." This endless title is exactly the same as that used by Philippe Jumaud in the October 1926 issue of *La Vie à la Campagne*. In addition, the photos of the Birman are also the same as in the previous publication, except for an additional image of Dieu d'Arakan inserted at the end of the article. On the other hand, with regard to the content, Crevoisier made revisions and redesigned the whole, while reproducing certain parts. He said, for example: "The Birman cat, which the English call gold cat (Golden cat), is well named so, although this name has rather to do with its coat. It is a valuable animal, and it is deserved. It is currently the rarest breeding cat there is." (p. 376). The paragraph on the origin of the cat no longer mentions Major Russel Gordon or Auguste Pavie; only the name of "Mrs. Thadde Hadish" remains:

The first subjects came to France around 1925 brought by Mrs. Thadde Hadish, in the form of a couple stolen, no doubt, from the Lao-Tsun Temple in Burma, where these divine beasts are jealously guarded. The male died on the boat, during the crossing, and the female, fortunately full, gave birth to Nice a litter including a perfect product, a female Poupée.

A new point appears in this text: the gradual desertion of breeders and their lack of perseverance: "It is up to the first breeders to have had the honor of maintaining this marvelous breed; unfortunately, none of them continued it. Some names, however, must remain in the annals of the Birman breeding: Mmes

Léotard [sic], Marcelle Adam and Brassard [sic] were the first to have these extremely rare Cats. "

We can conclude from this melancholy formulation that in 1932, the first three great flagship breeders of sacred cats from Burma were no longer active. Nevertheless, Baudoin-Crevoisier added two individuals, *Poupée de Rangoon* and *Zaquelle de Mandalay*, to the list of cats that he provided in March in his article of *Chasse, Pêche, Elevage* and valiantly concluded: "The last word is not yet said about the breeding of this breed."(p. 376).

In fact, at the exhibition "La Féline de Bruxelles," on November 6, 1932, I note that Lon Saïto de Madalpour and Djaïpour (which belonged respectively to Mrs. Brassart and to Mrs. Marigny) are now the property of Miss Rousselle (as of November 1932) of the *Cat Club of Liège* which hastens to expose its two new acquisitions. Then, at the cat show in Paris, at the end of the year, we learn that Djaïpur obtained his C.A.C., and that Mlle Rousselle alongside Lon Saïto de Madalpour, also presented Zaquelle de Mandalay. But there were new breeders: Mrs. Lasquin, who presented Mikette and Miki, Mr. L'abbé Chamonin, who presented Poupée de Rangoon, and Mrs. Hallot, who presented Marouf, Gabo and Greta. To report on this cat show, The *Journal* of December 3, 1932 and *L'Écho d'Alger* of December 12 published the same photograph, that of a Birman who appears to be Djaïpour. That same December 3, *Paris-Soir* added: "Beauty of Persian cats, like [...] Nostradamus, the wonderful Siamese; Djaïpour, the Birman with a squirrel tail. They look at the crowd and seem to exchange silent comments ... In all the cages, cat-kings and cat-gods, grave and closed, glances are heard." (p. 3). The same *Journal* number likens the Birman to ornamental cats, which Djaïpour must have been the inspiration for:

Villers de l'Isle-Adam who, like all poets, loved cats, liked to say that when he returned home one night very late, avoiding making the slightest noise, he surprised his cat, whom he loved very much, sitting in front of the chimney whose fire was out, distinctly meowing this sentence: "... Ah, how bored I am!

Nowadays, cats no longer speak (and still, what do we know?) But they understand us perfectly, there is no doubt about it. Any visitor to the Feline Exhibition in the Wagram hall can be convinced of this ... provided, however, that the pretty felines presented by their owner do not have an algebra problem.

Tell these "Siamese," these "Birman," these "Persians or these" Parisian kitties "that they are beautiful and you will see them engorged in purring with pride. If, on the other hand, you pass the fad of provoking it in by treating it for example of "cat of gutter," you will see it swearing and insulting you in the good manner. But "light and powerful" cats should not be hurt even lightly. [...] So, go today, to the Feline Exhibition in the Wagram Hall, because it closes this evening - and choose to decorate your home with a beautiful cat... a cat that will remind you [sic] by these attitudes of the beautiful sonnet by Charles Baudelaire... It will be the pleasure of your eyes and it will protect you from rats and mice. (p. 5).

The review *Chasse, Pêche, Élevage* in February reported to the Antwerp exhibition in Belgium at the beginning of 1933, the presence of these same Birman: "Miss Rousselle from Liège, had brought her beautiful Birman with a little Birman cat belonging to Father Chamonin, from Geneva. This beautiful breed, still little known in Belgium, caused a sensation. [...] Dora and Tao de Saint-Hubert, from Miss Rousselle's breeding, stood out particularly in Siamese."

Indeed, Miss Rousselle is rather known as a Siamese breeder; that year in April, Miss Rousselle created to replace the *Cat Club of Liège*, the *Cat Club Mosan*, affiliated to the *Belgian Féline Federation*, of which she became secretary. But it was Djaïpur who won all the prizes in 1933.

From the first days of January 1933, Manou, Madame Adam's favorite Birman became an editorial writer for the *Revue Féline de France* and wished readers, or rather readers, a happy new year in his own name: "We will tell you about the breeds of cats. They are countless and you don't know. [...] And the sacred cats of Burma, of which we do not have ten copies. [...] In short, Madam, our words are endlessly varied, in the section to which we affix our signature ([literally claw]." (p. 141-43).

Also in the same month, the journal *Minerva* published an article on "The Legend of the Sacred Cats of Burma," which would in fact become the main source of information on the subject. This article by veterinary doctor Fernand Méry, would be reproduced in *La Revue Féline Belge* a few months later. Here is the first paragraph, which announces the color:

Little is known about these precious cats which are, in general, the highlight of any self-respecting cat show. It is true that by counting well there might not be twenty in Europe. What do I say, not twenty? Not ten, not five ... Not one (as Marie Dubas sings) ... Let us be clear: not one who can boast of his authentic nobility ... Not one who can be said to come from a real couple of sacred felines directly imported from English Indochina. Those who currently exist with us, have only an ancestor of the Birman strain, "Poupée" which had to be mixed with a kind of Siamese: the Laos lynx, so that the Birman blood does not completely die out. What religious care and solicitude it has taken since to preserve through the generations of mixed blood, the gold fur and the sapphire eyes of these wonderful beasts, and especially the four immaculate gloves, symbol of their divine essence (p. 14).

Two photos of Birman are associated with the article, one more modern by Manou de Madalpour, and one of a hitherto unknown cat owned by actress Régine Marsay.

These cats were used in feline exhibitions and exhibited by more or less wealthy worldly perso-nalities as essentially prestigious animals; this is even more clearly the case with the Birman. But here in 1933, interest in the cat became more useful. The city of Paris planned to breed it to counter the invasions of rats in the sewers, as revealed in an article in the *Journal* dated January 11: "Will the Paris

lui méditait Sinh, son cher oracle, un chat tout blanc, dont les yeux étaient jaunes, jaune du reflet de la barbe d'or de son maître et du corps doré de la déesse aux yeux de ciel... Sinh, le chat-conseiller, dont les oreilles, le nez, la queue et les extrémités des membres étaient de la sombre couleur du sol, marqués de la souillure et de l'impureté de tout ce qui touche ou peut toucher la terre.

« Or, un soir, comme la lune malveillante avait permis aux Phoums maudits venus du Siam aborrhé, de s'approcher de l'enceinte sacrée, le grand prêtre Mun-Hâ, sans cesser d'implorer les destinées cruelles, entra doucement dans la mort, ayant à ses côtés son chat divin et sous ses yeux le désespoir de tous ses kittahs accablés...

« C'est alors que se produisit le miracle... le miracle unique de la transmutation immédiate : d'un bond, Sinh fut sur le trône d'or et se jucha sur la tête de son maître affaissé... Il s'arcbouta sur cette tête chargée d'ans, et qui pour la première fois ne regardait plus sa déesse... Et comme il restait à son tour figé devant la statue éternelle, on vit les poils hérissés de son échine blanche devenir soudain jaune d'or. Et ses yeux d'or devinrent

RÉGINE MARSAY et son chat sacré de Birmanie.
(Ph. G.-l. Manuel frères.)

Municipal Council raise cats to destroy rats? [...] this omnivorous brood which penetrates in the sheds and the best closed cellars and destroys annually several million cereals and foodstuffs ..." (p. 2). The text goes on to give the example of Doctor Adrien Loir, mayor of Le Havre and curator of the Museum of Natural History in that city, who raised these animals in a special cattery. He also published, in 1929, still in Le Havre, a 160-page book reissued in 1931 and entitled: "The Cat, its usefulness. The destruction of rats", here are some lines from the preface to the first edition:

ils vont tous à l'exposition féline internationale de paris salle wagram

21.22 avril 1933.

E Casthélan

Pour tous renseignements :
Téléphoner au Secrétariat Général, à Pereire 25-92, tous les soirs de 19 heures à 20 heures, ou s'adresser à M. GUINGAND.
Secrétaire Général, 16, avenue Anatole-France, à Clichy (Seine), le mardi de 18 h. 1/2 à 21 heures.

The rats are the Huns, the Vandals of the animal race, they sum up, they are the barbarians, the most barbarians - and by their destruction, their depredations - of the world of animals. [...] So what to do? Use this even smarter friend: THE CAT.

Adrien Loir has a tabby European cat, named Lilith, which is "a very good dobby cat;" his wife also seems to have raised Siamese for this function (in particular a certain Poupette whose photo appears in the book). (p. 112). In fact, a chapter of the book (pp. 177-128) is devoted to the Siamese cat who is described there as "the hunter par excellence" (p. 119). But, in his history of cats, Doctor Loir also mentioned Birman: "Let us also quote [...], the cat of the painter Laurent Gsell, the black cat by Mr. Paul Brulat, the Birman by Mrs. Marcelle Adam, the Siamese family by Paul Gsell" (p. 23).

If in Amiens, on April 8 and 9, 1933, we note the presence of Haydée and Hours which belong to Mrs. Hallot, the great annual exhibition which took place on April 21 and 22, in the Wagram Hall and was inaugurated by Mr. René Fiquet, whose purpose was to "ratify" the capital by using mainly the cat for this purpose. Overall, the articles reporting on the exhibition echo this concern, but that did not prevent the highlight of the demonstration from being an allegedly "winged" Belgian cat. Thus, *Le Journal* of April 22 humorously reports: "unexpected curiosity, a 'winged' cat or rather a six-legged cat whose two smaller ones are implanted in the back ..."

For its part, the *L'Œuvre* of April 22 gives a poetic and fun story about this event:

This exhibition is unique in that it is twofold. There are, on the one hand, cats, whose feline graces delight not only lovers and scholars but also artists, by the nobility of their attitudes, and, on the other ... their masters. With what tenderness do they strive to make the temporary prison where the pretty beasts will stay, in the ways of small boudoirs, decorated and furnished - yes, furnished - with a childishness that never fails to be moving. Here, a superb "sourabaya" has two rooms at its disposal: the first contains the essential dish filled with sawdust and a soft satin cushion; the second has a tiny bathtub, above which hangs a naturalized sparrow. Tango silk curtains, with their tiebacks, protect the precious sleep of the animal, to which its owner, probably unable to have a racing stable, gave the name of M. de Montherlant by play. A little further, the bouquets of lily of the valley decorate the niche with a white Persian flirt with blue eyes. Next to it, we finish decorating with celluloid flowers the background of pink lamé which lines the retreat of a nonchalant Siamese. But it is only to give in to habit that we have given the name of masters to the men and women who bear witness to the animals imprisoned here with inexhaustible and tender servility. The real masters, is it not true, are the cats rolled up in a ball on the kapok cushions, or coiled in a corner of the cage like sulky children, they seem to consider with a higher disdain the agitation of their entourage. Their eyes are emeralds or burnt topazes set with pale blue. But what kinship is there between the aristocrats, the great lords of felicity - the Siamese, the Persians - and the gutter cat, this "edible" thug, if we believe the legend, who is her majestic parents' descendants of the goddess Bast, what is the orchid of our royal orchid campaigns? And yet, how interesting this thug is! (p. 2).

The year 1933 is in fact a pivotal moment in the history of the Sacred Cats of Burma. Someone who will become an important actor in the breeding and the development of the breed came onto the scene, Father Marcel Chamonin, who often published under the pseudonym of Marcel Reney. Based in Switzerland, in Geneva, he organized from April (April 29 and 30, 1933) an exhibition in which subjects from his own breeding shine, in particular a certain Sinh de St Hubert, to which we will return. Then, in November 1933, he founded on November 17 the *Cat Club of Geneva*, of which he was immediately elected president and he announced at the same time the creation of a book of Swiss origins (LOS) where all the cats of the Swiss federation will be registered, pending the creation of other regional cats clubs. What is very interesting for the researcher is that Father Chamonin published in the journal *Chasse, Pêche, Élevage* a good part of the information concerning cats registered in the LOS, which provides valuable information on marriages and lines of the Sacred Cat of Burma. Father Chamonin is not only a Birman breeder, but he is also equally known in the feline world as a Siamese and blue Persian breeder. It seems that his interest in the Sacred of Burma was born in the years 1931 or 32, when he saw the Dieu d'Arakan in an exhibition and fell in love with this breed. Before producing his own cats, he would seize the opportunity offered to him by Baudoin-Crevoisier who complained of a slowdown in the development of the Birman breed and would in fact stop breeding and ended up selling his cats in Switzerland, Belgium, Germany, and Italy. An article published in July 1933 in the *Revue Féline de France*, and quoted by Chamonin testified to this disenchantment: "In Burma, alas, breeding does not win. The big effort that we made personally was not followed. And yet it allowed all hopes. Today, the same subjects of this unique breed are the only representatives of an easy breed now to breed and of which the French are alone or more or less having breeders."

In fact, we find as early as March–in the cattery of Abbé Chamonin who adopted the affix of "La Chesnaie "–several of the stars of the breeding of Baudoin-Crevoisier, in particular Poupée de Rangoon. Zaquelle de Mandalay stayed with Mlle Rousselle probably under the affix "St Hubert." The Abbé Chamonin exhibited in Geneva in April, a son of Zaquelle and Lon Saïto de Madalpour on January 30, 1933: Sinh de St Hubert which was one of the most awarded Birman of its generation.

The Abbé Chamonin was particularly interested in the origin of the breed and systematically researched it. In an article published in issue 197 of *Chasse, Pêche, Élevage*, he made the panegyric of the Sacred of Burma:

The sacred cats of Burma have been one of the best attractions of our cat shows for several years. Their half-long hair, their beautiful cream color, their white-gloved legs, their curious blue eyes, make them a dream animal. In addition, their mysterious origin and their very name make lovers of beautiful cats invincibly attracted to them. (p. 3931).

He was however quite skeptical about the legend and his research on the arrival of Birman in Nice logically concluded in a dead end. No data could be confirmed. All the people mentioned turned out to be imaginary and, in desperation, Chamonin called for information, be it about the so-called plaque No 4108 by Sir Russel Gordon, the existence of Mrs Thadde Hadich or the temple of Lao-Tsun or even about Mrs. Léotardi: "All these questions I propose to the sagacity of our readers hoping, by an investigation thus opened, to arrive at the truth." (Ibid). Incidentally, Chamonin is not entirely satisfied with Baudoin-Crevoisier's explanations, to the point of exclaiming about the latter's July article: "It is writing history in a singular way! ..." This did not prevent him from giving very interesting explanations on the cats' diaspora of his predecessor:

By the time Mr. Baudoin sold his kennel, his cats, Rose de Mogock and Reine de Rangoon hadn't produced anything for months. Lon Saïto was sold in Belgium [to Mlle Rousselle de Liège], Poupée de Rangoon and later Rose de Mogock, in Switzerland [at Chamonin himself], Reine de Rangoon and Dieu d'Arakan who was seriously ill, in Italy [to Princess Ratibor von Hohenlohe, as we will see below]! Djaïpour who belonged to Mme de Marigny also went to Belgium [also to Mlle Rousselle] Zaquelle de Mandalay also. In France, the remaining pure Birman are either castrated or unfit for breeding. Timour, who lived in Germany, died a few months ago, and was, moreover, a poor reproducer. This census may be incomplete: I would be delighted and this article would have proven its usefulness. As it stands, however, it shows what to believe from Mr. Baudoin's affirmations.

But if it is complete, we must raise a cry of alarm: the sacred Birman cat is in danger! Due to inbreeding, the females are fragile and the males' poor reproducers. All of them are in delicate health, aren't they Mr. Hasse [the great Belgian feline show judge of the time]? This breed, unique in its beauty, will disappear in the short term, if an energetic intervention does not react immediately.

For that very reason, it is necessary that the owners of sacred cats of Burma (let's keep this name: people like it and it is known), band in a special club which will aim to improve the breeding by facilitating the breeding, by checking the pedigree, keeping an original breeding book up to date and directing breeders to a strict observation of the laws of heredity... Many other questions, raised by Birman breeding and which concern only specialists, could be resolved by the Club. The foundation of an International Club of the Sacred Cat of Burma is a necessity for the future of the breed." (Ibid).

In the book he published in 1947 under his pseudonym Marcel Reney, *Nos Amis les Chats*, Chamonin said:

I took steps to obtain a photo of the piece mentioned by Sir Russel Gordon and the exact indication of the magazine or book where this text was published. They remained in vain. I sought to have new details on the existence of Mrs. Thadde Hadisch and on Mrs. Léotardi; it was in vain. Thus, the origin of the sacred cats of Burma remains enveloped in an impenetrable veil, as if to punish those who had desecrated, by their sacrilegious theft, the temple of Lao-Tsun. Besides, Baudoin, after having tried the breeding of Birman and affirmed that this breeding was easy, gave up on it in 1935, date on which he sold to the Princess Ratibor Hohenlohe, for nearly 30,000 French francs of that time, a splendid male who had won the votes of all audiences in France and abroad, Dieu d'Arakan, and the few five or six males or females he had left. In Switzerland and in Belgium, amateurs attached themselves to these cats without succeeding in saving the breed. In France, two or three breeders still owned half-Birman, poorly gloved, in early 1940. As for Princess Ratibor's cats, they had strange adventures. Bequeathed by the princess to H.R.H. the Duke of Aosta, they were hidden for a time. It was a cousin of the latter, Mrs. Countess Giriodi Panissera who, finally, succeeded in gaining possession of the cats. In the autumn of 1936, I had the honor of being the host of the castle of Francavilla-Bisio, near Novi-Ligure, and of seeing firsthand the results obtained thanks to the kindness and patience of the gentile lady. In addition to Dieu d'Arakan, and Reine de Rangoon, there were seventeen cats, including fourteen kittens, some of whom promised much. What has become of this magnificent collection of cats that I gladly call "the most beautiful cats in the world"? Since 1940, I have not received any news from Francavilla and I have, to console myself, only the nostalgic memory of the large courtyard of the castle in which my dear friends frolicked under the gentle gaze of the lady in her hands white ... (p. 180).

And he ends up lyrically regretting his own cats: "Also I cherish the secret hope one day of finding a couple who will give me back the caresses and the joy of the eyes which Sinh, Poupée de Mandalay, Kébir, Fakir et Fatma once filled me with ... the sweet Fatma, who allowed herself to languish after the sudden death of her unforgettable Fakir ..." (p. 184) [He lots all his cats in a house fire]. Around the same time (December 2-3), a feline exhibition held in the Wagram Hall in Paris and organized by the recently formed *Club des Amis des Chats*, did not seem to suffer from a shortage of Birman, from what *Le Journal* of December 2 indicated: "But here is a remarkable collection of luxury cats. Black, white, blue, tortoiseshell, cream Persians; admirable Birman like those of Mrs. Chaumont-Doizy [sic], whose most beautiful cat is accompanied by six admirable kittens" (p. 6).

Meanwhile, the interest in cats in general continued. On April 6 and 7, 1934, the "Société Centrale Féline pour l'amélioration du Chat," member of the *Fédération Féline de France*, organized its annual "Salon of the Cat" in the Wagram Hall. The numerous international judges and French representatives created the *Fédération Féline Européenne*, which will play a very important role in the promotion and development of cat breeds. Among the five Birman exhibited, we note the presence of Sinh de Saint-Hubert, whom we recently talked about.

The report of The *Intransigent* of April 8, 1934 does not specifically mention the Birman, but paints a picturesque image of the living room:

Like every year, the most beautiful animals were there. Siamese mortified to find themselves in cages, looked with resignation at the gloved fingers which passed through the bars, smelled them with their delicate muzzle and, disdainfully, turned their heads; lazy Persians, lost in their furs; cats from the island of Nam [sic Man], who pride themselves on not having a tail; noble and proud Chartreux; enigmatic Abyssinians; Argentines and how many others, all loved, all beautiful. Cats keep their traditional dress, but they wear white, black, tan, gray with superb. They like solid colors, but they are not loyal to them and they know the advantage that can be drawn, depending on the race to which one belongs, of ingeniously sown spots, chocolate boots and masks. (p. 3).

We actually have the point of view of an interior observer since Manou de Madalpour in his editorial for the *Revue Féline de France* in April commented on the evolution of feline standards:

A final word on fashion: For women, it seems, the chest is a little carried and the fashion is light blue. For Persian cats, the nose is no longer worn at all and the fashion is also light blue. Black is always dressed, all the more distinguished because it is rare. For the Siamese, the nose is long and strong. Putty overcoat, very clear. Dark gloves. For Birman, white gloves, very short. And cats, like women, manage to change up to date. (p. 203).

Indeed, *L'Écho de Paris* on the same day confirms the presence of Manou de Madalpour at the exhibition where it was declared out of competition. For its part, *Le Matin* of the following day was more interested in the economic aspect of the event by publishing an article, which highlighted the excessive prices of the cats presented: "About a Parisian. Our dear king of gutters!"

Certainly, the cat show offers as much beauty as the various painting salons. Many cats who deign to admire themselves are living works of art. Among others, the Persians with deep blue eyes, the Siamese, the mysterious Birman, offer an incomparable grace in resting, walking, jumping, playing. The "winged" cat, the sand cat, that of the Chartreux, the cat-panther, are attractive phenomena. The whole is of rare aesthetic value. These noble figures even cost so much that they no longer became the pride but the vanity of certain houses. We are sometimes too hasty not to let you ignore their considerable price, their pedigree, the awards obtained, etc. Will we admit that our intimate preferences go to the humblest of all, to the one who is not exposed, to the one who embodies the qualities and none of the faults of the feline breed, to the common short-haired kitty called "gutter." Its mother could not say which tomcat offered it to her; it takes over the whole neighborhood; it's the "total" cat. The old girl, the bachelor, the scientist, the writer, the priest, get this friend cheaply, just by saying to the baker or the creamer: "Keep me one of the next litter of your cat, don't drown everything!

It is made of robust health. Like angora, it does not obstruct its intestines by obstinately swallowing its hair. It is intelligent, funny, affectionate. Its cleanliness is meticulous. Until an advanced age, it plays - and without pulling out its claws. It understands and does not disturb the work of others. It is sober. It rewards us for our hospitality with a discreet, deep, caring affection. Salute, admire the cats grown in Asia. But let's not forget our good old French kitty. Perrault found It so witty that he made it save its poor master fool.

Just before the exhibition, Marcelle Adam herself published a new article in *Le Monde Illustré* on March 31, 1934, under the title "Here is the Feline Exhibition. French breeding is worth English breeding." She remarked: "Should we tell you about the Chartreux, imported, it is said, by the Reverend Fathers? Cats from the island of Malta [sic: Man] who are anurans, pink cats from Turkey, dawn color, cats from Burma whose wavy and long bristles have Siamese hues and whose sapphire eyes are unique?"

In July, the magazine *Chasse, Pêche, Élevage* proudly announced that Father Chamonin had obtained a litter of kittens produced from Poupée de Rangoon and Fakir de la Chesnaie without specifying the number, but he issued doubts about their survival, by mentioning the case of another litter born from Fatma de la Chesnaie who could not reach adulthood because of the problems of inbreeding (p. 4089). In addition, this same article reports an epidemic of "gastroenteritis" which has caused several deaths, in particular at *La Chesnaie*, where two blue Persians and a young Birman son of Lon Saïto died (p. 4088).

This sad news finds an echo which reached Marcelle Adam: Manou de Madalpour died suddenly, on July 9, 1934. In memory of her favorite cat, the writer composed a commemorative text in the form of dialogue from beyond the grave, which appeared in the *Revue Féline de France*,

"La Maison Vide" (The Empty Home):

- [Mme ADAM] - Where are you Manou?
- [Manou] - By your side. On the table where you eat, on the table where you work, on your bed when you sleep, in your arms ... everywhere, across the house, where you are. Can't you see me
- I see you, Manou, but your thin ghost escapes my caresses. I grieve.
- Me too. However, I love your grief. As long as it lasts, your thoughts will keep me close. I will not die until the day of your complete oblivion.
- That day will never come, dear little shadow.
- I think so, we held each other by so many links! –
  Very strong ties, yes, so much so that you took me a little. Your departure left the house empty and my heart empty. Your little departure, after the other great departures ...
- It was necessary. My hour had come.

- Too early. Always too early. You people, our beasts of choice, shouldn't you live as much as we do?

- Alas! Our brief lives cross yours, often without a trace, however they were entirely devoted to you. This is not my case, you loved me. I couldn't bear your absences. You can't stand mine.

- I think that each sentimental destiny has highlights: A friendship, a love, an animal tenderness, if I dare say it that way. I speak for normal beings. In my opinion, those who disdain beasts are not completely normal.

- They are, in any case, unjust. They despise us and we lavish on them a treasure that they are unable to return to us.

- For a long time, Jo, the gray cat, reigned over my heart, then, his memory ... And you came. Without erasing it, you took its place. Its jealous specter has turned pale. I beg your pardon. I've always been sick. Ten times, until the evening when she escaped me, quickly and painfully. Manou... Manou, bout-de-chat..., Manou, grand-god..., Manou, Lightweight..., Manou-Brisou, my Manou... Since then, I have been talking about the details of your brief story every day, as well as reread, without further action, the pages of a favorite book. Your brief story... Ten years, all the same, a chapter of mine. First, your arrival at home, the misery from which you came out, your thinness, the tail then in wire, and the rosary of your protruding spine, and the attention with which I watched your forehead where should appear, I was said, a puff quite similar to that of the cockatoo. And the delicious legend of the Sacred Cats of Burma... And my pride in front of the emerging beauty... And the tuft, especially the tuft!... We were still laughing at home, at that time...

- The extraordinary always appeals to humans. I was just a cat.

- Be silent, You were Manou, the-most-beautiful-of-cats. And the best. And the most cerebral. You were the one Jean-Paul Hippeau called the unreal Prince with sapphire eyes. Your eyes, your dear eyes, your immense eyes, of a dark blue iridescent of purple, your eyes lit by an interior light, your eyes whose deep water rested on a background nielloed by a divine goldsmith, your eyes that so many artists wanted to paint without ever succeeding, your incredible eyes whose gaze was so soft, so soft ...

- This gaze is still on you; he follows you.

- It haunts me, Manou. It populates my loneliness. It sustains my sorrow.

- It puts blue around you, pretty blue, blue tenderness, blue thoughts.

- Dear little specter! ... Your narrow grave, opening up to Jagny, in a friendly land has reopened other graves in my heart. My old mom loved you. Is it for this reason that, for three nights in a row, I had a strange dream where, coming out of a fog, she came to me, holding your inert body in her arms. "Manou is dead," she said, in a sorry voice. However, you seemed promised for long days. But a week later, you died suddenly. Poor mom! Did she receive you in her arms as I saw her? ... No more animal beasts she has touched. It's finish. Your image awakens hers and joins her. I remain alone and sad. - No. We are there alive in your heart. We are here.

- I know ... I know ... You are present by my side, oh my ghosts! I see you. Manou, on my table while I write. Your azure eyes look at my sorrow. I hear the silence of the house, I measure the emptiness. My tender comrade, your departure widens the silence and widens the void ... Your little departure, after the other great departures...

According to information provided by Marcelle Adam, Manou had just spent 9 years at his death since he was born on June 13, 1925. He was not very old for a Sacred Cat of Burma; it is interesting to learn how in a sad state he was when he arrived at Marcelle Adam's, from the Léotardi house. He was buried in Jagny-sous-Bois, not far today from Charles-de-Gaulle airport.

Laotian Cat			Birman Female
HIRAM-ROI			**POUPEE** de Madalpour
Father			Mother
Birth 13/06/1925	**MANOU** de Madalpour † 9/07/1934		

The melancholy impression aroused by this funeral was not dissipated by an article in the same issue of

La Revue Féline de France which was alarmed by the degeneration of the breed in the Milan International Exhibition:

The so-called "Burma" cats of French import (Dieu d'Arakan and Reine de Rangoon) redeemed their lack of hair only by their beautiful blue eyes. Their descendants (5 young: 3 of 9 months and 2 of 3 months) unfortunately lost the shape of the head and the marks; white spots disqualify some. Is failure already in the selection of this breed?

The two exhibitions of 1935 took place in the *Salle Hoche* which was the site of most feline exhibitions until 1939. About the first, from the *Cat Club of Paris*, took place January 13, 14 and 15, the *Feline Review of France* returned to the problems posed by the Birman.

Birman cats wear long, very pale creamy thick fur, dark brown mask and legs, perfectly white fingertips, blue-violet eyes. Their great rarity and their imposing beauty make them animals of real value. Some curious breeders have obtained, by calculated crosses and also sometimes, by chance, a variety of cats resembling Birman by the fur; but the shape of the head is missing, the legs are not gloved. We are still there only in experiments and nothing is fixed.

It is in fact the Khmer cat which would later be called Persian Colorpoint or Himalayan.

With regard to the following exhibition, that of *La Centrale Féline* which took place in April, the most interesting account can be found in the pen of Blanche Messis in the April 27, 1935 issue of the newspaper *Comœdia*. The journalist insisted on the presence of Mrs. Lebrun, wife of the President of the Republic, but also underlined the pecuniary advantages of breeding and continued to sing the praises of the rat cats:

Mrs. Albert Lebrun chairs this exhibition; and we are not surprised because the President of the Republic is a fervent of the most faithful friends that have been given to us.

She cannot be comforted by having lost her beautiful Siamese the same day that she entered the Elysée Palace. Besides, doesn't Miss Lebrun have a breeding of Persians of all colors?

Ms. Marcelle Adam, president of the Société Féline de Paris, explained to us yesterday the importance of this society.

- We want to protect the French breeders, and manage to equal the English breeders who, for the moment, are holding the lead.

It's not clear enough that cat breeding could be a very attractive source of income, for a small household, for example, which would have a very good breed couple. Weddings are very expensive ...

And the smallest Persian costs 500 francs. A couple can even reach 20 or 25,000 francs.

In addition, we also have a section of ratiers [rat killers] to help municipal catteries.

You know that Mr. Herriot, in Lyon, had a cattery installed? Because only cats can completely destroy rats. Thus, the port of Antwerp is almost entirely rid of its rodents thanks to a cattery where the animals are selected according to their vigor. "

Besides, whether rat or Birman, gutter prowler or luxury beast, the cat remains the very proud, very just animal - whatever the human disloyalty may have said - a little secret and always noble. Peasants, men of letters, artists, know this well, who their friends are. If Colette's cat is the most famous - not to mention that of Barbey d'Aurevilly - there are many others on the writers' tables: a black Persian at Lucie Delarue-Mardrus; a blue Persian at Claude Farrère and at Rosny; little alley cats that delight Arthur Bernède. Georges Bourdon is, it seems, "a fanatic of cats." We know that Poincarré had Siamese. Mary Marquet presents her Persian in La

Belle Aventure; Elisabeth Nizan and Véra Korène are great cat friends. Brunot cares for his gutter cat, and the sumptuous feline of Léon Bernard is called "Voyou." I will not list all the "fervent lovers and austere scholars." But do you want something to guide your sympathies in life? Love people who love cats; don't trust others too quickly! .... (p. 3)

The "Birmanian" neologism is a little disconcerting, but the rhetorical swaying of the sentence indicates that the Sacred Birman Cat is in a way emblematic of luxury cats. This is confirmed by the cover of the exceptional special issue devoted to the cat in 1935 by *La Vie à la Campagne* "His Highness the Cat." Next to a Siamese and a Persian, both great champions, is a photo of Dieu d'Arakan, "the most representative type of Birman Cats, obtained by Mr. Baudoin-Crevoisier."

Everyone in the feline world was involved in this special issue. Marcel Baudoin-Crevoisier wrote his last

«DIEU D'ARAKAN» vu de profil. Ce sujet, provenant de croisement, est supérieur au type ordinaire par sa beauté et sa rusticité.

LE MÊME, VU DE FACE, présente une silhouette unique. Admirez sa jolie collerette.

article while Ms. Chaumont-Doisy wrote the first of his on the Birman.

Baudoin-Crevoisier synthesized his knowledge on the Sacred Birman Cat:

The Birman cat or sacred cat. First cousins of the Siamese by their origin as by their appearance, the quality and very typical subjects of this breed are quite rare, which increases their value, while their originality and their beauty justify an amplification of their production. [...] The first copy imported into Western countries would have been in France. Currently, livestock production appears to be in decline; the majority of fine specimens produced over the past 10 years gradually disappear without always being replaced. This state of affairs justifies an effort at reconstruction.

It seems that Baudoin-Crevoisier had some doubts about the legend that he nevertheless continued to disseminate. In fact, he took the trouble to specify with regard to the origins of the Birman but with two new conditions: "The origins of the Birman Cat are discussed, despite its precise name. Several authors have made it a legendary animal, and it would be in the Temple of Lao-Tsun, in Burma, that the origin of these superb animals should be sought." He concluded: "After six years of personal research [note: 1929-35] and 10 years of Breeding in France, the Birman Cat remains as mysterious as to its origin, and no new imported product has been seen and, therefore, studied" (p. 19). The rest of the article is consistent with what he previously published.

In this same exceptional issue, Mrs. Chaumont-Doisy published an article entitled: "The Sacred Cat of Burma." But it is more of a story about his personal experiences with Birman, and is a beautiful testimony to the endearing personality of this cat:

In addition to its beauty, this Feline has a charming character. Its intelligence is as great as that of the Siamese; it is perhaps even more caressing, but not in the same way, and, if it has diverted, for its benefit, the admiration I had for the Siamese, it is because it does not cry and is less turbulent. It is very difficult to relate all the charm which is in him, one cannot even define it exactly; but for the past five years I have experienced this charm with ever new pleasure.

When I hold either Moses or Allah in my arms and very softly I whisper to him: "How beautiful you are! How good you are and how I love you!" Both of them hug as much as possible against me, and every day I love them more deeply, so deeply that I can no longer probe their bottom!

There are people who say that Cats do not think, that it is instinct that makes them act! Well, these people don't know animals at all. They think, and even when they are very small. A month and a half ago, I had a litter of 4 Birman kittens, 20 days old; they have been trotting for a few days in the kitchen, when one morning I caught them in the charcoal box! It was as much fun as possible! They certainly had to play who would be most unrecognizable; real charcoal burners! I plugged the tiny entrance where they entered with a cardboard box. Manoaster, the most rascal of the band, just returns to the spot and scrapes, with vivacity, the falling cardboard. You think how happy it was! I take it out, put the box back in and, so that it does not fall, I put a book and I release my little guy who has returned to the book; it camped on it and tried to knock it down.

On the other hand, animals are superior to us in affection. When I come back, if I'm late for dinner, the owner is not very happy, he sometimes makes more or less pleasant reflections.

Allah, when I come home late, does the opposite: it caresses my legs and waits with great impatience for the hat and the coat to be removed, and then it kisses me frantically, seeming to say to me: I was afraid you weren't coming back, that something had happened to you. And the more I am late, the more I receive caresses. Burmese Cats are therefore less selfish than men".

In addition to the aforementioned cover photo, this special issue includes the photos of Manou and Poupée already published in *La Vie à la Campagne* in 1926, joined with a new series with Moïse de

« MOÏSE DE MADALPOUR » très joli mâle, et quatre beaux Chatons âgés de 20 jours ; à Mme Chaumont-Doisy.

Madalpour, a very pretty male, and four kittens 20-days-old (probably the kittens mentioned above by

« HUELDÉDA DE MADALPOUR », belle femelle Birmane;
à Mme Chaumont-Doisy.

Mrs. Chaumont-Doisy). Additionally, there were Dieu d'Arakan, other unknown kittens, and another cat of Mrs. Chaumont-Doisy presented for the first time— Hueldéda de Madalpour. This iconography is accompanied by a laudatory comment:

LE CHAT DE BIRMANIE, first cousin of the Siamese, has been known in France since 1925; its qualities, its originality and its beauty make it very appreciated, but the subjects of quality are still extremely rare. 1 and 3 Manon [sic] of Madalpour; to Mrs. Marcelle Adam. 2. Madalpour Poupée; to Mrs. Léotardi. It is the crossing of this most perfect Birman type cat with a Siamese cat which is at the origin of the famous Madalpour strain. (p. 22).

It includes an old photo of Poupée with her four kittens born on June 20, 1926: Sinh, Lon Golden, Sita II, Nafaghi. Also included is a photo of 5 Birman cats of very Siamese appearance, which were said to belong to Mrs. Duym (unknown elsewhere).

Let us note in passing (as we have already said) that this same year, 1935, Mrs. Chaumont took over for her own cattery the affix of "Madalpour" which indicated a line different from the Madalpour's direct descendants of Doll. Mrs. Chaumont-Doisy continued to develop her breeding, as evidenced by this announcement published on December 15, 1935 in *La Vie à la Campagne*: "Birmans and Siamese kittens. From stallions in service. 'Moïse de Madalpour', two 1st Birman prizes; 'Champion Vichnou' two 1st prices of Siamese Championship: to Mrs. Chaumont-Doisy, 112, rue de Paris, Clamart (Seine). B. 371)."

The following feline exhibition, that of April 1936, still presented Birmans as confirmed by *Le Petit Journal* in its article of April 19 entitled "The most beautiful cats in the world are the hosts of Paris": "From some distance Isle of Man cats; of a Birman cat directly imported from Mandeley [sic], 17 French and foreign champions, and more than 400 subjects, Siamese, Chartreux, Persian of all shades, a whole family of Abyssinian cats, the father, mother and three cubs - this is the first time that "Abyssinians" have appeared in a feline exhibition" (p. VIII). Certainly, the information imparted is not very accurate. The Birman cat in question is actually Zaquelle de Mandalay (not Mandeley), and she was not imported from Burma since it was her matronymic. However, the emphasis on the family of Abyssinians announces a change of perspective which would be confirmed in the following years until the war; the Birman was relegated to the background and gave way to the Abyssinian cat. There are no longer any significant articles on the Sacred Birman Cat in magazines and newspapers.

Mrs. Chaumont-Doisy continued to breed Birmans in her new cattery of "Madalpour," and a certain Madeleine Boyer was doing the same on her side. It was not the usual newspapers that revealed Ms. Boyer's existence but the interview she gave much later to Mrs. Simone Poirier in the book *The Secrets of the Sacred Cat of Burma.*

According to this book, she began her breeding in 1928 by buying from Mrs. Gilles-Lénaerts Fly who became "de Kaabaa", her affix. This one born on May 10, 1928, was called "young angora," but also "Birman" (Simone Poirier, p. 73). Miss Boyer then acquired around 1935, the female Youla de Madalpour (who seems not to have been gloved) and obtained on May 5, 1936, from these two cats, her first litter of Birman kittens from which she kept Maïta de Kaabaa. Then, in 1938, she bought the semi-Birman Miarka I, ungloved, whose alliance with Fly produced Baker de Kaabaa, which in turn spawned the famous Orloff of Kaabaa. It was from him as well as from Mrs. Chaumont-Doisy's cats that all of the Birman descend today.

At least the disaffection of the press towards the Sacred Cat of Burma has spared it from being involved in a diplomatic pseudo-scandal. Indeed, in December 1938, the *Excelsior* du 3 in its report on the Chat Room—organized by the *Club des Amis du Chat* at the *Wagram Hall*—had the misfortune to caption the photos of white and blue Persians "When the Cat is King". This delicate allusion was apparently taken up by *Le Petit Parisien* as well as by a play on words by Pierre Dac in the satirical newspaper *L'os à mœlle*. However, Iran was using this pretext to announce the termination of its diplomatic relations with France.

The response was quick. In the January 2, 1939 issue of *L'Intransigeant*, the famous journalist Louis Latzarus published a caustic article which reviewed all the French proverbs containing the word cat that could shock that of Iran under the title "The Thorns of Ispahan":

— Attention ici, n'appelez pas le sha un chat !

Oh! My God, what a sad time! Now the Persian Shah himself is becoming quintile, susceptible and rascal. One day, he learns that *Le Petit Parisien* gave the title of the report of a feline exhibition this: "S. M. The cat receives [in his living room]." Immediately, he enters into fury. His Majesty the cat! It's about him. We want to make fun of him! We want to make fun of it. - No, sire! There are shah and chat. The cat is a domestic animal. - How? 'Or' What! The French take me for a pet! No way! Don't let your majesty get angry! But rather than considering foreign pronunciation ... - not sparing me. I have been told, I must take revenge!

Thereupon, the Shah of Persia breaks off all diplomatic relations with us. It's very funny. But don't say it, above all! In our time, everything that is comical becomes dangerous, Of course, we know that the shahs of Persia have never been very pleasant, and I remember that a music hall artist, in order to attract attention spectators, had baptized himself: the man who made the shah laugh, to signify that he has an irresistible gaiety. We easily believed it. Because the various shahs who came to visit Paris did

196

not seem to us to be cheerful or playful. We showed them everything. But they looked just as they would have looked at their own grave. One of them, before 1900, had heard of the guillotine. He wanted to see it. We couldn't refuse him this delicate pleasure. Mr. Deibler, under the hangar, mounted the machine, and lowered the cleaver several times, in a vacuum, of course. And the Shah disturbed this interesting demonstration, but a little bland. He asked for a man to be brought in and his head severed before his eyes. He was told that our laws forbid this kind of entertainment, so he turned his head towards the characters in his suite and showed one of them:

- Take this one, he said.

Between us, I am not sure that this story is authentic. Good stories are usually made up, or so arranged that you can't trust them. But I read this one twenty times, and the King of Kings took no shade, if he himself knew about it. You could talk, in those days, you could write without fear of falling out with Persia. Now, we will have to revise all our proverbs:

"Do not wake the sleeping cat" that is offensive. What does it mean, if not that the master of Persia is plunged into perpetual sleep, and that if he comes out of it, he will endanger honest people?

"At night, all cats are gray", it means that His Majesty abuses fermented drinks at dusk. There is no worse insult, and whoever utters it deserves to be impaled.

"To good cat good rat" is an undisguised threat. They try to imply that Her Majesty's enemies will be right, and we encourage them to put Her to death.

"Scalded cat fears cold water", what does that mean, except that the master of Persia is susceptible to fear and lives in disgusting filth?

"I call a cat [spade] a cat [spade]" is blatant rudeness. A cat is not a cat. It is a god.

"Buying a cat in your pocket", an expression that tends to prove first that the King of Kings is for sale, and then that you could repent of having bought it.

In addition, a tale by Perrault depicts a certain *Puss in Boots*, who is a simple swindler. A terrible allusion that Her Majesty rejects, but of which she remains justly indignant.

Even in French folklore, His Majesty is flouted. A certain shepherdess kills her kitten who has put her chin in a bad cheese. An awful way to signal to His Majesty that she has made bad alliances and that it will cost him his life.

I seem to be exaggerating. But it is not. As long as the Shah of Persia can be irritated by a perfectly innocent and harmless title, he can be irritated by everything, The roses of Isfahan, the roses of Shiraz, the roses sung by Saadi, leave us only their thorns Bah! We will console ourselves. But elsewhere, laughter and grace have also died out. Elsewhere, almost everywhere.

The same day, the newspaper *Populaire* put the finger on the diplomatic secrets hidden behind the feline pretext by comparing His Majesty the Shah with his European counterparts: "I have the same idea that it is much easier to get along with the Shah of Persia than with Lord Adolf and Monsignor Benito ".

However, the news grew darker and feline exhibitions became rare—it seems that the last of the *Cat Club of Paris* before the war took place from January 14 to 16, 1939 in the *Salle Hoche*. In the press reports there were final allusions to the Birman. In its February 5 issue, the first allusion to the Sacred Cat of Burma in *Nouvelliste d'Indochine* was not very friendly, despite the aesthetic admiration:

Cat lovers went to the Salle Hoche last Sunday to admire the magnificent felines that were exposed there. All the cats in the world meet there, from the vulgar Parisian gutter cat, so intelligent, so clever, to the sacred Burma cat whose title is equivalent to that of prince in the feline gent. They are animals of the highest arrogance, and contemptuous in the extreme, but very fine and elegant.

In any case, this was a fairly quick report compared to that of the *Petit Journal* of January 15 in which Maurice Coriem described in detail the exhibition of the Cat Club, with a strong quote from Baudelaire although Corien mentions among the fashionable breeds the "flexible and dreamy Birman" and he gives preference to "our beautiful gutter cats" who were not likely to trigger diplomatic incidents. The Iranian incident left a bitter taste in the memories even as the Cat Club devoted an entire gallery to "Iranian" cats.

Meow ... Meow ... This sweet plaintive song is exhaled from the basket where kitty awaits the hour of glory.

This is *Salle Hoche*, at the Cat Club's international cat show. This little solemnity has not only its grace, but also its usefulness. It is established for the benefit of the National Defense Committee against Tuberculosis. Good reasons for wishing him success. Vow, moreover, already realized.

Who doesn't like cats? Can we evoke them without the obligatory reminder of the immortal verses which are Baudelairian:

Thinking about noble attitudes
Large sphinxes lying at the bottom of solitudes ...

In fact, that's how I see these two gray striped cats, nonchalant, half-closed eyes, and as the poet once again said,

Who seem to fall asleep in an endless dream

I ignore their race and my eclecticism of admiration cares little. Incidentally, they are the most beautiful cats in the world here. To put it bluntly, their adventurous faces and the secret of their appearance, a whole repertoire of rare adjectives. Russian blues, Abyssinians from a single family (there are ten in France), supple and dreamy Burmese, all so wise, in their little cages with pretty cushions, precious silks ...

In their all-white nests, here are the wonderful pristine chinchillas. Alone, in this lilial symphony, their eyes have gleams of fatal colors of mystery. A whole floor is reserved for Iran. They are of all colors, all sweetnesses, all terrors. They have faces of female loves, warriors' muzzles with palikar mustaches, Mint, Kid, golden Iranians, mind-blowing strange humanity, are champions and Autocrates is champion of champions. It is the lord of the place, who is worth ten thousand pounds and deserves the charming smile of all the ladies.

Shall I dare greet this prince with a glitz of the East before whom everyone, suddenly amazed with such high beauty exclaims:

Oh!

And let's quickly come back to our good gutter cats with straight ears, high legs, real popular cats, sensitive, familiar, rat hunters, purring rooftops, and their simplicity keeps sovereign moods and diplomatic complications.

To finish our work, there remains to mention a final element which adds to the strangeness of the legend. Mrs. Marcelle Adam published in 1959 a book on cats (The Book of Cats) which became a worldwide success (with its many translations), and which reviews all the races, but, mysteriously, does not mention the Birman cat at all, when she was its main promoter! It was as if the Birman did not exist. Perhaps a late, silent recognition of its pure and simple invention unrelated to the historical reality of the feline world? Another possible explanation is the author's disdain for the re-creation of the Birman cat in the 1950s. During a cat show, Mrs. Simone Poirier reports that she reportedly said that the new Birman were not and did not look like the original strains.

EPILOGUE

Feline exhibitions slowly resumed after the war (1947) and there were occasional Birman cats, if we are to believe the few accounts given in the newspapers of the time. The great era of journalistic reporting has passed, but this does not prevent enthusiastic breeders from working to improve the breed. Over time, some create new colors, others refine or even modify certain elements of the standard. I was fortunate enough to be able to meet with Mrs. Michèle Lefrançois, from the Chatterley cattery, breeder of Birman since 1982, and I discussed with her the thorny questions of the silver gene and the Roman nose.

1. When did you first become interested in the Birman cat?

At an exhibition, the first I attended, 37 years ago. [1982]

2. How did you start your breeding?

First by taking a male when I knew nothing at all, I did not know the breed at all, and then I wanted a female who was in the standard, and I decided to produce a litter, but it wasn't really breeding.

3. What difficulties did you encounter when you started?

The first Birman I bought was not standard at all. I had to try to remedy the faults, he had very large gloves, he had socks. So, I wanted to compensate with a cat that had small gloves, thinking that it would be average, and in fact, I had a large glove and a small one. So, I saw that I did not understand at all that the distribution of white among the Birman is random.

4. What were your first successes?

The first success was the cat I bought, the second, after this male who was not in the standard, was unfortunately or fortunately what communicated to me the virus of exhibitions. The second Birman cat that I bought was a cat well in the standard which made a "Best in Show" in Baltard, during my first exhibition.

5. Did the breeders work more together than today?

Completely. We were looking for stallions; we had them. No one would ever refuse a stallion. We tried to be of service; we sold each other's cats. I started breeding by working with several people, and one day —for family reasons because my daughter 'de Chatterley' and my son-in-law 'de l'Oseraie' got married following an encounter at an exhibition—I worked in a more privileged way with this single cattery (Madame POULAIN) which only made Blue Birmans.

6. What colors were you interested in at the start and which colors are you interested in today?

At first, I was more for solid colors, in fact that's the only we had. The family was split in two, there were those who were more "Seal" and those who were more "Blue." Personally, because I had both colors, I was more attracted to blue, and then I found that the evolution of the family was as follows: those who liked the "Seal" liked the "Chocolate" and "Red," and those who had a predilection for "Blue," liked "Lilac" and "Cream." And the same for the "Tortie." I also raised "Tabby" and "Silver."

7. You are one of the first breeders to embark on the Birman Silver. What is its history and where does your interest in this color come from?

I heard about it from Mrs. Basquine, who was the first breeder and judge in France to have married one of her Birman with a Chinchilla Persian. The poor darling had twenty or thirty hybrid cats to place before Christmas. She was exhibiting, but unfortunately at the time, since I was working, I had not been able to offload one of her hybrids. I still found the idea of wanting to make a different color interesting. However, this presented the difficulty of producing hybrids that we didn't know what to do with, so it gave me the idea to help a little bit the people who made "Silver" and to associate myself with them. And then it was especially after seeing one of her "Silver" which was absolutely magnificent that I really got interested in the "Silver." This Seal-Silver-Tabby male from the 'Moulin de Busset' was spectacular, with a tail obviously much larger than the Birman had to this day. It was especially the tail of this cat that had interested me, without any joke at all, because the Birman had relatively small and fluffy tails, and this one had an absolutely gorgeous tail. He had to take it from the chinchilla which was among his ancestors.

8. You have been breeding Birmans for almost 38 years; Has the standard of the cat changed since the very beginning of your breeding?

It has changed enormously; Birman at the time were quite massive, with flat foreheads, straight noses, and we were mainly interested in gloves; it was the gloves that were really the major criterion, and also the chin, and they had pale blue eyes that we all found very pretty. It has evolved into a more Persian Birman. Currently, it tends towards the Persian, with more hair. This is where we lose this semi-long hair of silk, one of the most beautiful characteristics of the Birman. It has a forehead almost bulging like the Persians: its nose is totally different, this is called a "Roman nose," and this was the big news. It was Mrs. Marie-Anne Taranger from the *Srinagar* cattery, who literally invented the Roman nose: the nose had to "come down like a slide." She used the term "Toboggan," and that gave the typed cat that is sought after more than that in some clubs. The LOF attaches more importance to the Roman nose than the FIFE whose standard was: "Roman nose tolerated," while the LOF was "Roman nose required." As for the chin, it has not changed: the standard always says that a straight line is needed between the nose, the nostrils and the chin, but unfortunately, there are a lot of Birman who have lost their chin and who have a fleeing chin, and that is very difficult to recover.

9. What could we do to recover this chin?

Try to save cats that have chin and use them even if they do not have the other desired characteristics, but at least try to catch the chin, and then I also forget that in the evolution of the cat, the Birman eyes have changed enormously, because we mixed Chocolate Birman where the Siamese was closer and where the blue of the eyes was almost purple, thus really turning the eyes of the Birman; this is one of the major developments, I find, in this cat.

10. Lately we have seen the creation of new colors, such as Cinnamon and Fawn. What do you think of these new attempts?

Since I tried to make chocolate and lilac, I don't want to rebel against people who try to make Cinnamon and Fawn. Personally, I did not try because the Cinnamon and the Fawn that I saw have not convinced me for the moment, in particular, the Cinnamon appeared to me as neither beautiful red, nor beautiful chocolate, and there is something that bothers me.

11. What are the main difficulties encountered by Birman breeders today?

After the FeLV (Feline Leukemia Virus), there was and there is still the disease of FIP (Feline Infectious Peritonitis) which decimated a lot of Birman, and a lot of cats in general; we don't really know where it comes from, how it comes, and what to do. To date, we have not yet found the parade completely; there was leukosis before, but now we have a vaccine. There has also been PKD (Polycystic Kidney Disease) on the kidneys, but it turns out that Birman do not have many, though enough to find when a Birman has been married to a Persian. Another difficulty: there is the arrival of the other races, in particular the Ragdoll which made an absolutely extraordinary competition with the Birman, so that currently in TICA (The International Cat Association) there is practically no more Birman who compete, apart from one or two lost. But the exhibitors get discouraged very quickly, being in competition with an impressive number of Ragdolls: the Birman do not go out at all in TICA. Another difficulty: the world of Birman is fairly closed, and most breeders claim that they do not share their males studs, that they do not sell their stud, and also that they sell all their cats neutered. This is not entirely true, it is only partially true, those who say it do not necessarily do it, and those who do it do not necessarily say it.

12. What advice would you give to a young Birman breeder today?

To start small, to have very few cats, to try to find a cat that is roughly standard, and not to make too serious a selection by wanting beauty right away. It will not be found in other breeders because when a breeder has a very beautiful cat, he/she keeps it and does not sell it, so that is not what to look for. You have to look for a cat that is in the standard, which for example has beautiful eyes. I would take it in this order to reproduce: health, morphology, type, Roman nose, eyes and glove.

13. What is the goal you pursue today in your breeding?

My goal from the start was to make Birman better than I had from the start, and I continue to this day.

ANNEX

HERE YOU WILL FIND SEVERAL PERIOD ARTICLES REPRODUCED.

1. The text of Dr Vet Jumaud in *Vie à la Campagne* of October 1, 1926.

2. The first version of the Legend published in the serial *Le Matin*, January 9, 1926. "L'Amour qui Tremble", by Mrs. Marcelle Adam.

3. The (original) version of the legend published by S. R. in the review *Minerva* No 110, September 18, 1927.

4. The version of the legend published in December 1929 by Mrs. Marcelle Adam in the *Revue Féline Belge* No 5.

5. The final version of Dr Vet Fernand Méry, in the review *Minerva*, No 386, of January 1, 1933, p. 14.

6. The Crawford-Humbert Affair. Article from *La Justice*. May 2, 1902.

7. "Jo". Text by Marcelle Adam. *La Revue Féline de France*. No. 6. April 1931.

THE TEXT OF DR VET JUMAUD IN “VIE À LA CAMPAGNE” OF OCTOBER 1, 1926.

LE CHAT DE BIRMANIE, ANIMAL SACRÉ

RACE CARACTÉRISÉE, QUI SERAIT A L'ORIGINE DU SIAMOIS ET QUI SE DISTINGUE NETTEMENT DES RACES ASIATIQUES A POIL LONG, AVEC LESQUELLES LES SUJETS NE SYMPATHISENT PAS.

LE CHAT DE BIRMANIE est originaire de l'Extrême-Orient. Les sujets de cette race, élevés dans les temples, sont sévèrement gardés, et leur cession en est interdite. Cependant, voici quelques années, un couple fut importé par Mme Thadée Hadish (couple qui a donné souche à la famille de « Madalpour ») ; ce couple fut vraisemblablement dérobé par un serviteur du temple, ébloui par des promesses et qui aura pris la fuite pour éviter le châtiment, car, pour qui connaît le fanatisme des Hindous, jamais personne ne croira que des prêtres aient vendu, même à un prix fabuleux, un couple de leurs animaux sacrés. Le major Sir Russel Gordon, faisant partie des troupes britanniques chargées de protéger les Kittahs, eut, en 1898, l'occasion d'observer ces animaux sacrés. Il en dressa un standard qui corrobore celui établi en 1925 dans notre thèse de doctorat.

Mœurs. Le Chat de Birmanie est très sociable, intelligent, gai, caressant, obéissant au commandement, suivant son maître à la manière d'un chien. Ce Chat est peu joueur, ou bien joue avec calme. Hors la présence de ses maîtres, il est lointain, distant, nostalgique. C'est un animal d'appartement qui n'a pas la vivacité, la fougue du Siamois. Il semble avoir conscience de son origine sacrée.

CARACTÈRES ESSENTIELS. *Apparence et taille.* Plutôt de petite taille, il a le corps allongé, les pattes minces bien proportionnées. Les griffes sont acérées, recourbées, fortes mais fines et assez friables. Son poids à l'âge adulte varie entre 3 et 4 kg.

Tête. La tête est longue avec des oreilles dressées, couvertes de poils feutrés blancs. Le front est bombé, le nez légèrement camus, la lèvre inférieure forte donnant l'impression de la bouche entr'ouverte. Les moustaches sont drues et longues. Les sourcils sont particulièrement fournis. Les yeux, très mobiles, sont bleus de roi très intense, l'œil de saphir de la légende, profonds et mélancoliques. Si l'animal est menacé ou furieux, son regard devient féroce et révèle tout du petit fauve indépendant qu'il entend toujours être. *Queue.* La queue n'est jamais courte, ni tordue, ni nouée, ni déviée en aucune manière. A première vue, elle ne donne pas l'impression du panache de l'Angora ; elle est mince, non empâtée. On peut le comparer au « fouet » des Setters comme nature de poil et apparence. La prise de la queue, mince à la naissance des reins, va en s'élargissant. Au repos, la queue est portée tombante, légèrement retroussée à l'extrémité. Quand l'animal joue ou quand il est en fureur, la queue se met en angle droit avec le corps, se renverse même sur le dos en panache d'écureuil, hérissée, énorme.

Robe. Comme tous les Chats asiatiques, les poils du Chat de Birmanie sont longs et soyeux et de la longueur des poils des semi-angoras. Ceux de la queue sont touffus et forment un panache moins fourni que celui de l'Angora. *Couleur.* La couleur est, quant au masque, pattes, queue, celle des Siamois avec peut-être des tons plus bronzés sur l'échine. Vu en plein soleil, la robe du birman donne l'impression d'être mêlée de fils d'or bruni, d'où le nom de « Gold Cat » que lui ont attribué les Anglais qui ont pu les approcher. Les quatre pattes donnent l'impression d'être chaussées de mitaines loutre dont passent quatre doigts gantés de blanc, d'un blanc absolument pur jusqu'à la première phalange. Le blanc monte en pointe à l'arrière des pattes postérieures, ce qui donne l'impression de courtes bottes lacées.

ÉCHELLE DES POINTS. Robe, 20 ; couleur et marques, 20 ; tête, 15 ; yeux, 15 ; queue, 20 ; corps, 10. Total : 100.

REPRODUCTION, ÉLEVAGE. L'Élevage des sujets observés a été particulièrement difficile. Mme Léotardi, qui a eu l'occasion d'en élever plusieurs, affirme qu'il ne faut pas compter élever plus d'un sujet sur dix. Les Chats de Birmanie mâles ne s'accouplent pas avec des Chattes angoras. Mme Léotardi ayant présenté une superbe persane à un de ses mâles birmans, celui-ci entra dans une épouvantable fureur, et il fallut le recouvrir d'une couverture pour l'empêcher de mettre à sang et en pièces la pauvre bête, alors que le surlendemain, lui faisant le meilleur accueil, il s'accoupla avec une Siamoise chocolat. Les produits des Angoras avec des Chattes de Birmanie n'ont jamais donné de jeunes rappelant la race de Birmanie. Une femelle de Mme Léotardi, couverte accidentellement par un Angora tigré, donna d'affreux chatons, dont trois mâles tigrés, à poils ras, spécimen absolu du Chat Européen, et une femelle complètement noire, à poil semi-long. Dans cette portée, rien ne rappelait la mère, Chatte de Birmanie, ni comme poil, ni comme couleur, ni comme formes. Le Chat de Birmanie s'unit facilement avec le Siamois, ou avec le Chat lynx laotien, mais les sujets obtenus ainsi sont rarement gantés régulièrement et ont tendance à présenter le pelage de la forme du Siamois ou du Laotien.

Alimentation. Ces animaux se trouvent très bien de poisson bouilli et de salade cuite ; d'autres n'acceptent que de la viande crue ; ils sont particulièrement sujets à la constipation.

Pour compléter cette étude sur le Chat de Birmanie, voici quelques notes de Sir Russel Gordon, démontrant que les *Siamois* proviennent du croisement de Chats annamites et de Chats de Birmanie. « Réellement, je pense, et le savant explorateur Auguste Pavie le pense avec moi, que le Chat de Siam est un croisé du Chat sacré de Birmanie et des Chats annamites importés au XVIIe siècle dans l'empire Khmer, au moment où le déclin de cet empire rigoureusement fermé eut lieu sous l'action des Siamois et des Annamites. Déjà, au VIe siècle, les « Thaï » (Siamois) envahirent les Khmer (Cambodgiens et Birmans) et développèrent leur puissance à leurs dépens. Les *Khmer* furent, de tout temps, réfractaires à l'influence de l'Inde Brahmique. Leur religion absolument fermée, très secrète au bas peuple et aux profanes, était consacrée par des prêtres tout-puissants et très vénérés les « Kittahs ». Ces prêtres furent impitoyablement massacrés et traqués par les brahmanes lors de la seconde invasion Thaï, au début du XVIIIe siècle. Ceux qui purent échapper se réfugièrent dans la Haute-Birmanie du Nord, parmi les montagnes inviolables, et y fondèrent le Temple souterrain de Lao-Tsun (habitation des dieux).

Le temple de Lao-Tsun est incontestablement une des curieuses merveilles de l'Inde que de bien rares mortels ont été appelés à contempler. Situé à l'est du lac Incaougji, entre Magaung et Sembo, dans une région quasi désertique de barrière de monts infranchissables. Là, vivaient encore en 1898 les derniers Kittahs, et il me fut, par extraordinaire faveur, permis de les observer quelque peu avec leurs animaux sacrés. A la suite de rébellion et lors de l'occupation anglaise, base de Bhamo, base très isolée en raison de son éloignement de Mandalay, nous vînmes à protéger les Kittahs contre une invasion brahmane, et nous les sauvâmes d'un massacre et d'un pillage certains. Leur Lamah-Kittah, le Votagi, me reçut et me fit présent d'une plaque représentant le Chat sacré aux pieds d'une divinité bizarre dont les yeux sont faits de deux saphirs allongés (pièce 4 108 de ma collection de Mildenhall) et après m'avoir, faveur insigne, permis de contempler les Chats sacrés, au nombre d'une centaine, me fit expliquer leur origine.

La légende est jolie, mais elle n'explique rien scientifiquement. Il est certain qu'une race de Chats annamites aux yeux jaunes, aux formes graciles et élégantes, de petite taille, à la queue courte naturellement, a été, à un certain moment, introduite en Birmanie avec l'invasion. Des études rattachent ce Chat à celui de l'île de Man (Chat sans queue), et cet animal aurait été importé par des caravelles anglaises aux Indes, vers le XVIIIe siècle.

Ceci à remarquer : Tous les Chats asiatiques ont une fourrure touffue. Chats d'Angora de toutes teintes, Persans, Chats écureuils, Bengalis, Chats chinois, Chats nains de l'île Formose, dits « Chats pêcheurs » ou Japan-Cat, etc. La nature les a pourvus, comme il a incité l'Arabe et l'Indou à se protéger du soleil brûlant avec de vastes et épais vêtements. Seul parmi ses frères d'Asie, le Siamois est de fourrure rasée. J'opine donc à croire avec quelque vraisemblance que le Chat de Birmanie à longs poils est l'ancêtre d'un Siamois par un croisement avec le Chat annamite sans queue importé par les Anglais. Il se trouve, du reste, pas mal d'exemplaires, parmi les Siamois, d'individus à yeux jaunes, pelage chocolat plus ou moins bringé et dont l'appendice caudal est réduit à quelques centimètres. Tous les Siamois ont une brisure ou une nodosité sur la queue lorsque celle-ci est longue. On peut trouver là encore un indice de jonction de ces deux races certainement très distinctes au début. Cette hypothèse est justifiée et répond d'avance à celle émise par plusieurs, prétendant que le Chat de Birmanie est dû au croisement du Siamois et du Chat Angora blanc. Hypothèse inadmissible, ainsi que le démontre l'impossibilité d'obtenir des résultats pour l'accouplement du Siamois et de Chats d'autres races.

Docteur-vétérinaire Ph. JUMAUD,
Secrétaire général du Cat-Club de France.

LE CHAT-TIGRE.

De dimensions remarquables, chasseur et sauteur de premier ordre, il est très caressant et affectueux.

IL EXISTE EN FRANCE un exemplaire curieux de Chat-Tigre, importé de la République Argentine et appartenant à Mme F. Marie. Ce Chat, qui ne semble pas le produit d'une race spéciale, sélectionnée, est né de l'accouplement probable d'une très belle Chatte avec un Chat sauvage d'une des provinces du Nord de la République Argentine. Ce Chat-Tigre, âgé de quatre ans, pèse 8 kg. environ. Malgré ce poids respectable, son pelage ras lui donne plutôt un aspect fluet. Contrairement à l'aspect des Chats qui ont le museau court et arrondi, celui-ci l'a allongé et quelque peu pointu, légèrement creusé sous les pommettes. Tout petit, son nez avait un profil amusant et semblait partir du sommet du crâne. Sa tête est admirablement tachée, présentant des lignes noires très nettes, qui se détachent sur un fond jaune-sépia très brillant. Ses yeux, très vifs, à demi fermés pendant le jour, sont très ouverts et paraissent très grands le soir.

Très haut sur pattes et d'ailleurs assez long de corps, il est parfaitement proportionné. Ses pattes sont très nerveuses et possèdent une détente incroyable. En jouant, il peut franchir d'un bond, sans élan et sans effort, une hauteur de 2 m. 50. Il ne se lasse pas de répéter ce saut, à la grande admiration de qui l'observe. Sa démarche, au pas, est tout à fait caractéristique : il a une façon de faire « rouler » ses omoplates qui rappelle tout à fait l'allure du fauve ; lorsqu'il court, il a l'allure d'un cheval de course au galop. Il porte la queue basse et horizontale, au ras du sol.

Son agilité est telle que, souvent, apercevant un oiseau sur une branche éloignée du tronc et à 2 ou 3 m. du sol, au lieu de chercher à grimper au tronc, il rampe sur le sol et bondit sur sa victime, qu'il manque bien rarement. Il chasse avec passion. Son naturel sauvage apparaît par périodes irrégulières et s'assouvit sur les oiseaux de basse-cour en particulier. Il apporte le produit de sa chasse avec satisfaction et même orgueil, et les corrections qu'il reçoit n'apaisent pas sa soif de sang.

D'une intelligence exceptionnelle, comparable à celle d'un chien et d'un chien particulièrement intelligent, il semble réellement comprendre. Très obéissant et docile avec ses maîtres, il ne se laisse guère approcher par les étrangers. Non pas simplement caressant, il est affectueux. Il prodigue ses caresses plus qu'il n'en recherche, bien qu'il aime à être caressé, mais pas avec excès. Les corrections, même sévères, que ses maîtres peuvent lui infliger n'atteignent en rien l'affection qu'il leur porte.

Th. E.

LE MARCHÉ DES CHIENS.

TANDIS QUE LES COURS élevés se maintiennent pour les races de Chiens d'agrément, très en vogue, les Chiens d'utilité restent demandés et leur prix assez fixe. Par contre, une baisse marquée s'affirme pour les Chiens de chasse. On a vu dernièrement 3 Cockers noirs pour 900 fr., alors que chaque sujet aurait été payé au moins 1 000 fr. il y a 2 ans. Aussi beaucoup d'éleveurs et de dresseurs sont-ils dans le marasme. Pendant ce temps, les Anglais vendent leurs Chiens très cher. Ajoutons qu'en commerçants avisés ils font de la publicité pour les faire de plus en plus connaître. Et c'est précisément lorsqu'ils prévoient une stabilisation, un arrêt, une régression des demandes, qu'ils accentuent celle-ci. De plus, aucune personnalité, si haut placée soit-elle, ne considère déchoir lorsqu'elle vend des Chiens.

C. de M.

(402)

FIRST VERSION OF THE LEGEND.

MRS. MARCELLE ADAM (1925)

- Long before the coming of the Buddha, long before the birth of Brahmanism, even before Vyâsa had dictated the immortal words of his divine books, the Khmer people jealously guarded their temples, where the Kittahs lived, venerable priests so close to perfection that their spirit, before conquering the eternal ecstasy, passed only in the body of a sacred cat, the time of its animal existence. But from the origin of the worlds the saints disapproved of those who did not sanctify themselves in their own way. So did the Brahmans who attacked the Kittahs and piously massacred them. However some of the venerable escaped through the unbreakable mountains of northern Burma and there they founded the underground temple of Lao-Tsun, which means dwelling of the gods.

- This temple is a wonder among the wonders of Indochina. Not far from a lake, it is lost in a chaos of immense peaks, and if, by an extraordinary favor, my English friend was able to enter it, it is because he happened to protect the last Kittahs from the ruthless Brahmins. He was therefore able to contemplate the hundred sacred cats of the cult and learn about their history.

- When with the malevolent moon, came the "phoums" or, if you prefer a clearer language, the cursed Siamese-Thais, when these barbarians came in the mountains of Lugh, in the mountains of the Sun, was at the temple of Lao-Tsun the most precious of the precious: the one whose golden beard the god Song-Hio himself had braided. The Venerable had always lived in the contemplation of Tsun-Kyanksé, the Sapphire-eyed goddess who presides over the transmutations of souls, the number of which is numbered. He never looked away from his sculpted image. His name was Mun-Hâ. He had an oracle without which he made no decision: his cat Sinh, whom the other Kittahs revered with fervor. "

- Sinh, seated near his dreaded master, also lived in the contemplation of the goddess. The beautiful animal! Its eyes were yellow as gold, yellow from the reflection of Mun-Ha's metallic beard and the amber body of the sapphire-eyed goddess. One evening, at moonrise, the Thais approached the sacred precinct. So, invoking the threatening Fate of his own, Mun-Hâ died charged with years and anguish. He died before his goddess, having his divine cat with him. And the Kittahs mourned such a cruel loss, under threat of invasion. At that moment, the miracle of immediate transmutation took place. Sinh leaps to the holy throne, braced on the head of its sagging master, facing the goddess. And the hair of his white spine turned golden and his eyes, his eyes yellow from the golden yellow of Tsun-Kyankse, yellow from the yellow of the beard woven by the god Song-Hio, its eyes turned blue. Huge and deep sapphires, like the eyes of the idol. Its four paws the brown of the earth, its four paws that touched the venerable skull turned white, to

215

the tips of the fingers purified by the touch of the mighty dead. It turned its precious gaze towards the southern gate, which read a harsh, imperative order, which, driven by an invincible force, the Kittahs obeyed. Thus they closed the bronze doors of the holy temple against the ancestral enemy. Then, passing through their underground passages, they routed the profaners. Sinh, refusing all food, never left the throne. It remained standing, facing the goddess, mysterious, hieratic, fixing his azure eyes on the sapphire eyes whose flame and softness he took. Seven days after the death of Mun-Hâ, upright on the paws purified of white, without lowering the eyelids, it died, carrying towards Tsun-Kyanksé the soul of Mun-Hâ, too perfect for earthly life. But one last time, its gaze slowly turned to the southern gate from which later the Annamese and Cambodian hordes came in number.

- Seven days after Sinh's death, the Kittahs assembled before Tsun-Kyanksé to decide on Mun-Hâ's succession. So, oh wonder, they saw the hundred cats coming slowly from the temple. Their paws were gloved in white, their snowy coats had a golden sheen, and the topazes in their eyes had turned to sapphires. The Kittahs bowed down in an attitude of devout dread. And they waited. Did they not know that the souls of their ancestors inhabited the harmonious forms of sacred animals? These, serious and supple, surrounded Ligoa, the youngest of the priests who thus knew the will of the sky.

THE LEGEND OF THE SACRED OF BURMA BY S. R. REVUE MINERVA NO 110 (1927)

When with the malevolent moon came the army of the phoums, the army of the cursed Thai Siamese, then lived, in the mountains of the sun, the precious among the precious, the one whose beard the god Song-Hio himself had braided. of gold: the lamah Kittah Mun-Hâ.

The venerable had always lived in contemplation of Tsun-Kyankse, the sapphire-eyed goddess who presides over the transmutations of souls whose number is numbered, and had never looked away from it.

The revered Kittah Mun-Hâ had an oracle without which he made no decision: his cat Sinh, whom the other Kittahs revered with fervor. This magnificent cat was pure white: only its ears, its nose, its tail as well as its four legs, all its ends, finally, were of brown earth color, in order to demonstrate that everything that touches the earthly impurity must hide its filth under a dark shade.
Sinh also lived in the contemplation of the goddess, seated near his dreaded master. Its eyes were yellow as gold from the reflection of Mun-Ha's golden beard and the golden body of the sapphire-eyed goddess.

Now, one evening, at moonrise, while the "Thais" approached the sacred enclosure, and invoked with all his soul the threatening destinies, the venerated died, laden with years and anguish, in front of his goddess and having near him his divine cat. He died, leaving his Kittahs overwhelmed by the loss of their great master amid the

217

cruel ordeal of the invasion. Then the miracle of immediate transmutation took place.

Sinh leaped onto the golden throne, bent over its slack master's head, facing the goddess. Then the hair on its white spine turned gold and its eyes turned blue, immense and deep sapphires, like the eyes of the goddess. Then it turned its gaze to the southern gate, and its four paws, the brown of the earth, turned white to the spot that had dug in the silks of the sacred garments. It turned its precious gazes to the southern gate, bright, harsh, imperative, and the Kittahs, obeying an unseen force, rushed forward just to close the bronze doors on the Brahmin enemy. By passing through their undergrounds, they were able to exterminate them and rout them, thus saving their temple from desecration, plunder and destruction.

Sinh never left the throne, refusing all food; facing the goddess, eye to eye, sapphires within sapphires, mysterious and hieratic. Seven days after the death of Mun-Hâ, upright on its paws purified of white, its precious eyes riveted on the goddess, Sinh died at the time of the opening of the temple, carrying to Tsun-Kyanksé the soul of Mun-Ha, too perfect, therefore, for the earth. One last time, its sapphire gaze slowly turned and fixed forever on the North gate, from which, later, the Annamese and Cambodian hordes came in number. And when, seven more days later, the Kittahs were gathered before Tsun-Kyanksé, to decide on the succession of Mun-Hâ, they saw all the cats of the temple advancing little by little, and, in great astonishment and respectful terror, noticed that their paws were gloved in white, that their white coat had gold reflections, and that their golden eyes had turned into sapphires. The cats surrounded Ligoa, the youngest of the Kittahs, and all the kittahs thus knew the designation of their ancestors reincarnated in the body of the sacred cats by the will of the goddess.

So when a sacred cat dies at Lao-Tsun temple, it is the soul of a Kittah that returns forever to the mysterious Heaven of Song-Hio, the golden god. Woe to him/her who, even involuntarily, hastens the end of these dreaded and revered felines: the worst torments are reserved for him/her to appease the soul in pain, separated from his body before the term fixed by the gods.

THE LEGEND OF THE SACRED CAT OF BURMA; BELGIAN FELINE REVIEW NO 5.

MRS MARCELLE ADAM (DECEMBER 1929).

Here is the holy legend, as it was told to me by those who entered the land of my little feline god.

Long before the coming of the Buddha, long before the birth of Brahmanism, even before Vyâsa had dictated the immortal words of his divine books, the Kmer people jealously guarded the temples where the Kittahs, venerable priests, lived so close to perfection that their spirit, at the moment of conquering the eternal ecstasy, passed only in the body of a sacred cat, the time of its animal existence.

But from the origin of the worlds, the saints disapproved of those who did not sanctify themselves in their own way. So did the Brahmans who attacked the Kittahs and piously massacred them. However, some of the Venerables were able to escape through the unspoiled mountains of northern Burma and there they founded the Underground Temple of Lao-Tsun, which means Dwelling of the Gods!

This temple is a wonder among the wonders of Indo-China. Not far from a lake, it is lost in a chaos of immense peaks and if, by an extraordinary favor, Auguste Pavie and Major Russel-Gordon were able to penetrate there, it is because it happened to them to protect the last Kittahs against the relentless Brahmins. They were therefore able to contemplate the hundred sacred cats of the cult and learn about their history.

You know that Auguste Pavie, this hero, conquered us, step by step, Cambodia and that his great benevolence, born of his intelligent kindness, brought us more victories than the force of arms.

From Cambodia he went to Burma and the Kittahs informed him of this legend:

When, with the malevolent moon, came the Phoums, or if you prefer a clearer language, the cursed Thai Siamese, when these barbarians came in the mountains of Lugh, in the mountains of the Sun, Mun-Hâ remained at the temple of Lao Tsun . Mun Hâ the most precious of the most precious, the one whose golden beard the god Song-Hio had braided. The venerable had always lived in the contemplation of Tsun-Kyanksé, the sapphire-eyed goddess who presides over the transmutation of souls, whose number is numbered. He never looked away from it.

He had an oracle who dictated his decisions, his cat Sinh whom the Kittahs fervently revered.

O wisdom to choose an oracle who does not speak!

Sitting beside his dreaded master, Sinh also lived in the contemplation of the goddess. The beautiful animal! Its eyes were yellow as gold, yellow from the reflection of Mun-Ha's metallic beard, yellow from the amber body of the sapphire-eyed goddess.

One evening, at moonrise, the Thais approached the sacred precinct. So, invoking the threatening fate of his own, Mun-Hâ died charged with years and anguish. He died in front of his goddess, having near him his divine cat. And the Kittahs mourned such a cruel loss.

At that moment the miracle of immediate transmutation took place.

Sinh leaps to the holy throne, braced on the head of its master slumped in front of the goddess. And the hair on his white spine were the color of gold. And its eyes yellow from the golden yellow of Tsun-Kian Kse, yellow from the golden yellow of the beard woven by the god Song-Hio, its eyes turned blue, immense deep sapphires, like the eyes of the goddess. Its four paws of the brown of the earth, its four paws which touched the venerable skull were made white from the nails to the tips of fingers purified by the contact of the powerful dead.

Sinh turned its precious gaze towards the southern gate, which read a harsh, imperative order, which, pushed by an invincible force, the Kittahs obeyed. Thus they closed on the ancestral enemy the bronze doors of the holy temple. Then passing through their underground passages, they routed the profaners.

Sinh, refusing all food, never left the throne. It remained standing, facing the goddess, a mysterious hieratic, fixing his blue gaze on the sapphire eyes whose flame and softness he took.

Seven days after the death of Mun-Hâ, upright on its paws purified with white, without lowering its eyelids, it died, carrying to Tsun-Kyanksé, the soul of Mun-Hâ, too perfect for the earth. But, one last time, its gaze slowly turned to the southern gate from which, later, the Annamite and Cambodian hordes came in number.

Seven more days after Sinh's death, the Kittahs assembled before Tsun-Kyanksé to decide on Mun-Hâ's succession.

So, oh wonder, they saw the hundred cats slowly coming in herds from the Temple, their paws were gloved in white, their snowy coats had a golden sheen, and the topazes in their eyes had turned into sapphires.

The Kittahs bowed down in an attitude of devout dread. And they waited. Did they not know that the souls of their masters inhabited the harmonious forms of sacred animals? These, serious and supple, surrounded Ligoa, the youngest of the priests who thus knew the will of heaven.

When a sacred cat dies in Lao-Tsun temple, the soul of a Kittah returns forever to the mysterious Heaven of

Song-Hio, the golden god. Woe to those who hasten the end, even involuntarily of these feared and revered felines, the worst torments are reserved for him/her, in order to appease the soul in pain.

THE LEGEND OF THE SACRED CATS OF BURMA

(MINERVA REVIEW. NO 388, JANUARY 1, 1933)

BY DR. VET FERNAND MÉRY

Little is known about these precious cats which are, in general, the highlight of any self-respecting feline show. It is true that if we counted we might not find twenty in Europe. What am I saying, not twenty? Not ten, not five... not one (as Marie Dubas sings)... do we hear! not one who can boast of his genuine nobility ... not one that can be said to come from a real couple of sacred felines directly imported from English Indochina.

Those who currently exist here have only one ancestor of Birman "Poupée" origin that had to be mixed with a kind of Siamese: the Laos lynx, so that the Birman blood does not completely die out. What religious care and what solicitude it has taken since, to preserve through generations of mixed blood, the golden fur and the sapphire eyes of these wonderful beasts, and especially the four immaculate gloves, symbol of their divine essence.

But if we know little about the Birman cats because they are rare, we know even less the beautiful legend that told us one summer evening near the Spanish border by a blonde friend of animals and poets ... Would I know, now, tell it to you in my turn as it should ...

"At that time," our friend began gently, in a temple built on the slopes of Mount Lugh, lived in prayers the very venerable kittah Mun-Hâ, great lama precious among the precious: the one whose god Song-Hio himself had braided the golden beard ... Not a minute, not a look, not a thought of her existence that was not devoted to the worship, to the contemplation, to the pious service of Tsun-Kyanksé the goddess with the eyes of sapphire, the one-which presides over the transmutation of souls, that which allows the kittahs to relive in a sacred animal the duration of its animal existence, before taking up a body crowned with the total and holy perfection of the high priests. Beside him was meditating Sinh, his dear oracle, an all-white cat, whose eyes were yellow, yellow from the reflection of the golden beard of his master and the golden body of the goddess with the eyes of the sky ... Sinh, the advisor cat , whose ears, nose, tail, and limb ends were the dark color of the ground, marks of the filth and impurity of anything that touches or can touch the earth.

"Now, one evening, as the malevolent moon had allowed the accursed Phoums from abhorred Siam, to approach the sacred enclosure, the high priest Mun-

Hâ, without ceasing to implore cruel destinies, entered gently into the dead, having at his side his divine cat and under his eyes the despair of all his overwhelmed kittahs ...

"It was then that a miracle happened ... the unique miracle of immediate transmutation: with a leap, Sinh was on the golden throne and perched on the head of his sagging master ... It leaned on this head laden with years, and which for the first time no longer looked at his goddess ... And as it remained in its turn frozen in front of the eternal statue, one saw the bristling hair of its white spine suddenly turn golden yellow. And its golden eyes turned blue, huge and deep like the eyes of the goddess. And as it gently turned its head towards the southern gate, its four paws which touched the venerable skull became a dazzling white, until the place covered by the silk of the sacred vestments. And as its eyes turned away from the southern gate, the kittahs obeying this imperative gaze charged with hardness and light, rushed to close the heavy bronze doors on the first invader ... The temple was saved from desecration and plunder ... Sinh had not yet left the throne, and on the seventh day, without having made a movement, facing the goddess and looking into her eyes, it died, mysterious and hieratic, carrying to Tsun-Kyankse the soul of Mun -Ha, too perfect now for the earth ...

"And when seven days later the assembled priests consulted each other in front of the statue to decide on Mu-Hâ's succession, one saw all the cats from the temple come running ... And all were dressed in gold and white gloves, and all had changed. in a deep sapphire the yellow of their eyes... And all surrounded,

226

in silence, the youngest of the kittahs, which thus designated the ancestors reincarnated by the will of the goddess.

....

"And now," the storyteller clarified, "may a sacred cat die in Lao-Tsun temple, it is the soul of a kittah that takes its place forever in the paradise of Song-Hio, the golden god." But woe too, she concludes, to anyone who hastens the end of one of these sacred beasts, even if he/she did not want to. He/she will suffer the most cruel torments until the pained soul He has disturbed subsides ... "(p. 14)

THE CRAWFORD-HUMBERT AFFAIR

(JUSTICE. MAY 2, 1902.)

"Probably between 1878 and 1883, and in a country we don't yet know, died an extremely wealthy American who would have borne the name of Robert-Henry Crawford. His fortune estimated at 120 million must have been very portable since no one has ever found traces of castles, estates, lands, dunes or boats that belonged to the deceased. All he left is a will of about two lines, dated Nice, September 6, 1877, instituting as universal legatee Mlle Thérèse d'Aurignac, who became Mme Frédéric Humbert only ever produced a copy, although that she claims to own the precious original.

However, Mrs. Humbert thanks to this inheritance or rather to the loans which she made, bought a hotel, avenue de la Grande-Armée, the castle of Vives-Eaux, near Melun and the property of Céléran, at the gates of Narbonne. Happy with her new situation, she was preparing to conscientiously enjoy the new luxury in which she was plunging, when one day, two strangers saying to each other: one Robert Crawford and the other Henri Crawford, both supposedly nephews of the mysterious testator, sent the following document to the daughter-in-law of the former Minister of Justice:

"This is my will.

After my death, I want everything I own to be divided into three: a third to Marie d'Aurignac, a third to my nephew Henri Crawford, a third to my nephew Robert Crawford, with the responsibility of the latter to place in France a capital taken from their share, sufficient to serve Thérèse d'Aurignac a life pension of 30,000 francs per month.

Nice, September 6, 1877.

H. R. CRAWFORD "

Consequently, we were in the presence of two wills having the same date and the same origin.

Mme Humbert was appalled: she fell from 100 million in capital to 360,000 francs in a life annuity, and it was her sister, Marie d'Aurignac, who came as a third person to inherit in her place.

But the older Crawford had reassured her with a gesture.

He and his brother owned hundreds of millions in fortune. They did not want to increase their number. But they wanted to fulfill their uncle's supreme wish by mingling the blood of the Crawfords with the blood of the Aurignacs.

In short, by means of a small marriage, they offered their withdrawal. But Mme Humbert was married. So they fell back on sister Marie. This one was minor. So they agreed that until the marriage the fortune would remain in sequestration and that Thérèse Humbert would deduct from the income the 360,000 francs of annuity which is acquired to her in any event. As for the rest, it would be reused in French annuities to be put, capital and interest, in the wedding basket.

The safe was then opened, an inventory of the securities made, sealed in the name of the Crawfords, and it was stipulated that Mrs. Humbert would only be the keeper of the treasure. Madame Humbert could still look, but she could no longer touch, and the slightest indiscretion on her part, the slightest additional levy would entail her irreparable downfall.

The situation is still going on, the capitalized millions have grown and Miss Marie's Aurignac does not want to marry any Crawfords. Now she is in her late forties, and the billionaire who wanted her and who has never been seen again is still advertising her, but only by bailiff. For twenty-two years the trial has continued. But Ms. Humbert did not remain inactive. She simply borrowed nearly $42 million, secured against the stranger in her safe, and repayable at the end [sic] of her trials. Because, as you can imagine, the trials are in full swing around this case.

We had moving pleadings from Mr. Pouillet, calling for the court's heartache over the love misfortunes of these elusive Crawfords. [...]

They went to court; the Humbert spouses summoned the Crawford heirs before the Seine court to have it said that this allegation of a secret clause is not serious, that there is a writing, a transaction, that it is valid and that therefore there is no need to stop at such expedients.

They encountered very strong resistance from the Crawford heirs which resulted in numerous procedural expedients: but finally, on October 27, 1886, the First Chamber rendered a fully reasoned judgment in which it declared that the transaction was good, that it is excellent, it is all that there is more solid and consequently the Humbert spouses, in return for the payment of nine millions to the two brothers Crawford, will have, said the court, the free and entire disposal of all the succession of which they were instituted universal legatees.

This is, gentlemen, a great victory, and one which must have truly delighted those whose loans, whose advances were subordinated to the decisions of justice.

The Crawford heirs appealed; there again, a lot of procedure was done; but finally it took hardly more than four years, from October 25, 1886 to January 3, 1890, to obtain the confirmation of the judgment which the tribunal of the Seine had rendered. The Crawford heirs went to cassation, it goes without saying, their appeal was dismissed. So here it is that all is said and I believe that the most defiant, the most skeptical, the most mocking, confronted with a judgment like that of October 1886, giving, abandoning the succession to the Humbert spouses on the condition of paying nine million, this judgment once confirmed by the Paris Court of Appeal, will not be in doubt. It is quite clear that now the Humbert spouses will finally be able to dispose of this large fortune and will therefore be able to pay off their creditors.

They had, gentlemen, at that time, an infinitely honorable scruple, but they will allow me to say, infinitely excessive. The authority of *res judicata* left them this situation that by paying nine million, they kept the difference, they wondered whether they could pay the nine million by taking them from the Crawford estate or whether it was not appropriate to ask them elsewhere, and this scruple was based in their reasoning on the following consideration: we are sequesters on condition that nothing is distracted from the inheritance; there is indeed a judgment which sends us into possession, which declares that this succession is ours in return for the payment of nine millions, but could it not happen that these cunning Crawfords came to say afterwards: "Pardon, you took the nine millions? on the heirloom. So you are fallen! "

So the Humbert spouses went to the Seine tribunal, they explained their case of conscience to him, they said to him: "Yes, you told us: take all this succession, give nine million to the Crawfords and everything will be said. Well, we dare not, we come to ask you to judge, not that we can give those nine million, you said. But that we can take them from the disputed estate itself.

This claim, gentlemen, was so legal, it was so obvious, that it was upheld by the judgment of May 7, 1896, which said to the Humbert spouses: "Go in peace, have no more worry or remorse; By telling you that the estate is yours for nine million paid to your opponents, I heard that you would take those nine million from the estate. And, in truth, any other interpretation was not very reasonable.

The Crawfords have appealed; they went to cassation; they came back and, on their way, they found something else to have the pleasure of starting over.

Note that I am not exaggerating anything, that I only want to take from this presentation and this account one proof, that the Humberts are in no rush to win their case.

I imagine they know where the Crawford brothers live, that there are many Crawford brothers, that they are very rich in the hundreds of millions all of this, they know it, they keep it to themselves, it is theirs. case; but what is confusing is that, when one has only one gesture to make and these three words to say to have the free disposal of the millions that one has inherited, instead of pronouncing these three words and pay our debts, we accumulate and multiply the requests for dismissal and dilatory expedients.

The ironic doubt of Me Waldeck-Rousseau has today assumed the proportions of a general concern, to such an extent that a few months ago, President Beaudoin exclaimed in court: "I want to see the Crawfords," Brought them to me at the bar! "

And well, they did not bring anyone to the stand, and things are going so far that today we are talking about a dramatic turn, imminent arrests, unless they are warned by rushed leaks or sensational suicides.

Indeed, on Wednesday, at the public hearing, The First President Forichon asked Mr Bazile, the lawyer of the Crawford brothers, if the domicile chosen by his clients really existed. And Mr Bazile declared that he could not affirm anything, having contented himself in his conclusions to repeat those of his colleague at first instance.

In short, the lawyer does not know the homes of his clients.

- This is serious, said the first president. We must end it. - This has been going on for long enough.

And he ordered the two attorneys for the opposing parties to come to his office to provide him with the necessary explanations of the situation.

The interview with MM. Forichon and attorneys Canuel and Bazile lasted more than twenty minutes.

We do not know the results. But an evening sheet speaks of seven arrest warrants allegedly seen on the desk of a senior magistrate. (pp. 1-2).

In the meantime, on May 17, 1893, the Humberts had created "La Rente Viagère de Paris," a limited company with a capital of 10 million. On May 11, 1902, the safe was opened and nothing was found. The

Humberts are on the run and have left the country. They were arrested in Madrid on December 20, 1902.

"JO"

MARCELLE ADAM

(REVUE FÉLINE DE FRANCE NO 6. APRIL 1931)

"I'm telling you, Ma'am, that Jo's swelling has a very natural cause. Your cat will soon have little cats.

- I, doctor, tell you that it is impossible.

-        Impossible ?

- Absolutely impossible. The virtue of Jo is housed on the fifth floor of our Ivory Tower. She never gets off it, I can attest to that. There are a lot of pigeons on my roof, but they don't have the faculties of the Holy Spirit.

-        So ?

- So, I'm sure Jo is keeping her dress of innocence. How could she have lost it?

- This is not my business, Madame. You are consulting me about Jo. Alfort's smallest pupil would tell you that she is in a state of advanced pregnancy.

- Impossible ... It's impossible. Let's see, doctor, to have children, it takes two.

- Two, at least, yes Madam.

- Ah! ... Well, Jo is one. I am not counting Pussy, nor Manou, which you skillfully reduced to 0. It is true that a zero to the right of one unit increases it tenfold. Do you think that Pussy or Manou...

- Certainly not, Madam, I do not think so.

- So you are wrong to accuse Jo.

- I'm not accusing her I see. See how the hair on the belly are dividing. And then, gently palpate this belly, these swollen breasts. We smell the kittens. They are already fat. And they stir.

- I'm afraid, alas, it's a tumor, several tumors ... I'm sorry.

- Rest assured, Madam, in two weeks, Jo will give birth to these tumors.

- You are -obstinate, doctor. You attest to a miracle, yes, a miracle, since Jo remains inaccessible, on her fifth floor, the door of which remains closed to any indiscreet.

- I am here to certify the effects and not to explain the causes.

- So, doctor, no surgery?

- The operation will be done on its own, hopefully without anyone needing it. Bye Madam.

- Goodbye, doctor.

I was angry with this man of science, the third one I had seen in a week. He, too, was getting bogged down in error. He persisted there against all logic: "How can we suppose that the virtue of Jo was, from a dwelling so high up, fell into the garden of my Montmartre building?" I returned to my little pussy. She was sitting on the narrow box that usually served as her plinth. By what miracle did she reduce her buttocks to the dimensions of this plinth? It doesn't matter. She was succeeding. It seemed to me that she was looking at me ironically. Under her half-closed lids, filtered the golden light of her eyes. She climbed down from her pedestal, stretched her bloated body, shrugged and sneered.

"So much ado about nothing! Who are these strangers to whom you allow touching me that I cannot qualify? "

She sketched, on the tips of her four slippers together, a few steps of the sacred dance dear to ancient Isis. Then she fell back heavily braced. Its sides spread out like a half-full skin bottle. She gave a hoarse purr, half pleasure, half fatigue, not unlike the crackle of a T.S.F. on stormy days. My concern grew even more.

"What's going on in there?" Who will know? "

My suspicions, still vague, dared not become clear.

Jo didn't like animals. She liked people even less. She only loved me. She loved me with jealousy, with tyranny. Like a Valkyrie, I was guarded by a little dragon who warned of any approach by breathing fire and uttering roaring threats. We hardly left each other. I had no recollection that our mutual supervision was at fault. But, going back through my memories, I came to recall certain mistakes into which Jo's malice had led me.

Did you forget that she was imposed on me by fraud? A ball of gray velvet, holding entirely in one hand, a ball in which were pricked twenty steel needles. I said to the one who offered it to me, "I don't want that pussy. "

She replied, "It's a cat. He's a little monk, He's a Chartreux. "

This was the first imposture of which Jo was guilty. I was fooled for six months. What do you want? Ms. de Tencin tells us the story of a young woman who lived, under the frock, in the monastery of La Trappe, with the one she loved. The naivety of the Reverend Monks equaled mine, isn't it? Chartreux dress, Trappist dress, the story is similar. You see, novelists don't invent anything.

This time, however, it seemed improbable to me that Jo would have played the comedy of persistent candor on me. Did I have any secrets from her? Love has wings, I can believe it, but Psyche, lighting his lamp, recognized him, before he took off. However, I had not opened the door to him and Jo-Psyche never came out.

Ah! my friends, with what tender care I enveloped Jo during the following days. My indecisive anxiety multiplied in kindness, which she abused.

One evening, she demanded to enter the cupboard where my linen rooms are.

"Brrou... Open that door. Don't close it. I will be well on this department which keeps your scent a little. You should sit there next to me. I manage to become smaller in the dimensions of the small spaces that I like. You are unable to do the same. You leave? What a pity! Do you go out without a collar and bells? Don't get lost and come back quickly. "

Her authority, at that moment, seemed to me even more impetuous than usual.

Two hours of absence. And on the way back, in the anteroom, Pussy and Manou, who, alone, are waiting for me, with a look borrowed from people in possession of too important a secret.

"Jo... Jo... where are you my daughter?"

- Brrrou... brrou... where... on your bed. " So what do I see there on my bed? A little gray thing, wailing in high tones. And, at his side, my friends, a Jo, standing, with a triumphant air, her back arched, her tail raised like a bottlebrush, a Jo who chokes on laughter, her mouth slit, her eyes drawn towards the temples, two thin flames in his devil's face.

- "Huh! Here is a surprise! That's not all. Hold on."

With a bound, she is in the cupboard and pulls out another kitten, this one, spotted white.

"They are two. I give them to you. Two, I'm telling you... two tumors... "

They are now flapping, side by side, on my comforter.

Jo, obviously, continues to laugh. And I end up laughing too. Think about it! Two plump kittens, in good health; it is indeed very funny, compared to the illness of which I was terrified. But, without admitting it, I am a little upset to have played, in this farce, the classic role of the duenna that the ingenuous scorn.

The ingenuous? ... Has Jo ever been ingenuous?

Imagine that I am not alone in asking myself this. Pussy and Manou are on the bed. They lean with growing astonishment at the newborns. They seem to say:

"How the hell did she do that? We are certainly not responsible for it. However, it's just us at home. Then then ?..."

*

* *

I didn't understand until two years later. Love had no wings, but he was an acrobat, rather poorly dressed, moreover, in a livery of misery, white and gray. He would enter through the window and visit Psyche. Eternal history!

Alas he was seen by Manou who fiercely used his alarm signal. They have no pity for the weaknesses of others, those whom an inflexible law compels to virtue.

"Hou ... or ... or ... Hou ... or ... or ..."

Believe me, it sounded like the sinister siren call of our firefighters. Was this how the sirens of the Ionian seas sang for Ulysses?

Either way, I lit the lamp that my hypocrite Psyche wished to be extinguished forever. As in the legend, my friends, Love was gone, with a great crash of terror.

And we never saw him again.

Jo remained sad about it until her death.

As for her son, who resembled her, I regarded him as a female cat for six months, the time it took to prove to me that, indeed, I was unswervingly simple. (pp. 58-59).

BIBLIOGRAPHY

"À l'Exposition féline." L'Écho de Paris, 8 avril 1934, p. 5.

"À l'Exposition Féline. Trois des animaux exposés: Chat tigré du Brésil - Chat sacré de Birmanie - Chat sans poils." Le Petit Journal, 26 avril 1930, p. 1.

"À la Salle Wagram. Le Triomphe des chats exotiques." L'Intransigeant, 2 avril 1932, p. 4.

"Arts et Lettres: Carnet de Lettres." Le Rappel, 11 juin 1926, p. 3.

"Au Club du Faubourg. Ce soir: Colette sur "Les Chats"." La Lanterne, 9 mai 1927, sec. La Vie Littéraire Artistique, p. 3.

"Au milieu des chats les plus rares." L'Écho de Paris, 26 avril 1930, p. 2.

"Avec une pierre précieuse un prince hindou, hypnotisait naguère, Mme Léotardi!" Le Petit Journal, 5 janvier 1923, 5 heures ed., p. 4.

"Cat Club de Paris." Chasse, pêche, élevage, 1925, p. IV.

"Cat Club de Paris. L'Exposition des CHATS à la Salle Wagram. Compte rendu officiel." Chasse, Pêche, Élevage, 15 mars 1929, p. 4.

"Ce matin s'est ouverte à la Salle Wagram une Exposition féline." Paris-Soir, 23 avril 1930, 2nd ed., p. 1.

"Chats." Chasse, Pêche, Èlevage, 15 novembre 1927, p. 2.663.

"Chiens et Chats." Figaro, 28 mai 1927.

"Classement des chats exposés." La Revue Féline de France.7 (1931), p. 7.

"En Marge du fantastique héritage. Comment M. Delbost désirant vendre le château de la Ferté-Vidame a miss Fair Heller fut excroqué de 23,000 francs par les époux Léotardi." Le Petit Parisien, 9 janvier 1923, 5 heures ed., p. 2.

"Exposition Féline Internationale." L'Homme Libre, 1926, 14 Mai ed., p. 2.

"Fence saves Express from being ditched. Seven Hurt When New Haven Train Is Derailed." The NewYork Herald, 19 Décembre 1922, p. 6.

"L'Exposition Féline à la salle Wagram." Le Petit Journal, 1926, sec. 14 Mai, p. 3.

"L'Héritage Mystérieux. Multiplications sans produit. Car, par malheur, Mme Léotardi ne touchait jamais ce qu'elle devait toucher." Paris, 29 décembre 1922, 3e ed., sec. Dernières Nouvelles, p. 1.

"L'Exposition Féline." Comœdia, 27 mai 1927, p. 2.

"L'Exposition Féline a distribué ses récompenses." Le Petit Parisien, 16 Janvier 1927.

"L'Exposition Féline à la Salle Wagram. Chats de Luxe." L'Œuvre, 22 avril 1933, p. 2.

"L'Exposition Féline Internationale." L'Écho de Paris, 2 avril 1932, p. 1.

"L'Exposition Internationale Féline de Paris. Comment un mouvement progressif est enregistré par cette deuxième compétition mettant en présence les principales races de "Tigres d'appartement"." Vie à la Campagne, 1er février 1927, p. 56.

"L'héritage de 9 milliards. Les époux Léotardi protestent de leur bonne foi." Le Journal, 25 décembre 1922, 5 heures du matin ed., p. 1-2.

"L'Héritage Fabuleux. Les petits papiers de Mme Léotardi." La Presse, 29 décembre 1922, 3e ed., p. 1.

"L'Héritage Fabuleux. Mme Léotardi a été entendue hier par le juge d'instruction." Le Populaire. Journal Socialiste du Matin, 22 décembre 1922, sec. Dernière Heure, p. 3.

"L'Héritage fantastique. Les investigations officielles sur cette étrange affaire vont commencer." Le Journal, 27 décembre 1922, 5 heures du matin ed., p. 1.

"L'Héritage-Fantôme de l'Américaine. Mme Léotardi s'explique devant les juges sur les millions de dollars qui devaient lui tomber ... du ciel." Le Petit Journal, 13 novembre 1924, 5 heures du matin ed., p. 2.

"L'Histoire du Laos, ce joyau méconnu de l'Indochine Française." Le Petit Marseillais, 9 Janvier 1924, sec. Page Coloniale, p. 5.

"La Gloire!" Paris-Soir, 2 avril 1932, p. 8.

"La Race Féline est superbement représentée à l'Exposition ouverte hier matin." Le Petit Journal, 9 février 1929, p. 5.

"Le Chat. La IIe Exposition Internationale Féline de Reims. Les 11 et 12 avril 1931." Chasse, Pêche, Élevage, Mai 1931, p. 3.381-82.

"Le Concours de Chats. Palmarès." Le Petit Courrier d'Angers, 14 Juin 1925, p. 4.

"Le fabuleux héritage." Le Petit Parisien, 24 décembre 1922, p. 3.

"Le Fabuleux héritage de Mme Léotardi ou les milliards qui s'envolent." La République Française, 29 décembre 1922.

"Le Laos." La Croix, 12 Juillet 1921, p. 3.

"Le Milliard qui roule. Un dossier qui contient le gotha de la noblesse et celui de la faune." Paris, 22 décembre 1922, 3è ed., sec. Dernières Nouvelles, p. 1.

"Le Mystère du collier de Mme Léotardi est éclairci." L'Œuvre, 13 mars 1931, p. 2.

"Le Petit Chat très photographié." L'Intransigeant, 24 janvier 1932.

"Le Salon du chat." Le Journal, 3 décembre 1932, 5 heures du matin ed., p. 1.

"Les plus beaux chats du monde sont les hôtes de Paris." Le Petit Journal, 19 avril 1936, p. 8.

"M. Vanderbilt." Le Journal, 22 août 1924, p. 3.

"M. Vanderbilt." Le Gaulois, 14 Octobre 1922, p. 2.

"Mme Léotardi condamnée pour escroquerie." Le Journal, 29 novembre 1931, p. 4.

"Mme Léotardi qui disait avoir hérité d'une milliardaire imaginaire est arrêtée." Le Journal, 7 novembre 1923, 5 heures du matin ed., p. 1 & 3.

"Mme Léotardi s'explique devant le juge au sujet du fabuleux héritage." Le Journal, 29 décembre 1922, p. 1-3.

"Nos Échos. On dit que ... L'Exposition féline." L'Intransigeant, 19 mai 1931, sec. Nos Échos, p. 2.

"On arrête à Paris Mme Léotardi la pseudo-héritière de l'américaine invisible." Le Petit Journal, 7 novembre 1923, 5 heures ed., p. 1.

"Police of Paris Scoff at Story of Fair Estate. Say Marcel Leon Tardi Is a Joke Victim or a Dreamer." New York Herald, 23 décembre 1922, p. 7.

"Quand le Chat est Roi." L'Excelsior, 3 décembre 1938, p. 8.

"Quelques Chats particulièrement remarqués à la Salle Wagram." L'Excelsior, 6 décembre 1930, p. 6.

"Serait-ce une nouvelle affaire Humbert ? Un Héritage d'un milliard et demi qui pourrait bien n'être qu'un beau mirage." La Petite Gironde, 23 décembre 1922, 18è ed., p. 1.

Smud Khoi. 17 Peintures de chats. Bangkok.

"A-t-on substitué au greffe du tribunal des perles fausses aux perles précieuses du collier de Mme Léotardi." Le Journal, 14 janvier 1931, p. 1.

"Une Exposition Féline." L'Ouest-Eclair, 28 Mai 1927.

"Une Nouvelle Affaire Humbert. Le juge écroue la pseudo héritière à la prison de Saint-Lazare." La Libre Parole, 7 novembre 1923, p. 2.

"Vendredi et Samedi." L'Intransigeant, 3 mai 1928, p. 2.

A. H. "La IXe Exposition Féline s'est ouverte ce matin à Paris... au profit du Comité nationale de défense contre la tuberculose." Paris-Soir, 3 décembre 1932, p. 3.

Abbé Chamonin Marcel. "Pour les Chats de Birmanie." Chasse, pêche, élevage, Novembre 1933 1933, p. 3.932-32.

Adam Marcelle. "Deux Magnifiques Races de Chats exotiques. Dondoca, Maracaja du Brésil. « Manou » Chat Sacré de Birmanie." La Vie à la Campagne, 1 Juillet 1929, p. 284-85.

---. Eros Vaincu. Paris: Albin Michel, 1926.

---. "L'Amour qui Tremble. Roman de Marcelle Adam. Deuxième Partie. La Gloire dans les myrtes. I." Roman. Le Matin, 9 janvier 1926, sec. Feuilleton. 55, p. 5.

---. "L'Amour qui Tremble. Roman de Marcelle Adam. Première Partie. L'amour dans les myrtes VI." Roman. Le Matin, 27 décembre 1925, sec. Feuilleton 43, p. 4.

---. "L'Amour qui Tremble. Roman de Marcelle Adam. Première Partie. L'amour dans les myrtes. V." Roman. Le Matin, 26 décembre 1925, sec. Feuilleton 41, p. 5.

---. "L'Amour qui Tremble. Roman de Marcelle Adam. Première Partie. L'amour dans les myrtes. VII." Roman. Le Matin, 28 décembre 1925, sec. Feuilleton 43, p. 5.

---. "La Maison Vide." La Revue Féline de France.20 (1934), p. 223.

---. "Le Tigre dans la Maison." L'Intransigeant, 16 mai 1931, p. 11.

---. "Les Chats Sacrés de Birmanie. La Légende du chat Sacré de Birmanie " La Revue Féline Belge.5 (1929), p. 1-2.

---. "Voici l'Exposition des chats. L'élevage Français vaut l'élevage Anglais." Reportage. La Monde Illustré, 31 Mars 1934, p. 257.

Adam Marcelle, and Lédoire Eugène Lépinay. "Société Féine Centrale de France." Revue Féline de France. Littéraire, artistique et scientifique 1.1 (1930).

B. G. de. "Chats de Salon." Paris-Midi, 12 mars 1930, sec. Page de la Femme, p. 7.

Bard Louis (rédacteur). "À quelques millions de dollars près... Le fabuleux héritage de l'Américaine. Ce que raconte Mme Léotardi, la légataire universelle." La Liberté, 23 décembre 1922, 2e ed., p. 1.

Barnay Gisèle, and Simone Poirier. Les Secrets du chat sacré de Birmanie. [Paris]: Bornemann, 1987.

Baroche Jacques. "Chronique Parisienne. Paris le 23 janvier." Le Nouvelliste d'Indochine, 5 février 1939, p. 8.

Bart Paul de. "Mme Vanderbilt." L'Éleveur (1899), p. 278.

Baudoin-Crevoisier Marcel. "Le Chat de Birmanie." Chasse, pêche, élevage.177 (1932), p. 3.554-55.

---. "Le Chat de Birmanie, animal sacré. Race caractérisée, qui serait à l'origine du Siamois et qui se distingue nettement des races asiatiques à poil long, avec lesquelles ces sujets ne sympathisent pas." Jardins et Basses-Cours, 20 Août 1932, p. 376-77.

---. "Le Chat de Birmanie. II." La Revue Féline Belge IV.2 (1931), p. 6-7.

---. "Le Chat Sacré de Birmanie." La Revue Féline Belge.11 & 12 (1931), p. 4-6.

---. "Son Altesse le Chat. Le chat de Birmanie ou chat sacré. Cousin germains des siamois par leur origine comme par leur aspect, les sujets de qualité et très typés de cette race sont assez rares, ce qui en fait monter la valeur, alors que leur originalité et leur beauté justifient une amplification de leur production." La Vie à la Campagne, 15 Avril 1935, p. 19.

Brassart L. "Élevage de Maritza. La Plus grande chatterie Française. Chatterie Unique des Birmans. Chatons au sevrage." Jardins et Basses-Cours, 20 Octobre 1927, p. CCCXC.

---. "Le Chat de Birmanie Standard." La Revue Féline de France.2 (1930), p. 15.

C. P.-E., and André Galland. "Une réception chez les Chats." L'Illustration. Journal Hebdomadaire Universel, 20 Décembre 1930, p. 580.

Causse Pierre. "Nos amies les bêtes. Aujourd'hui le Cat Club expose. Persans bleus, Siamois..." L'Intransigeant, 15 Mai 1926, p. 1.

Chamonin Abbé Marcel. "Cat Club de Genève, Naissance." Chasse, Pêche, Élevage, Décembre 1933.

---. "Cat Club de Genève: Nouvelles des Chatteries." Chasse, Pêche, Elevage, Juillet 1934, p. 4.088-89.

---. "Pour les chats Sacrés de Birmanie." Chasse, Pêche, Élevage, 1er Novembre 1933, p. 3931-32.

Chauffard Émile. "Les Populations Indigènes du Cambodge et du Laos." Les Actes du Congrès Colonial Français et les Comptes-Rendu des conférences. Paris 1908. 339-44.

Chaumont-Doisy. "Les Bonnes adresses: Chatons Birmans et Siamois issus des Étalons en service." Vie à la Campagne, 15 décembre 1935.

---. "Son Altesse le Chat. Le Chat sacré de Birmanie." Vie à la Campagne, 15 Avril 1935, p. 19-20.

Cheminaud Guy. "Du chat Siamois et de sa queue nouée." Chasse, Pêche, Élevage, Mai 1932, p. 3.807-08.

Condroyer Émile. "L'Exposition Féline et sa Majesté Fourrée." Le Journal, 16 Mai 1926, p. 1.

Coriem Maurice. "Des Chats... des chats... des chats... À l'Exposition féline internationale du "CAT-CLUB"." Le Petit Journal, 15 janvier 1939, p. 4.

Coupin Henri. "Les Chats de Siam." L'Illustration, 31 août 1895.

D. A. "Les Millions de l'Américaine. "Mme Léotardi a une imagination délirante", dit le rapport médical." Le Gaulois, 5 janvier 1923, 5 h. du matin ed., p. 3.

D. R. "L'exposition féline." Le Journal, 3 décembre 1932, 5 heures du matin ed., p. 5.

---. "Le Conseil municipal de Paris va-t-il élever de chats pour détruire les rats?" Le Journal, 14 janvier 1933, p. 2.

Dartois Yves. "Quand S. M. le chat reçoit en son salon." Photo. Le Petit Parisien, 3 décembre 1938, p. 1 & 4.

Dautun Yves. "L'exposition féline s'est ouverte hier." Le Petit Parisien, 26 avril 1930, p. 1.

de la Gombaudière Boilève. Nos compagnons.... Les chats. Paris: Éditions Nilsson, 1932.

Delly. "Le Maître du Silence. Le Secret de Kou-kou-noor." Roman. Le Journal de Roanne, 1920, sec. Feuilleton, p. 3.

---. Le Maître du silence... par Delly. Paris: Plon-Nourrit et Cie, 1919.

Derys Gaston. "La Gastronomie et les Littérateurs." Minerva. Le Grand Illustré Féminin que toute femme intelligente doit lire, 16 janvier 1927.

---. "La Littérature et a Gastronomie." Minerva. Le grand illustré féminin que toute femme intelligente doit lire, 3 avril 1927, p. 7.

---. "Les Chats des Gens de Lettres." L'Ère Nouvelle, 14 octobre 1927, sec. Feuilleton, p. 2.

Dorsenne Jean. "Au jour le jour. Exposition Féline." Journal des Débats Politiques et Littéraires, 16 Mai 1926, p. 1.

Dr. Schwangart F. "Classification des races de chat." La Revue Féline de France 1.6 (1931), p. 61.

Farnoux-Reynaud Lucien. "La Vie qui Passe: Plaisir Félin." Le Gaulois, 15 janvier 1927, 5 heures du matin ed.

Férard A. "Exposition Féline de Paris." Vie à la Campagne, 1er juin 1928.

---. "Pour aider à la Classification des Races de Chats." Vie à la Campagne, 1er Mars 1927, p. 108-10.

Frantel Max. "Le Japon sera-t-il le régulateur des quatre Chines?" Comœdia, 27 février 1927, p. 2.

Gilbert Gile. "Mme Léotardi romancière. Elle avait de grandes idées...." L'Intransigeant, 12 janvier 1923, p. 1-2.

Giraud Madeleine H. "Au Cat-Club. Cages fleuries et chats de luxe." Le Siècle, 17 janvier 1927, p. 2-3.

Guingand Germaine. "Les diverses variétés de chats." Revue Féline de France.21 (1935).

Horatio. "Échos de la Ville et des Champs." Comœdia, 18 juillet 1932, p. 3.

Howard Robert Ervin, Patrice Louinet, and François Truchaud. Conan traduit de l'anglais (États-Unis) par Patrice Louinet et François Truchaud. Paris: Milady, 2011.

Interim. "Propos d'un Parisien. Notre cher roi des gouttières!" Le Matin, 9 avril 1934, 5 heures du matin ed., p. 1.

Jumaud Philippe. "Élevez et sélectionnez rationnellement le chat. Pourquoi il faut vous intéresser aux races et variétés de qualité de ce félin domestique, en constituer des lignées et quels profits pouvez-vous tirer de cet élevage." Vie à la Campagne, 1er Février 1925, p. 66-67.

---. "Le Chat de Birmanie, animal sacré. Race caractérisée, qui serait à l'origine du siamois et qui se distingue nettement des races asiatiques à poil long, avec lesquelles les sujets ne sympathisent pas." Vie à la Campagne, 1926, p. 402-3.

---. "Le Chat Siamois, race de luxe. Intelligents et très fidèles, les sujets de cette race demandent des précautions pendant l'Hiver et la femelle ne peut être impunément croisée avec des étalons de race commune." Jardins et Basses-Cours, 5 mai 1928, p. 210-12.

---. Les Races de chats thèse présentée à la Faculté de médecine et de pharmacie de Lyon et soutenue publiquement le 25 mars 1925 pour obtenir le grade de docteur vétérinaire. Saint Raphaël: Édition des Tablettes, 1925.

---. Les Races de Chats. 2éd ed. Saint Raphaël: Ed. des Tablettes, 1926.

---. Les Races de Chats. 3éd ed. Saint Raphaël: Ed. des Tablettes, 1930.

---. Les Races de chats. 4e éd. refondue et complétée ed. Saint-Raphael: Éd. des Tablettes, 1935.

L. L. "En Vrac: Chat et Shah." Le Populaire, 2 janvier 1939, p. 2.

Lara René. "La Saison d'Hiver. De Cannes: sont arrivés:." Le Gaulois, 9 Mars 1926, p. 2.

Larieux E., and Philippe Jumaud. Le Chat races, élevage, maladies Ph. Jumaud, docteur-vétérinaire, lauréat de l'École vétérinaire de Lyon, diplômé de physiologie de la Faculté des sciences de Lyon, secrétaire général du Cat-Club de France et de Belgique. Paris: Vigot frères, 1926.

Latzarus Louis. "Les Épines d'Ispahan." L'Intransigeant, 2 janvier 1939, p. 2.

Loir Dr. Adrien. Le Chat. Son Utilité. La Destruction des rats. 2nd ed. Paris: Librairie J-B. Ballière et Fils, 1931.

Louvet Louis-Eugène. La Cochinchine Religieuse. Vol. I. Paris: Ernest Leroux, 1885.

M L. "L'Exposition Internationale Féline de Paris." Vie à la Campagne, 1er Juillet 1926.

M. A. "Salon du Chat." L'Intransigeant, 8 avril 1934, p. 3.

M. C. de. "Ce qu'il faut retenir des Expositions et Concours. Exposition Féline de Reims." Vie à la Campagne, 1er février 1932, p. 80.

Magog H. G. "Coureur de Dot. Première Partie. Le Voyage Imprévu." Le Matin, 18 août 1929, sec. Feuilleton, p. 4.

Malardot Paule. "Les Dimanches de la Femme: L'Exposition Féline." Mode du Jour, 12 Juillet 1931, sec. Supplément de la Mode du Jour, p. 5.

Malève André. "Salle Wagram. L'exposition féline est inaugurée." L'Intransigeant, 26 avril 1930, p. 3.

Manou Mme Marcelle Adam &. "Le Salon du Chat." La Revue Féline de France.18 (1934), p. 203.

Martin Georges. "Une mission. Ce que M. Robert Chauvelot va faire au Sahara." Le Petit Journal, 1926, 17 Novembre ed., p. 4.

Marton Francis. "Chats." Chasse, pêche, élevage, 15 Juillet 1924.

Méry Fernand. "À la Salle Wagram. L'Exposition Féline." L'Intransigeant, 16 février 1930, p. 2.

---. "Chats d'écrivains & Chats d'artistes." Minerva. Le grand magazine illustré que toute femme intelligente doit lire, 24 Juillet 1927, p. 7.

---. "Chats de Birmanie." La Revue Féline Belge (1933), p. 4-5.

---. "La Femme et les Animaux." Minerva. Le grand illustré féminin que toute femme intelligente doit lire, 15 avril 1928, p. 7.

---. "La Femme et les Animaux." Minerva, 1929, p. 7.

---. "La légende des Chats Sacrés de Birmanie." Minerva, 1 Janvier 1933, p. 14.

---. Sa Majesté le chat. Paris, Denoël (Mayenne, impr. de Floch)1956.

Messis Blanche. "De l'exposition féline aux chats célèbres." Comœdia, 27 avril 1934, sec. La Vie des Femmes, p. 3.

Milloué M. L. de. "Le Temple d'Angkhor." Conférences du Musée Guimet. Paris 1908. 94-95.

Montherlant Henry de. "Passe-Temps. Exposition Féline." L'Intransigeant, 29 mai 1929, p. 1.

Moorcock Michael, et al. Elric intégrale 1 préface inédite de Jean-Luc Fromental. Pocket Science-fiction fantasy. Paris: Pocket, 2013.

Mortillet Adrien de. Chat Sans Queue de l'île de Man. Bulletins de la Société d'anthropologie de Paris. Vol. IV. Paris 1893.

Mortillet M. A. de. "Chats sans queue de l'île de Man." Le Bulletin de la Société Nationale d'Acclimatation de France (1893).

Normand Suzanne. "Les Chats Puissants et Doux...." Paris-Soir, 23 mai 1931, p. 2.

Ostroga Yvonne. "Philantropie et Commerce." Le Figaro, 20 juillet 1932, p. 4.

Paris Cat Club de. "1ère Exposition de la Féline de Bruxelles." Chasse, Pêche, Élevage, novembre 1932.

---. "Exposition d'Anvers." Chasse, Pêche, Élevage, Février 1933, p. 3.755.

---. "Palmarès de l'exposition de Paris." Chasse, Pêche, Elevage, mars 1933, p. 3.770.

---. "Palmarès Exposition Féline de Paris: 2-3 décembre 1932 (CCP)." Chasse, Pêche, Élevage, janvier 1933, p. 3.727.

Paris Cat Club de, and Mme Marcelle Adam & Manou. "Année Nouvelle." La Revue Féline de France.13 (1933), p. 141-43.

Pavares Somdet Phra Maha Samana Chao Krom Phraya. Tamra Maew (Good Luck Cats). Drawings. Bangkok.

Pavie Auguste. Mission Pavie. Indo-Chine. 1879-1895. Zoologie. Études diverses. Recherches sur l'histoire naturelle de l'Indo-Chine Orientale. Vol. III. Paris: Ernest Leroux, 1905.

R. D. "Les plus beaux Chats du monde." Le Journal, 2 décembre 1933, p. 6.

---. "Les plus beaux chats du monde à la Salle Wagram." Le Journal, 22 avril 1933, p. 4.

R. S. "À la salle Wagram. Les plus beaux chats viennent-ils d'Asie?" Reportage. Comœdia, 15 Mai 1926.

Ravon Georges. "L'Exposition Féline s'est ouverte hier." Le Figaro, 25 mai 1930, p. 3.

Reney Marcel, and Marcel Abbé Chamonin. Chats. Petits Atlas Payot Littérature. Vol. 23. Lausanne1957.

---. Nos Amis les Chats. Genève: Ch. Grasset, 1947.

Rol Agence. "14 Mai 1926, salle Wagram, exposition féline organisée par le Cat Club de France. Chat Sacré de Birmanie à Mme Marcelle Adam " BNF. Ed. Photo Mme Adam et Manou de Madalpour. Paris: Agence Rol, 1926. Print.

Ross David. "Notes and Queries: Manx Cats." Hardwicke's Science Gossip (1865), p. 142.

S. H. "La VIe Exposition féline de Paris. Salle Wagram." L'Œuvre, 15 février 1930, p. 6.

S.R. "À la Salle Wagram. Les plus beaux chats viennent-ils d'Asie?" Comœdia, 15 mai 1926.

---. "L'Exposition Féline: Chats d'Europe et chats d'Asie." Comœdia, 28 mai 1927, p. 1.

---. "La Légende du Chat Sacré de Birmanie." Minerva. Le grand Illustré Féminin que toute Femme Intelligente doit lire, 18 Septembre 1927, p. 14.

Sanvoisin Gaëtan. "La Vie qui passe. Le Club des Chats." Le Gaulois, 15 Mai 1926, p. 1.

sciences Association Française pour l'avancement des. "Le Chat de Birmanie. Dr. Jumaud." Conférences. Compte rendu de la 50e session. Lyon 1926 (1927), p. 426.

Simoni Henri. "Princes des Attitudes... Des chats sont exposés à la Salle Wagram." L'Œuvre, 9 février 1929, p. 1.

Simpson Frances. The Book of the Cat. With 12 coloured plates and nearly 350 illustrations in the text, etc. London: Cassell, 1903.

---. Cats for Pleasure and Profits. 1909. London: Sir Isaac Pitman & Sons, LTD, 1928.

Taskin Dr Vet. "Ce qu'il faut retenir de l'exposition Féline de Paris." Vie à la Campagne, 1 Juillet 1929, p. 293.

Trévières Pierre de. "L'Amour des Bêtes." La Femmes de France, 12 Jujllet 1931, p. 22.

Tzigane La. ""La Ruche". l 946. Amies des félins." La Femme de France, 13 Juillet 1930, p. 792.

V. H. de. "Chez les Bêtes. Leurs altesses les chats." Je Suis Partout, 30 mai 1931, p. 10.

Vanderbilt William Kissam II. 15,000 Miles Cruise with Ara. New York: Privately Printed, 1927.

---. Taking One's Own Ship Around the World: A Journal Descriptive of Scenes and Incidents Together with Observations from the Log Books Recorded on the Voyage Around the World of the Yacht Ara. New York: Privately Printed by William Edwin Rudge, 1929.

---. To Galapagos on the Ara. New York: William Rudge, 1926.

---. A Trip Through Sicily, Tunisia, Algeria, and Southern France. New York1918.

Vautel Clément. L'Amour à la Parisienne. Paris: Albin Michel, 1927.

Wherry Edith. "La déesse de la lanterne rouge." L'Humanité, 26 avril 1921, p. 3.

---. The Red lantern being the story of the goddess of the red lantern light. New York: J. Lane, 1911.

ABOUT THE AUTHOR

Born in Menton in the Alpes-Maritimes, Doctor Alain Lescart is professor of literature and French at an American university in San Diego, California. A 19th-century scholar, he has a master's and an aggregation in theology, a master's degree in family therapy, and a doctorate in French literature from the University of Connecticut in the United States. His doctoral thesis on the emblematic figure of the grisette has been published by *Champion editions* as well as various articles in literature and poetry.

Books published:

Lescart Alain. « L'Extraordinaire Aventure du Chat Sacré de Birmanie. » Les Trois Colonnes. Paris. 2020. [The original text of this book in French].

Gorrillot Bénédicte & Lescart, Alain. "Les Actes de San Diego. L'Illisibilité en Questions." Collectif. Septentrion. Lettres et Arts. 2014.

Lescart Alain. Prince, Sue Ann. « Of Elephants & Roses. French Natural History: 1790-1830.» An Egyptian Giraffe and Six Osage Indians: An Exotic Plea Against the Censorship of 1827. The American Philosophical Society of Philadelphia Museum. 2013 (Ch. 18 : pp. 214-222.)

Lescart, Alain. Faire du Nouveau avec de l'Ancien. Le recyclage de la grisette fossilisée dans "Les Misérables" de Victor Hugo. Revue des Sciences Humaines- No 302 – Avril-Juin 2011.

Lescart, Alain. Splendeurs et Misères de la Grisette : Évolution d'une figure emblématique. Paris : Honoré Champion, Romantisme et Modernité no 113, 2008 (332 pages).